MAGIC

AND

SHOWMANSHIP

MAGIC AND SHOWMANSHIP
A HANDBOOK FOR CONJURERS

Henning Nelms

DOVER PUBLICATIONS, INC.
Mineola, New York

Published in Canada by General Publishing Company, Ltd., 30 Lesmill Road, Don Mills, Toronto, Ontario.

Bibliographical Note

This edition of *Magic and Showmanship: A Handbook for Conjurers,* first published in 2000, is the unabridged republication of the work originally published in 1969 by Dover Publications, Inc.

Library of Congress Cataloging-in-Publication Data

Nelms, Henning, 1900–
    Magic and showmanship : a handbook for conjurers / Henning Nelms.
        p. cm.
    Originally published: 1969.
    Includes index.
    ISBN 0-486-41087-0 (pbk.)
    1. Magic tricks—Handbooks, manuals, etc. I. Title.

GV1547 .N43 2000
793.8—dc21

99-052791

Manufactured in the United States of America
Dover Publications, Inc., 31 East 2nd Street, Mineola, N.Y. 11501

To My Wife

CONTENTS

FOREWORD

Drama and conjuring are both arts of illusion. The techniques which enable an actor to persuade his audience that he is Hamlet or Falstaff are equally useful to a conjurer who wants to persuade his audience that he can take a rabbit out of an empty hat.

Unfortunately, as few people practice both arts, even the most elementary methods employed by actors are largely unknown to conjurers. Nor is that all, for the conjurer must also be his own playwright and director, though he has few opportunities to learn from specialists in either field.

For example, conjurers give much thought to misdirection. They tend to regard it as a mysterious art in which each problem must be solved separately. Actually, misdirection is only a special application of the techniques used by stage directors to control attention. Any conjurer who makes a serious study of these techniques will find that most problems of misdirection solve themselves.

This book attempts to explain those methods of the legitimate theater which are most useful to conjurers. It makes no pretense of originality, but merely applies the lessons I have learned in the theater to the conditions under which the conjurer works. I have devoted much space to devices for increasing the comic or dramatic impact of conjuring routines, because these offer the greatest opportunities for improvement. However, there is much more, ranging from the actor's technique for picking up something from the floor to devices for increasing applause.

The sixty-odd routines in the book are intended primarily as examples. I shall be flattered if you use some of them, but you will do better to take them as models and invent routines of your own. Chapter 16 describes the procedure for invention.

You may need a little practice to get the knack. But once you do, you will find that invention comes easily.

Conjurers are the nicest people! Whenever I tried to invent a routine and found that either my ingenuity or my technical knowledge was inadequate, some friend generously supplied the idea I required. As this often involved hours of thought and experiment, my debt is far from light.

In acknowledging assistance from particular friends, I am keenly aware that many others would have been willing and able to supply equally helpful advice. I appreciate this deeply and wish that the list of potential contributors were not too long to print here.

My chief debt is to Louis Bertol, who is the world's foremost inventor of simple accessories for making conjuring apparatus work. Some of his creations appear in the illustrations for "The Haunted Conjurer" and "The Consolidated Guinea Pigs." You may not like my routines, but you can probably find uses for his devices in routines of your own.

Robert Tilford supplied nearly all the material in Chapter 5. If you work with an assistant you can almost certainly find places for at least one of his creations in your act.

Asking Richard Gray for suggestions has its hazards. He usually finds at least six answers for each of my problems. I then face the difficult task of deciding which one is best.

William Adamson deserves special mention. I devised an original, highly entertaining, impromptu, cup-and-ball routine. As manipulative conjuring is far from my field, I asked Bill to work out the required moves. After spending hours in research and experiment, he reported that the routine had built-in flaws which only the most expert manipulator could overcome. This verdict forced me to abandon the routine. However, it increases my indebtedness to him.

Maj. Winton A. J. Carroll, Alfred Cohen, Jimmy King, Ed Mishell, and the late Samuel (Sabar) Shapiro all made valuable contributions which are acknowledged at the appropriate points in the text.

My gratitude is also extended to the Carlance family. Joseph took the photographs upon which many of my illustrations are based, and Bonnie, Ella, and John posed for them. John also added to my knowledge of conjuring and helped to prepare my drawings for reproduction.

I have used a number of ideas from men with whom I am not personally acquainted. These include Theodore Annemann, Al Baker, George Blake, Darrel Fitzkee, Karl Germain, U. F. Grant, Otis Manning, and Orville Meyer. I have expressed my obligation in the text, but it is only fitting that I also confess it here.

The quotation on p. 3 from Harlan Tarbell appears on pp. 34 and 35, Vol. 2 of *The Tarbell Course in Magic*. Louis Tannen, the present owner of the copyright, graciously gave me permission to use it.

Chapter 1
THE TWO MAGICS

The art of conjuring consists in creating illusions of the impossible.

In 1856, French North Africa was as disturbed as it is today. However, the agitators were not Communists but marabouts—Mohammedan fanatics who worked the Arabian mobs into superstitious frenzy by pretending to possess magical powers.

The French Government displayed imagination almost unique in official circles and sent a conjurer, Robert-Houdin, to discredit the marabouts by outdoing their magic.

One of Robert-Houdin's feats is probably the most perfect example of conjuring ever performed. The marabouts had a trick which apparently proved that no pistol aimed at them would fire. The French conjurer countered by letting a marabout shoot at him and catching the bullet in an apple stuck on the point of a knife. However, Robert-Houdin had announced publicly that his "magic" consisted entirely of tricks, and the shrewder marabouts guessed that his bullet-catching feat could be performed only with his own gun.

Some time later, while the Frenchman was stopping in a native village, a marabout drew two pistols from his burnoose and challenged Robert-Houdin to a duel in which the marabout claimed the right to the first shot! Robert-Houdin protested but finally agreed to fight the duel under the marabout's conditions at eight o'clock the following morning.

The meeting took place in an open square surrounded by whitewashed buildings. The square was packed with Arabs who hoped to see the Frenchman killed. The marabout produced his pistols which he loaded with powder. He offered Robert-Houdin a handful of bullets. The Frenchman chose two, dropped them into the weapons, covered them with paper wads, and thrust them into the barrels with a ramrod.

The marabout had watched every step and felt sure that his adversary could not escape. He took careful aim and pulled the trigger. Robert-Houdin smiled—and displayed the bullet between his teeth.

The marabout tried to seize the other pistol, but the French conjurer held him off, saying, "You could not injure me, but you shall see that my skill is more dangerous than yours. Watch!"

He fired at the nearest wall. Whitewash flew. Where the bullet had struck, a gout of blood appeared and dripped down the masonry.

The art of illusion is at least 95 per cent applied psychology. In the duel with the marabout, psychology accounted for 98 per cent of the effect. The underlying trick was simple. If it had been used alone, it might have puzzled the Arabs, but the dramatic impact would have been lost.

In those days, duelling pistols were provided with bullet molds. Robert-Houdin cast two hollow balls of wax which he rubbed with graphite to make them look like lead. One ball was left empty; the other was filled with blood drawn from his thumb. He *switched* these for the real bullets by sleight of hand. The empty ball went into the marabout's gun and was rammed home with enough force to break the wax into small bits. The blood-filled bullet in the conjurer's pistol was merely pushed into the barrel. It was strong enough to hold together until it struck the wall and splashed it with blood.

Robert-Houdin was able to overcome the Arabs because he followed the formula adopted by the most successful wonder-workers down the ages. Witch doctors, pagan priests, spiritualist mediums, and confidence men have impressed their dupes by making the least possible use of trickery and applying all the psychology they could muster. Modern conjurers can profit from following the same rules. When they use more than one part of trickery to nine parts of psychology, they cannot hope to create the maximum impression.

DRAMA AS MAGIC

Drama, like conjuring, is an art of illusion. A play does not take place on the stage but in the minds of the spectators. What really happens is that a troupe of actors repeats a carefully rehearsed routine before an obviously artificial setting. The audience, however, misinterprets this as a series of exciting events in the lives of the characters.

Forcing spectators to interpret what they see and hear in ways which they know are false comes as close to genuine magic as we are likely to get. The everyday illusions of the legitimate stage put all but the best conjuring performances to shame. Even a second-rate play convinces spectators of "facts" which they know are not true. It can go further and use these imaginary "facts" to wring real tears from the eyes of the audience. Everyone is aware that a leading lady on Broadway receives a salary which puts her in the upper tax brackets. Nevertheless, this knowledge does not keep audiences from sobbing over her poverty when she impersonates a homeless waif.

The magic of drama is infinitely more powerful than the magic of trickery. It is as available to the conjurer as it is to the actor. The only difference is that actors take it for granted, whereas few conjurers are even aware that it exists. You need not accept this on my testimony. Here is evidence from Harlan Tarbell, one of the greatest conjurers of the twentieth century:

What magical showmanship can do was brought home to me forcibly when a party of twelve magicians, including myself, went to see the play *The Charlatan* in which Frederick Tilden was playing the leading role of Cagliostro, the magician. We sat delighted at the magic and illusions that he presented from time to time in the play. When he produced a rosebush from a seed which he planted into a bit of sand in a clear glass flower-pot, we were completely mystified. Here, truly, was a great magician whom we had hitherto missed. After the show, we went back stage, met Tilden and invited him out to dinner. . . .

As is customary at dinners, some of the boys performed a few miracles. This was no exception. When Tilden was called on to perform, he said, "Why, boys, I'm no magician. I do not do tricks. You have me all wrong. I am just an actor."

"Oh, no," said we, "You are a magician. Didn't we see the wonderful magic you performed in the theater this afternoon? . . ."

He leaned back and laughed. "Do you mean to say those simple tricks fooled you?"

Then Tilden gave us an excellent talk. He said that when he was chosen to play the part of a noted magician, Cagliostro, he determined to make himself feel like a great magician and act the part. He studied what he thought a man like Cagliostro would do and what he would say in the emergencies which the play brought forth. . . .

He decided that things could be produced and vanished from places which an audience would least suspect. In this instance, the man who appeared most innocent of helping him was the villain, a lawyer who tried to expose Cagliostro and prove him to be a faker. So Tilden thought his best helper would be this disturbing lawyer, a skeptic who sought every way possible to undo the magician. In the eyes of the audience, this lawyer and the magician were bitter enemies. In reality, it was the lawyer who helped create the illusions. When the lawyer lifted up the paper cone from the flower-pot to see that there was no trickery, he put the flowers into the cone himself in readiness for the production a moment later. And Tilden, in his mastery of showmanship, put his effects over as though he were the greatest magician in the world.

The bullet-catching routine provides another example. As far as the trickery was concerned, Robert-Houdin's feat was merely another version of stage effect that was old even in his day. But from the standpoint of the audience, there was no comparison. The stage performers challenged their audiences to discover how the gun was *faked* so that no bullet came out of the muzzle. Sometimes the device actually lay elsewhere. However, as that possibility did not occur to the spectators, it could not affect their reactions. The Arabs in Robert-Houdin's audience, on the other hand, did not think of him as doing a trick. From their viewpoint, he was staking his life in a duel for the control of North Africa—a duel in which only the power of his magic could protect him from certain death!

Actually, the stage versions are extremely dangerous. At least ten performers have been killed by them, and there have been twice as many nonfatal accidents. But most theatergoers do not know that and would not believe it if they were told. Hence, the men who have presented the trick on stage were taking a tremendous risk without making a corresponding impression on their audiences. This illustrates a basic principle. *What occurs on the stage is of no consequence except as it affects the thinking of the spectators.* All that matters is what they think and see and hear.

Tricks vs. Illusions

Stage bullet-catching is a trick. It makes the audience wonder how it is done, but it does not persuade anyone, even momentarily, that the performer's magic renders him invulnerable to rifle fire. Robert-Houdin, on the other hand, created an illusion. He persuaded his audience that no bullet could harm him.

Unfortunately, conjurers have formed the habit of referring to any large trick as an "illusion." The term is used as a description of size. If the equipment is big enough, the trick is called an "illusion" even though a ten-year-old child can see through it. This careless use of language is likely to confuse our thinking. We shall not follow the custom. Instead, we shall call anything a "trick" which challenges its audience to discover how it was worked. We shall reserve *illusion* for those feats which actually convince the audience. In most cases, the conviction will be neither deeper nor more lasting than the conviction of an audience at *Hamlet* that the prince has been killed in a duel. However, this is all the theater needs to create drama—and it is all a conjurer needs to fascinate his audience instead of being content to provide a little amusement.

There is a tremendous difference between even such short-lived illusions and none at all. If a play fails to create any illusion, it is worthless. On the other hand, if it succeeds in creating an illusion, the fact that the spell of the drama is broken with the fall of the curtain does not diminish its effect in the slightest.

Fortunately for conjurers, a routine that fails to create an illusion is better than an unconvincing performance of a play. It may still be highly entertaining as a trick. Nevertheless, as illusions have far more appeal to most audiences, there is no reason why we should not gratify them and ourselves by providing the additional interest.

The difference between a trick and an illusion depends largely on the conjurer's attitude. Illusions take many different forms. But, in the most typical examples, the performer claims some specific, supernormal power and makes this claim as impressively as possible. He then indicates that the purpose of his performance is to demonstrate the power. He provides this demonstration, and it appears to prove his claim.

The conjurer who presents a trick usually begins by admitting that it is a trick. On the rare occasions when he pretends to have some remarkable power, he does it half-heartedly as though to say, "We all know that this is pure hokum, and that I only talk about magic, telepathy, or what not because it is part of the act." Such an attitude cannot create an illusion. If one actor in a play treated his part in this fashion, the play would fail. Furthermore, even when the man who performs a trick does claim a power, he usually leaves it vague; the trick is not treated as a demonstration of the power, and the *effect* does not prove the claim. He cannot expect to create an illusion, because neither he nor his audience knows what illusion he is trying to create.

THE MAGIC OF MEANING

No matter how astonishing a trick may be, it suffers from one major fault—it has no point. Suppose you could work miracles. Suppose that, without coming near me, you simply gestured toward my pocket and told me to put my hand in it. I did so and took out a ham sandwich. This would no doubt amaze me, but after I had recovered from my surprise my only feeling would be, "So what?"

But suppose I say, "I'm hungry," and you reply, "I can fix that. Look in your left coat pocket." When I do so, I find a sandwich. This has a point. It makes sense. You cannot work that sort of miracle, but you can add meaning to your conjuring.

Even the celebrated classics of conjuring have no point. The spectator may say, "Marvelous." However, he then shrugs his shoulders and adds mentally, "But what of it?" This is why many people find tricks dull. They feel that any form of entertainment should have meaning. When they can find none in a trick, they yawn.

Consider the well-known *Four Ace Trick* for example. The Aces are dealt on a table. Three *indifferent* cards are placed on each Ace. A pile is chosen by a spectator. When it is turned over, it is found to contain all four Aces and the other piles are shown to consist of indifferent cards. The audience may be amazed, but the trick makes little impression because it has no significance. If you could perform real magic, even very minor magic, would you waste it on an effect like that?

An illusion is entirely different. The fact that the performer claims a supernormal power, and proposes to demonstrate it, arouses attention. It gives the spectators a definite idea on which to focus: *Can this man substantiate his incredible claim?* The mental attitude of the audience watching an illusion is far removed from that of one watching a mere trick.

Interest depends entirely on meaning. The degree of interest that spectators take in any performance is in direct proportion to its meaning for them. The more meaning you can pack into a presentation, the more interest it will excite. An illusion creates interest because the conjurer gives it meaning by proposing to demonstrate some remarkable power. A typical trick has no meaning beyond the fact that it presents a puzzle and challenges the audience to find a solution.

Many people find puzzles dull. Even the enthusiast is bored by some types of puzzles. Conjuring puzzles are not likely to fascinate anyone who is not a conjuring-puzzle addict.

Conjuring puzzles have a special weakness. When a spectator meets the challenge by solving the puzzle, the conjurer loses. When the spectator fails, he regards the conjuring puzzle like any other puzzle; he gives up and feels entitled to be told the answer. This places the performer in an insolvable dilemma.

If he refuses to divulge his secret, the spectators feel frustrated and resentful; if the conjurer yields, the explanation seems so trivial that they feel let down.

When we supply a meaning, we eliminate the challenge, and the puzzle becomes secondary. After the climax, the spectator may wonder how it was achieved. But even then, the puzzle element is greatly weakened. In fact, if the meaning is made strong enough, many spectators may not realize that there is any puzzle to solve. With a competent performance and a not-too-skeptical audience, the following illusion will be accepted as a genuine demonstration of telepathy.

DIAL INFORMATION

Start a conversation on the subject of extrasensory perception. Try to have each spectator express his views. This arouses interest in the subject before you even suggest your intention of exhibiting any supernormal phenomenon.

Remark that a friend of yours claims to be telepathic. You have seen him do some remarkable things with ESP cards, but you suspect he is a fake. Your friend claims that distance is no barrier, and that he can read minds ten miles away as easily as those in the same room. In fact, he says people call him up on the phone and ask him to read their minds as a stunt. This happened so often that he had to get an unlisted number. However, he let you have his number and promised to give you one demonstration of his powers. This seems as good a time as any to take him up on his offer.

As you have no ESP cards, you will have to use something else. Why not coins ? Take a handful of change from your pocket and have someone choose a coin. Let us suppose that he chooses a quarter.

Your telepathic friend has given you a card bearing his unlisted number. Read this to yourself to refresh your memory, but before you dial say to a second spectator, "After I get him, you do the talking. My friend lives alone, so he's the only one who can answer and you won't have to call for him by name. Just tell him I said he can read your mind, and ask him if he knows what you're thinking about. Don't say it's a coin."

Dial the number and wait until the telepath answers. Do not speak yourself; simply hand the telephone to the person who is to do the talking.

When the telepath is asked to read the speaker's mind, he replies that the group must all think of the same thing. After a pause, he announces that the object is round and metallic, probably a coin. He then adds, "Tell Joe (you, the conjurer) that he's in this too. If he'll get his mind off the blonde in the red dress and focus it on the coin, I may be able to give the demonstration." As there actually is a blonde in a red dress and you have been eyeing her during the test, this comes as a shock to everyone—including you.

DIAL INFORMATION

When the telepath answers your call, signal him by clicking your fingernail across the groove of the telephone (*A*, Fig. 1). This assures him that the call comes from you. He then says slowly, "Penny . . . nickel . . . dime . . . quarter . . . fifty cents." Click again when he names the chosen coin. This tells him both the denomination and the date. He then checks the guests by saying, "Man . . . woman. . . ." If both of those whom you have described are present, do nothing. But if either one failed to attend, signal at the appropriate moment. If possible, call your friend secretly after the guests arrive and give him last minute information, such as the fact that the blonde is wearing red. Of course, if you can make this secret call, the telepath will not need to have you confirm the presence of particular guests when you dial him again.

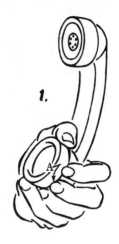

After another pause, the telepath says that the coin is silver, and he gets the number "five." However, he cannot say whether it is a quarter or a fifty-cent piece because there is interference from a large gentleman connected with the law—"a policeman, or perhaps a judge." As one guest is actually a fat lawyer, this is highly convincing.

"Tell him to stop trying to guess how the trick is worked," the telepath continues, "there isn't any trick. And if you'll all concentrate on the date of the coin by repeating it over and over to yourselves, I'll try to tell you what it is." There is a longer pause this time. After it, the telepath says, "The date on the coin is 1962. Don't be so skeptical about things you can't understand," and hangs up.

Dial Information is actually an improved and dramatized variation on an old trick known as *The Wizard*. In this version, you prepare yourself by having all your pennies the same date, all your nickels the same date, and so on. Make a card like this and give it to the telepath.

| 1¢ | 1951 | 10¢ | 1948 | 50¢ | 1963 |
| 5¢ | 1964 | 25¢ | 1962 | | |

He knows in advance that the object will be a coin. If he is told its denomination, he can announce this and read the date from his card. You also give him advance descriptions of one man and one woman whom you expect to be present.

You mention the "unlisted" number to keep anyone else from offering to dial or from trying to call the telepath later. Do not stress this. Merely work it into the conversation so that you can refuse to give the number if anyone asks for it.

The method of signaling is explained in Fig. 1.

MEANING, SHOWMANSHIP, TECHNIQUE

Meaning creates drama. Houdini's escapes made him the most famous wonder-worker of all time. His reputation did not depend on any one feat, no matter how daring or how apparently impossible it might be. What counted was the fact that he seemed able to escape from every sort of restraint that his challengers could devise. He amazed multitudes less by the feats that he actually showed them than by the countless other escapes which they believed he had performed. It was this reputation for being able to get out of *anything*, plus the fact that escapes are fundamentally romantic, which gave meaning to Houdini's performances. In later years, when he turned to straight conjuring, he was much less impressive. His fame still provided him with audiences, but all that the spectators saw was another entertainer doing meaningless tricks.

Showmanship brings out the meaning of a performance and gives it an importance that it might otherwise lack. The telepath in *Dial Information* could say, "I get an impression from two minds. A large, heavily built lawyer is thinking of a coin. The thought which comes to me from a blonde young lady in a red dress tells me that this coin is a quarter. If you will look at the date, you will find that it is 1962." This is actually more marvelous than the version given above, but it is much less impressive because it is completely lacking in showmanship.

When showmanship is carried far enough, it can even create an illusion of meaning where none exists. Houdini's showmanship was developed to glamorize his escapes, and he had little success in adapting it to his performances as a conjurer. There was, however, one exception—*The Needle Trick*. That consists in placing a packet of needles and a length of thread in the mouth and then pulling out the thread with the needles strung on it.

This does not even make sense. Is the performer supposed to thread the needles with his tongue? If so, the way the thread is handled makes the idea absurd. Or does he swallow both thread and needles and make the latter thread themselves magically in his stomach? In that case, the stomach is merely a container; it would be safer and more convincing if the magic took place in an ordinary box. Few spectators go through this reasoning in detail. However, most of them realize instinctively that the trick itself is trivial. When the average conjurer presents it, the interest of the audience is largely confined to the question, "will this rash idiot swallow a needle and require surgery?" Sometimes he does.

In Houdini's hands, however, this meaningless bit of leger-demain became a minor miracle simply through his superb showmanship. That began with his costume. For matinees, he wore formal afternoon clothes like an ambassador going to pay a call at the White House. At evening performances, he wore tails. He invited twenty or thirty spectators to come up onto the stage. This has no real significance, but it gave the impression that he was performing a large-scale "illusion." When calling for volunteers, he made a special point of requesting a dentist. If one consented to assist, Houdini asked him to examine his mouth—and provided a dental mirror for the purpose. Most performers use one packet of needles; Houdini used two. Most performers are content with six feet of thread; Houdini used thirty. When the thread was drawn out, it stretched all the way across the stage. This action was accompanied by music from the orchestra, with the trap drummer striking a bell so that it tinkled as each needle appeared between Houdini's lips.

These things may seem trivial in cold print, but they held Houdini's audience spellbound for ten or twelve minutes. I remember every detail after forty years, whereas much better (but less well presented) tricks have long since faded from my memory.

Technique has two elements. The first is the method of deception. Compare, for example, *Dial Information* with *The Wizard* on which it is based. In *The Wizard*, a spectator is asked to choose a card and display it. The performer then dials the "wizard's" telephone number. When the latter answers, he begins naming the suits. When he reaches the right one, the conjurer asks, "Is the wizard there?" This tells the "wizard" the suit of the chosen card. He then starts counting. When he reaches the number of the chosen card, the performer says, "Hello, Wizard," and hands the card to someone else. The "wizard" then names the card.

Dial information improves this technique in several ways: (1) It uses coins instead of cards; that tends to make the audience accept it as a serious demonstration of telepathy instead of just another card trick. (2) The performer seems unaware of the date of the coin until after he has left the telephone. (3) He apparently does nothing which can possibly be construed as a signal. (4) Even if the performer is suspected of knowing the facts and signaling them in some way, it seems that he must transmit the denomination and date of the coin and a description of two spectators indetectibly in the few seconds that he holds the receiver. As this is actually impossible, few people will accept it as an explanation. That leaves only telepathy.

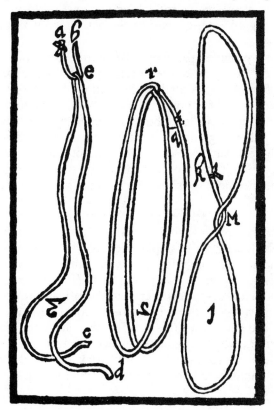

2. STRING TRICK FROM HOCUS POCUS, JR.
Published in 1634

Technique also covers the conjurer's manner of presentation —how he moves, how he speaks, what he says, his timing, and the skill with which he conceals any devices that may be necessary.

In an ideal performance, the spectators should be able to follow the ideas of the illusion, step by step. Nothing should be allowed to divert their attention to anything else. In most cases, any lack of polish on the part of the performer becomes a distraction. An awkward movement or an inaudible word interrupts the smooth flow of thought and leads the minds of the audience away from the illusion. Nevertheless, there are exceptions. In *Dial Information*, for example, noticeable polish would be a mistake. You want everything to seem impromptu, and you do not want anyone to look on you as a performer. If the audience regards you as part of the act, most of the mystery will be lost.

Meaning provides the magic of drama. Showmanship intensifies or exaggerates the meaning. Technique keeps the meaning from being diluted by distractions.

If we are to add the powerful magic of meaning to the magic of conjuring, we must learn how to dramatize our presentations by making them significant. That is not merely the first step, it is also the fundamental one. When a routine has a built-in meaning, we find many opportunities for showmanship; when there is no meaning, the showman has little with which to work.

Adding the Meaning

The procedure for providing a routine with a meaning is best explained by an example. Let us start with one of the oldest and least meaningful effects in conjuring, the cut-and-restored string. Fig. 2 was taken from *Hocus Pocus, Jr.*, the second book on conjuring ever printed in English. Instead of cutting the string in the center, the performer merely cuts off one end. He gets rid of this in some way and then shows the main portion, which he claims has been restored.

Countless improvements on this trick have been devised. The best one is based on an idea of Karl Germain's. We shall call it:

THE INSEPARABLE STRING

Figs. 3–5 show the preparation. The performer begins by taking the loop of string and offering to present a trick. He puts his hands through the loop to reveal it clearly. No one can suspect that a string is continuous at Point *B*, Fig. 4. Next, he takes a pair of scissors from his pocket and snips off the glued bit (Point *A*). He puts this in his pocket with the scissors. He then unties the knot and drops the string on the table—where it looks like Fig. 6.

"We now have two lengths of string and four ends. Choose either pair of ends." If the spectator selects the real ends, the performer adds, "Take one in each hand." If the spectator selects the joined ends, the performer remarks, "All right, I shall now proceed to join the ends you chose together." In either event, he takes the twisted "ends" (actually the center) in his fist and has the spectator hold a real end in each hand—or each of two spectators may hold an end (Fig. 7).

The conjurer then says, "I will now restore the string by saying a few magic words. However, while I do so, you must help me by pulling on both ends of the string. Are you ready? Pull. Hocus pocus, abracadabra, alakazam!" The pulling has untwisted the fake ends and twisted them again to re-form the original center of the string. When the conjurer removes his hand, the string is seen to be completely restored and will stand the closest examination.

THE INSEPARABLE STRING

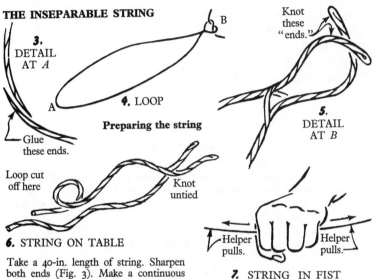

3. DETAIL AT *A*

Glue these ends.

4. LOOP

Preparing the string

B

Knot these "ends."

5. DETAIL AT *B*

Loop cut off here

Knot untied

6. STRING ON TABLE

Helper pulls.

Helper pulls.

7. STRING IN FIST

Take a 40-in. length of string. Sharpen both ends (Fig. 3). Make a continuous loop (Fig. 4) by joining these ends with white glue (Elmer's is the best known brand). Untwist the strands of the section opposite the joint. Divide these into two parts and retwist them to make two short "ends" (Fig. 5). Tie these together loosely with an overhand knot (*B*, Fig. 4). The result looks like a plain loop with its ends tied in a square knot.

This is a brilliant trick. It avoids all false moves and will fool spectators who either know the *Hocus Pocus, Jr.* method or are shrewd enough to see through it. Nevertheless, it is just a trick. The spectators may be impressed by its cleverness, but they are not convinced even for an instant that the string has been cut and restored. Instead, they have been challenged to solve a puzzle. It is a frustrating puzzle because the conjurer refuses to supply the answer even when they "give up."

Although *The Inseparable String* fools spectators who would see through the older method, many people are fooled by either method. As far as these people are concerned, both methods are equally good; in fact, they are both the same trick.

Can we give the continuous-loop method a meaning that will retain its deceptive qualities and still create a convincing illusion? We might find a cut-and-restored meaning, but this line of thought is hardly promising. Also, our illusion could be mistaken for merely another version of an old trick. However, when I first saw the continuous-loop method performed, I did not know that the string would be restored. For a moment, I thought I was witnessing a strong-man feat in which the performer held the ends of two pieces of string in his fist and defied the spectators to pull them free. This supplied a fresh meaning. It also furnished, temporarily, an effect which I believe is entirely new to conjuring. Of course, restoring the string destroyed the strong-man effect, but the following version eliminates this anticlimax.

The Strong Man's Secret

While chatting with a small group, you "happen" to find a loop of string in your pocket. Take this out and play with it. Casually introduce the subject of side shows. Work in any bit of lore you may have—such as the fact that the performers themselves no longer speak of "side shows" but of "freak shows" and that the old-time "spielers" and "barkers" are now called by the more dignified title of "lecturers." Handle all this merely as interesting items of conversation with no hint that you are leading up to anything more.

State that the strong men have always been your favorites. They are genuinely powerful, but they fake their acts so that they seem to perform feats which are actually impossible. Indeed, some of their demonstrations, such as tearing a telephone book in half, require more knack than strength. At this point, the string reminds you of one strong-man's stunt that you can do yourself. Unfortunately, you are not free to explain it because the performer who taught you made you promise not to reveal his secret. However, you are willing to demonstrate it if anyone is interested—and if you can remember just how it works.

The procedure is almost the same as that for *The Inseparable String*, but there are a few changes.

The natural way to divide a piece of string is to cut it at one spot, but you must snip off the glued loop. The best method of doing this is with a sharp penknife (Fig. 8). Although this is not quite natural, a knife is much less noticeable than a pair of scissors. Also, the technique in Fig. 8 permits you to sever the string without looking at it. If you make the cut that way, few people will pay any attention to the action.

Do not offer a choice; merely take the twisted ends in your fist (Fig. 7). Give one cut end to a spectator on your right and the other to one on your

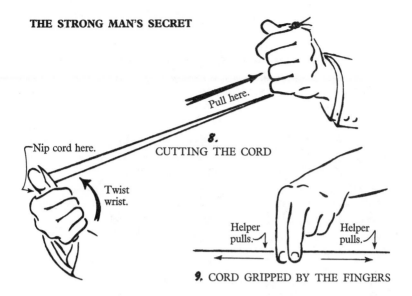

8.
CUTTING THE CORD

9. CORD GRIPPED BY THE FINGERS

left. Tell them to pull hard but avoid jerking "as that might yank the loose ends out of your hand and spoil the stunt."

Holding two pieces of string in your fist against a strong pull is quite a feat in itself, but you can do better. Ask for a little slack. Carefully work the string down in your hand until it is held between two fingers and your thumb (Fig. 9). Tell the spectators to pull again. You can still hold the string. When they let go, gather it up and drop it into your pocket.

This routine introduces the important principle of *conservation*. You could hold the string with your thumb and *one* finger. However, this is so incredible that the audience may suspect something more than a mere strong-man stunt and guess that the string had been restored. This would still be a good trick, but it would confuse the issue. The impression made on the minds of the spectators would be seriously weakened.

The Strong Man's Secret offers only a minor example of conservation. We shall find more important applications of the principle as we proceed. The Japanese define an artist as "one who has the ability to do more and the will to refrain." This definition covers showmanship as well. Showmanship adds glamor and drama. However, if we try to give any routine more importance than it will bear, we destroy the illusion and may reveal the secret.

The Strong Man's Secret provides much more entertainment than *The Inseparable String* because it has much more meaning.

The preliminary information about freak shows takes your audience behind the scenes of a world that most people regard as strange and mysterious. If you read up on the subject, you can hold the interested attention of the group for five minutes or more before you even mention strong men. This introduction also gives significance to the routine. It ceases to be just another cut-and-restored-string trick, or even just another conjuring trick. It is something brand-new, a demonstration from the exotic world of carnivals and freak shows. Finally, where *The Inseparable String* convinces no one, *The Strong Man's Secret* convinces everyone. They are convinced merely of a trick, but the trick they think they saw bears no relation to the trick you actually performed. This is as genuine an illusion as Robert-Houdin's demonstration of *invulnerability*.

TRICKS PREFERRED

What I have written is not intended to imply that tricks are dull. I enjoy them immensely. However, as illusions are more entertaining, have greater impact, and are equally easy to perform, conjurers miss a great deal when they fail to take advantage of the magic of drama. In spite of this, there are important exceptions to the rule. Situations exist in which tricks are definitely better than illusions.

Children are highly entertained by tricks. They regard the conjurer as a glamorous figure and enjoy matching wits with him. They are convinced that they can almost grasp his secrets, and that they could do his tricks themselves if they could get hold of his apparatus.

This does not mean that convincing illusions would fail to impress children. On the contrary, they would succeed only too well. Overimaginative youngsters might accept the conjurer as a genuine magician and become afraid of him. Even those with harder heads could mistake a routine like *Dial Information* for proof of the occult. That would be bad for the children. It certainly would not please their parents—who pay the performer's fees.

Salesmen who use conjuring to gain attention and good will are in much the same position as the man who entertains children, though for different reasons. A good salesman uses a trick just as he would a joke. The trick is more effective because the prospect hears many jokes, but a trick is a refreshing novelty. In both cases, however, the salesman is acting as Court Jester to His Majesty the Prospect.

A salesman who allowed himself to present convincing illusions would give evidence of extraordinary powers or unusual skill. That would make him seem superior to the prospect. The wise salesman does not flatter his own ego. He wants the prospect to feel superior. Hence, he offers his tricks simply as tricks and says, or at least implies, "There is really nothing to it. You could do the same thing yourself if you could spare the time to practice." This kind of conjuring sells goods. It is not, and is not intended to be, a convincing display of mystification as a fine art.

Torture routines, such as *Sawing a Woman in Half*, provide a third instance where illusions are undesirable. When these routines are offered frankly as tricks, they create no illusion, but they can be highly entertaining. If a foolish performer dramatized them to the point where the audience could almost feel the blade tear through human flesh, they would become violently unpleasant.

CONJURING FOR CONJURERS—AND LAYMEN

Membership in a conjuring society offers many advantages: encouragement, suggestions, criticisms, and unparalleled opportunities for studying the art of deception. Nevertheless, performing for conjurers is the worst possible way to test the value of your presentations. Everything you do, literally everything, has a different value for conjurers than it has for laymen. Conjurers are fascinated by subtle devices and difficult sleight of hand. Laymen are incapable of appreciating either the subtlety or the difficulty. In fact, if the performance succeeds, the layman cannot even guess what methods have been used. On the other hand, laymen are easily impressed by illusions, whereas conjurers are immune except in rare cases like *The Charlatan*. If you try to dramatize a routine for a brother conjurer, you will merely bore him—unless he sees something in your routine that he can use in his own act.

When you work out a routine for laymen, test it on a friend who knows nothing about conjuring. Ask for his detailed criticism. Then try your routine on another friend and get his opinion. If several laymen find fault with the same spot in your routine, it is bad.

A layman's diagnosis of what is wrong will usually be false and will often be absurd, but he almost always puts his finger on the point where the trouble lies. When lay friends criticize your presentation of *The Strong Man's Secret* "because you held your hand in a funny way while the string was being pulled," you need not pay much attention to their reasons. Perhaps your face provided a clue, or it may have been something you said. On the other hand, you can be fairly sure that *something* went wrong at the point they criticize.

This is true no matter what you think and no matter what your conjurer friends think. It is true whether your lay critics are intelligent or stupid. You are preparing a routine for the public, and the public contains a large percentage of fools. The only way to gauge audience reactions in advance is to find out how laymen actually react. If you are concocting a new dog food, the opinion of a battery of French chefs is worthless—you must try it on a jury of dogs.

Your friends' criticisms may hurt your feelings, but never let them suspect it. If they do, they will stop telling you the truth. On the other hand, do not put much weight on one layman's opinion. Get several to criticize your routine. Individuals may have freak prejudices. You cannot hope to please everyone.

This book deals with methods of creating illusions by the magic of drama. Some of these methods, especially those concerned with showmanship, can be adapted to tricks as well. If you are primarily interested in appealing to children, sales prospects, or conjurers, you must decide for yourself how far my suggestions apply. On the other hand, if you are interested in entertaining the general adult public, I feel confident that convincing illusions will be far more successful than any collection of tricks, however puzzling.

Chapter 2

DECEPTION VS. CONVICTION

A trickster's chief aim is to deceive his audience about the way his tricks are done. With rare exceptions, a stage director makes no attempt to deceive and could not hope to succeed if he tried. Everyone knows that actors wear makeup, that the scenery is painted canvas, and that the offstage thunder, battle, or train wreck is merely a sound effect. Nevertheless, the fact that the whole audience recognizes these things as fakes does not keep them from being convincing.

Conviction differs fundamentally from deception. Successful deception results in unquestioning belief. Conviction requires only what is called "suspension of disbelief." The playgoer never regards the events of a drama as real; he merely fails to disbelieve in them. This may seem like a weak basis for illusion, but the result can be overwhelming. If the minds of audiences did not permit a suspension of disbelief, there would be no drama.

Although conviction normally vanishes within a few seconds after the routine ends, this need not be the case. Many people accept *Dial Information* as evidence of telepathy, and *The Strong Man's Secret* will leave most observers with the belief that you can hold two pieces of string together no matter how hard spectators pull on the outer ends. A trick which lacks meaning rarely achieves any conviction at all.

Conviction can occur without deception. When someone is shot in a play, the spectators are convinced that the *character* is killed but they are not deceived into believing that the *actor* is dead. A ventriloquist's audience is never deceived; it does not think the dummy is alive. Nevertheless, the conviction of life is irresistible.

Conviction without deception is not confined to actors and ventriloquists. Thousands of fortune-tellers and spirit mediums do nothing more deceptive than speak in a normal tone of voice. In spite of this, they are able to convince their dupes that they are oracles of fate or that they can make contact with the happy dead.

Unlike these illusionists, the conjurer must employ some deception. He needs it to disguise his device. Thus, Robert-Houdin deceived the Arabs when he made them think his hollow balls of wax were solid lead. But he merely convinced them that he was bulletproof.

Even when an illusion requires no trickery, we must deceive the audience in order to disguise the fact that no device exists. For example, most bridge players are convinced that singletons (only one card of a suit in a hand of thirteen) are comparatively rare. Actually, at least one singleton will appear in five deals out of six. If you merely demonstrate your ability to deal singletons, astute spectators will realize that they were wrong in believing singletons to be rare. We can avoid this by applying the principle of conservation and weakening the effect through hinting at other explanations. In such cases, I like to suggest two possibilities, one magical and one rational. Even though the magical one is incredible, it helps to divert attention from the true solution.

THE SINGULAR SINGLETONS

This is based on an idea by George Blake which first appeared in *Magic Magazine*, an English publication. The routine is wasted on those who do not play bridge. They would not be surprised if a singleton appeared in every hand. However, those who do play bridge usually find it completely astounding.

After a card game, take a small object from your pocket and finger it. When someone asks about it, explain that it is a "toad stone" and quote Shakespeare's words from *As You Like It*,

> Which like the toad, ugly and venomous,
> Wears yet a precious jewel in his head.

Actually, the "stone" is a flattish pellet of plastic wood dyed green with food color.

Inform your listeners that such "stones" are extremely rare. "Not one toad in ten thousand has one." Sorcerers used to call such a stone "stelon," "crepaudia," or "batrachos," and wealthy noblemen had them set in rings as "antivenins" or defenses against poison. You doubt if they gave much protection, but they undoubtedly bring luck and have helped you to win money on bets.

At this point you say, "For example, how often do you deal a singleton ? Once in ten hands ? A dozen ? Twenty ?" Let everyone guess. Few will

THE SINGULAR SINGLETONS

Place stone on back of deck. Take packet of cards from the face. Shuffle some on top of stone and some under it. Do this several times. Whenever stone works its way to face of deck, return it to the back and continue shuffling.

Stone

10.

guess under ten, and some may guess over twenty. When they have given their opinions, offer to bet that with the aid of your toad stone, you will deal at least one hand with a singleton.

Without waiting for the bet to be covered, shuffle the deck around the stone using an *overhand shuffle* (Fig. 10). Return the stone to your pocket. Hand the deck to the person who showed the strongest belief in the rarity of singletons. Tell him to deal four hands, face up. While he does so, remind him that he claimed a singleton would turn up, say, in only one out of fifteen deals and that he should therefore be glad to give you odds of at least ten to one.

Once in six deals, there will be no hand with a singleton. When this happens, say, "That was just a come-on. Would you like to bet now?" and repeat the process. Occasionally, no hand will show a singleton, but one will have only three suits. In this case, remark that the shuffle must have rubbed too much luck off onto the cards.

Although the "stone" has no effect on the cards, it has a profound effect on the minds of the audience. It deceives even the shrewdest spectator into believing that the singleton appeared because of something that you did during the shuffle. No one who thinks along those lines has any hope of discovering the true secret.

REALISM VS. FANTASY

Conjuring imitates the impossible, but some impossibilities are plausible enough to make at least part of the audience accept them as true. Few people who witness *The Strong Man's Secret* doubt that the performer is really holding two strings against a strong pull. Such illusions are *realistic*. They are offered as authentic phenomena, and the spectators may take them seriously without being unduly credulous.

Plausibility varies with the performer, the situation, and the individual spectator. People may be so impressed with Dunninger's personality that they accept his telepathic powers, whereas they would be highly skeptical if a less commanding *mentalist* presented precisely the same act. You can convince many spectators with *Dial Information* in your own home, but only the most gullible would take it seriously as part of a club performance that included taking a rabbit out of a hat and *Sawing a Woman in Half*. Again, some spectators who accept

The Strong Man's Secret without question may be merely entertained by *Dial Information* or vice versa.

Realistic illusions are comparatively rare. Most routines come under the head of *fantasy*. Fantastic conjuring lulls an audience into the frame of mind in which we view fantasy in the theater. No one questions the magic in Shakespeare's *Tempest* or *A Midsummer Night's Dream*. We simply accept it. Spectators cannot be expected to take fantastic conjuring seriously, but they should be entertained rather than incredulous.

In many cases, you can present the same basic illusion as either fantasy or realism. The choice depends partly on your personality and partly on the type of audience. The two routines that follow employ the same device and have the same fundamental pattern. In spite of this, they will impress the layman as two separate illusions—although you should not offer both at the same sitting.

I SCRY

Place the cards in front of a spectator and tell him to give you approximately one third. Take this packet, but do not look at it. Tell your victim to lift off another third and to count the cards in the remaining pile. Count your own cards one at a time onto the table so that their order is reversed. This leads the helper to count in the same way. Have him put his packet beside the one on the table. Place yours so that his packet is in the center (Fig. 11). Tell the spectator to turn the cards on the end packets face up.

Announce that you are a "scrier," one who is able to divine unknown facts by staring at a drop of ink. Scrying originated in Scotland and is a kind of poor man's crystal gazing. It works just as well and costs almost nothing.

Squeeze a drop of ink from your fountain pen onto a white saucer. Stare at it while you put your fingers lightly on the two outside packets. Mumble to yourself for a few seconds and then name the top card of the center packet.

Have someone choose either outside packet. If he selects the one with the second known card on its face, "scry" the card. If he takes the other packet, turn it face up, rest your fingers on the exposed card and "scry" the second known card.

To work this you merely note the top and bottom cards before you begin. The *business* of counting the cards confuses the spectators and keeps them from remembering the location of the cards in the deck. As you know the top card of the middle packet and the bottom card on one side packet, you are able to "scry" both cards.

I Scry will be regarded as fantasy unless your audience is unusually gullible. The next version is realistic and will be

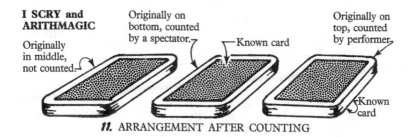

I SCRY and ARITHMAGIC

Originally in middle, not counted.

Originally on bottom, counted by a spectator.

Known card

Originally on top, counted by performer.

Known card

11. ARRANGEMENT AFTER COUNTING

taken seriously by many people—especially those who stand in awe of mathematics. It requires some mental agility and a little talent for mental arithmetic. However, it employs an extremely useful principle and one which has been entirely neglected in modern times. Casanova, the great lover, supported himself in luxury for years by using arithmetic to spell out the answers to the questions of his dupes. If you learn to handle such calculations in your head, you will be able to invent illusions on the spur of the moment. All you need is five or more numbers to start with and an answer which is known to you and which can be expressed in numerical form.

ARITHMAGIC

Proceed exactly as in *I Scry* until the cards are in the positions shown in Fig. 11. Talk constantly while the cutting and counting are being done. Explain that no matter how well the cards are mixed, they are related to each other by mathematical formulas. Announce that Jacks count as 11, Queens as 12, and Kings as 13. Let us assume that one end packet contains 16 cards and has a four face up on top. The other face up card is a Jack, and there are 19 cards in its packet. You then have eight numbers that you can use:

4 for the four.	17 for the uncounted pile.
11 for the Jack.	52 for the whole deck.
16 for the pile with the four.	4 for the four suits.
19 for the pile with the Jack.	3 for the three piles.

These numbers can be added, subtracted, multiplied, or divided. If necessary, you can halve one, double it, or take its square root. With all these possibilities, you can always arrive at any result from one to thirteen. This lets you appear to determine the denomination of the card on the center packet by arithmetical calculation. Thus:

IF KNOWN CARD IS:	SAY:
Ace	"11 plus 4 equals 15. Subtract this from 16 for the four pile. That leaves 1."
2	"11 plus 4 equals 15. Subtract this from the 17 for the center pile. That leaves 2."
3	"11 plus 4 equals 15. Subtracting 3 for the three piles

23

	gives you 12. Divide by 4 for the four suits, and you get 3."
4	"11 plus 4 equals 15. Subtract this from the 19 for the Jack pile. That leaves 4."
5	"11 plus 4 equals 15. Divide by 3 for the three piles, and you get 5."
6	"11 plus 4 equals 15. Subtract 3 for the three piles. That leaves 12. Half of 12 is 6."
7	"4 from 11 is 7. Adding 3 for the three piles makes 10. Subtract that from the 17 in the uncounted pile, and you get 7."
8	"11 plus 4 equals 15. Subtract 4 for the four suits and 3 for the three piles. That leaves 8".
9	"11 plus 4 equals 15. Divide by 3 for the three piles and add 4 for the four suits. That gives you 9."
10	"4 from 11 is 7. Add 3 for the three piles, and you get 10."
Jack	"11 plus 4 equals 15. Subtracting 4 for the four suits leaves 11."
Queen	"11 plus 4 equals 15. Subtracting 3 for the three piles gives you 12."
King	"11 times 4 is 44. 19 plus 16 equals 35. Subtracting that from 44 leaves 9. Add 4 for the four suits to get 13."

After you announce the denomination of the known card, have a spectator turn over the top card of the center pile to prove you are right.

Offer to repeat. Tell a spectator to choose either of the end packets. You know the card on the bottom of one of these. If he picks it, say that you will compute the denomination of its bottom card. Then have him turn the other outside packet face up to reveal its bottom card. If he chooses the outside packet with an unknown card on its face, tell him to turn this over. Then proceed to compute the denomination of the card on the bottom of the remaining outside packet. You cannot use the same "formula" that you did before. If anyone notices this, say, "There are twenty-six different cases depending on which cards are exposed, and you have to remember them all. That's why so few people do this stunt. Theoretically, I could name the suit, too, but that requires a hundred and four different formulas. I never took the trouble to memorize them."

CONVICTION AIDS DECEPTION

Conviction not only makes your performance more impressive, it makes deception much easier. This is why Frederick Tilden was able to fool the conjurers who saw him in *The Charlatan*. Their conviction that the lawyer was trying to expose Cagliostro kept them from suspecting the actor who played the lawyer of being Tilden's assistant.

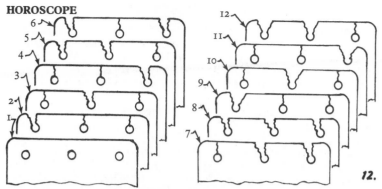

12.

Code notebook sheets by tearing small bits from around certain holes. Make a central tear at each hole to avoid ripping off bits of paper by accident. Dog-ear the unprepared sheet behind the last one coded. That makes it easy to locate the first uncoded sheet. Tear out this uncoded sheet along with the coded ones. As the first and last sheets are actually torn, no one will suspect preparation. Distribute sheets to the spectators in the order of their seats. This is natural and makes it easy to remember which person got which sheet. Note that each sheet can be identified even if some spectators write on the backs of their sheets.

When a conjurer performs a trick, he usually says, or at least implies, "I'll bet you can't guess how I do this." That presents the trick as a puzzle and challenges the spectators to solve it. Some spectators accept the challenge. The harder they try to find the answer, the more likely they are to succeed.

On the other hand, when we claim a supernormal power, we deny that a secret device exists. If we can convince the audience of this, even momentarily, all suggestion of a puzzle disappears and there is no thought of a challenge.

In the following example, many people will accept the astrology as genuine. Even the skeptics will not regard the routine as a challenge. They may begin to feel puzzled after you have given a few "readings." But, by that time, it is too late for them to have any chance of penetrating your secret.

HOROSCOPE

This goes best with a party of eight or ten people, including some whom you have just met. It should be introduced at a moment when conversation lags.

Mention the subject of astrology. Remark that you have no faith in its ability to predict the future, but it does seem to provide a good deal of information about a person's character. "For example, I've never known a Sagittarian who wasn't a bit odd. No two of them were odd in the same way. Some were geniuses, some were screwballs, but each one was peculiar in his own fashion."

If you are asked to give astrological readings at this point (and you probably will be), say, "I know most of you so well that you'd think I was cheating if I just asked your birthdays. So let's work it this way. Each of you write your birth date on a slip of paper." Distribute slips from your notebook and add, "Mix them so that I can't tell who wrote which slip."

Take the leaves from the person who shuffled them. Pick up one at random and say, "May 3rd, that's Taurus the Bull—about the middle of the sign."

Go on to describe the person's character. If you are doing this before a group of friends, they will recognize the person after the first few items that you mention. If the person described is a stranger, he will soon begin to show signs of self-consciousness. Grin at him and remark, "You're May 3rd, aren't you?"

Give several more "readings" but stop as soon as your audience will let you. After three readings, everyone except the person who is being "read" begins to be bored.

The secret lies in the fact that the leaves from the notebook are coded as shown in Fig. 12. This lets you identify each spectator with his sheet, and you can read his birthday from the sheet. Once you have that information, you merely describe the person concerned and dress up the description in astrological terms.

SIGN	STARTS	SIGN	STARTS
Aries, the Ram	Mar. 21st	Libra, the Balance	Sep. 23rd
Taurus, the Bull	Apr. 20th	Scorpio, the Scorpion	Oct. 24th
Gemini, the Twins	May 21st	Sagittarius, the Archer	Nov. 22nd
Cancer, the Crab	Jun. 22nd	Capricorn, the Goat	Dec. 22nd
Leo, the Lion	Jul. 23rd	Aquarius, the Water Bearer	Jan. 20th
Virgo, the Virgin	Aug. 23rd	Pisces, the Fishes	Feb. 19th

Ascribe any quality you like to any sign. If you state that generosity is typical of those born under Leo, and someone says, "I thought Leos were supposed to be stingy," reply loftily, "You've been misled by the nonsense of the Neapolitan school. Read Anstruther's *The Stars in Their Courses*. He'll set you straight." Few people will argue against a printed authority—even one that you invent on the spur of the moment.

When a birthday falls near the beginning or end of a sign, ascribe some influence to the nearest sign. Thus, August 27th is in Virgo, but it is near Leo. You can therefore say that the spectator's character is basically determined by Virgo but affected by Leo. This avoids problems in case two people are born under the same sign. If a man and a woman have the same birthday, give a different reading for each sex. If they are both of the same sex, do not give either one a reading if you can avoid it. When you are forced to say something, try to find qualities which they have in common.

The most superficial conviction is enough to keep spectators from feeling challenged and to divert their minds from the puzzle. Furthermore, when you dramatize a routine, people are so absorbed in what you are doing that they have little or no attention to spare for how you do it. Obviously, an audience which is not trying to see through your deceptions is easier to fool. Compare the trick in the next section with the illusion which follows it.

PASSE-PASSE DICE

The performer displays two silk hats and two large dice. One die is black with white spots, and the other is white with black spots. The dice are so large that they just fit the hats. The performer raps them together to prove that they are solid. He places a die in each hat, says a few magic words, and removes the dice. They have changed places. He again raps them together to show their solidity. Figs. 13 and 14 reveal the secret.

PASSE-PASSE DICE

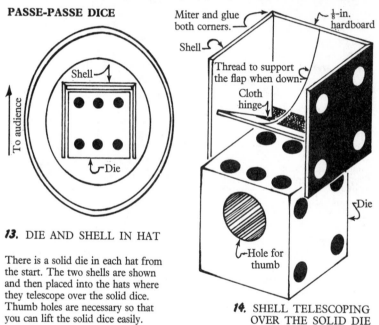

13. DIE AND SHELL IN HAT

There is a solid die in each hat from the start. The two shells are shown and then placed into the hats where they telescope over the solid dice. Thumb holes are necessary so that you can lift the solid dice easily.

14. SHELL TELESCOPING OVER THE SOLID DIE

In this trick, the performer seems to have achieved the impossible, but the impossible is rather dull. The only real interest lies in his implied challenge. The spectators feel that they are engaged in a contest with him; he tries to fool them, and they try to detect his method. If they succeed, they are disappointed in the trick; if they fail, they feel frustrated.

Let us now convert this into an illusion. The conviction will not be very deep. Nevertheless, it minimizes the puzzle, denies the existence of a challenge, and keeps the spectators so busy wondering what is going to happen that they are not even curious about how it will be achieved.

Our new version will not stand by itself. The whole act must be built around a single idea of which this is only one example. However, that is an asset, not a liability. Each routine will strengthen both conviction and interest. That will make the later illusions much more impressive than they could possibly be as separate items.

THE HAUNTED CONJURER

The stage is set for a second-rate conjuring act with conventional apparatus. Present your opening number in a hesitant manner as though expecting something to go wrong any minute. Something does go wrong in a funny way. Grin sheepishly and apologize for your nervousness. You have a good excuse for it. Last night, you attended a musician's jam session and criticized the horn player. Unfortunately, he turned out to be a voodoo obeah man from New Orleans, and he put some sort of mumbo-jumbo whammy on you. "Of course," you insist, "I don't really believe it, but . . ."

Soon, a trick goes wrong in a way which must be due to the obeah man's magic rather than to your simple conjuring. You struggle valiantly on, getting more and more upset and funnier and funnier. Do not let the obeah man interfere with every trick, but he should play at least three jokes on you. This version of *Passe-Passe Dice* is typical:

Proceed as in the earlier version up to the point where you put the dice into the hats. Make sure that the audience remembers which die is in which hat by saying, "White on your right." Or you might have one white hat and one black one.

Announce that you will make the dice change places. Mumble your magic words. Glance apprehensively into the hats to make sure that the dice have really changed. Raise your head with an assured smile. Reach into both hats at once without looking and bring up—two guinea pigs! The one on the left of the audience is a white guinea pig with black spots and the other is a black guinea pig with white spots. You changed the dice, but the obeah man turned them into guinea pigs.

The guinea pigs take the places of the solid dice and are in the hats from the beginning. You will need to make little containers for them (Figs. 15–20). Otherwise they will not be in the right positions for you to slip the *shells* over them (see Fig. 14).

ATMOSPHERE

The first step toward conviction consists in inducing a suspension of disbelief. That is done by establishing an *atmosphere* in which the illusion will seem plausible. In a play,

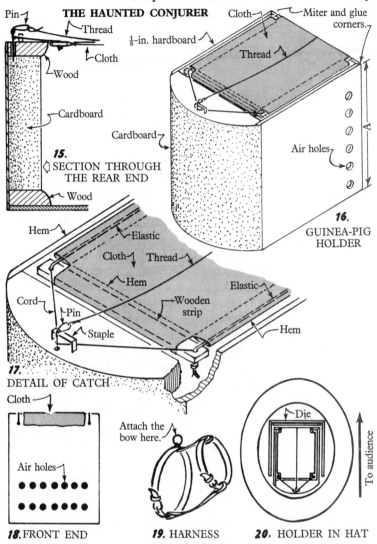

THE HAUNTED CONJURER

Pin

Thread

⅛-in. hardboard

Cloth

Wood

Cloth

Miter and glue corners.

Thread

Cardboard

Cardboard

Air holes

A

15.
◁ SECTION THROUGH THE REAR END

Wood

16.
GUINEA-PIG HOLDER

Hem

Elastic

Cloth

Thread

Hem

Elastic

Cord

Pin

Wooden strip

Hem

Staple

17.
DETAIL OF CATCH

Cloth

Air holes

● ● ● ● ● ● ●
● ● ● ● ● ● ●

18. FRONT END

Attach the bow here.

19. HARNESS

Die

To audience

20. HOLDER IN HAT

Dimension *A* is ⅛ in. greater than the height of the shell. When the threads are lifted, they pull the pins clear. This releases the cords, and the elastics flip the cloth tops back giving instantaneous access to the guinea pigs. These must wear harnesses like that in Fig. 19 so they can be lifted out of the containers without fumbling. Hide the harnesses with bows of ribbon.

the scenery and lighting provide atmosphere almost automatically. However, unless a conjurer is fortunate enough to have a big stage production, he must supply his own atmosphere.

Atmosphere controls the state of mind in which the spectators view your performance. Anything that makes them think about the strange power you are about to manifest will help to create or maintain the proper atmosphere. Thus, talk about freak shows prepares your audience for a strong-man stunt, and a discussion of telepathy, even by a skeptical group, establishes a mental attitude that finds *Dial Information* hard to resist.

LENGTH

Obviously, you cannot create atmosphere in a moment—especially for a realistic routine where you hope to secure fairly deep conviction. This means that illusions are normally much longer than tricks. *The Wizard* rarely lasts over three minutes. *Dial Information* may run for twenty, counting from the first mention of telepathy to the moment when the "telepath" hangs up and the spectators turn to some other topic.

Many conjurers will regard this as a fault. In fact, "the briefer the better" has become a maxim with both professionals and thoughtful amateurs. Hence, anyone who advocates greater length must be prepared to present powerful arguments.

To some extent, the belief in brevity is based on a failure to distinguish between the nature of a routine and the nature of an act. I agree that most acts are too long. However, we can remedy this by using fewer routines; it does not follow that the individual routines should be shorter.

The brevity-is-best rule seems to be supported by a much sounder maxim which reads: "Always send them away wanting more." But that is a one-sided view. We can observe this maxim by giving them less than they want; we can also observe it by making them want more than we give them. The latter policy is clearly better.

Finally, I agree that most tricks are too long. However, this does not mean that length is bad in itself, but rather that the length of a dull trick is due to padding it with dull material. If all the material were interesting, it could be ten times as long and still make the spectators want more. One of the best ways to make them want more is to eliminate padding and add meaning. Atmospheric material adds meaning. It can also be interesting in its own right.

As far as "impromptu" routines are concerned, I submit that *The Strong Man's Secret* and *Dial Information* prove my point. If you have enough interesting material to contribute, you and your friends can discuss a subject like freak shows or extrasensory perception for ten or fifteen minutes merely as conversation and find it pleasant and stimulating. This would be true even if you stopped without doing the string stunt or calling your "telepathic" friend. In both cases, the conjuring adds an exciting climax. Nevertheless, the fact that the conversation can be thoroughly entertaining without the conjuring shows how little reason we have to cut our routines short at all cost.

Horoscope proves the same point. In this case, the character readings come after the conjuring. Nevertheless, they can hold your audience spellbound. Of course, the readings must interest everyone. If they are dull, or appeal only to the individual whose character is being analyzed at the time, you will be a bore.

Far from feeling that routines should be as short as possible, I am convinced that we should try to find interesting material which will make them longer. No really short routine can arouse a high degree of interest. Suppose I could perform a genuine miracle. Suppose I could bring a troop of elephants into each ring of a circus and then make them all vanish in the twinkling of an eye. That would be astounding. No one who saw it would ever forget it. But it would not be entertaining. The crowd would watch the elephants come in. It would wonder what was going to happen. Then, suddenly, the elephants would be gone. The whole thing would be over before anyone had time to work up much interest.

Interest, like atmosphere, must be built up. If you need more proof, get a volume of *The Best Plays* series from your local library. This contains synopses of all plays produced in New York. Read the synopses of a few hit plays. You will find that although the plays themselves ran for years and entertained thousands, the synopses are deadly dull. The reason is that a synopsis gives only the bare bones, and the bare bones of a play are no more attractive than an X-ray picture of a beautiful girl.

Most tricks strip a routine to the bare bones. An illusion rounds these out with flesh. However, the flesh must be firm and smooth. Padding and digressions should be thought of as fat and warts, and should be ruthlessly eliminated.

CREATING ATMOSPHERE

The process of establishing the appropriate atmosphere for an "impromptu" illusion can almost be reduced to a formula. Arouse interest in some topic connected with the illusion. Encourage spectators to increase their interest by contributing to the conversation. Try to start an argument between the spectators. Bring the discussion around to the specific power that you plan to exhibit. If possible, lead someone to challenge you. *Although conviction is weakened when you challenge the spectators to see through a trick, it is strengthened when one of them challenges you to display your powers.*

All the "impromptu" illusions described so far follow the formula. *Dial Information* begins with a general discussion of extrasensory perception and leads up to a specific experiment designed to test the "telepath's" ability. *The Strong Man's Secret* introduces the broad topic of freak shows and works around to a point where the performer is urged to exhibit his stunt. In *Horoscope*, the preliminary conversation first deals with fortune telling in general and becomes more and more specific until the "astrologer" consents to give character readings.

This formula for building atmosphere has many virtues. It tends to lull spectators into the frame of mind which suspends disbelief. It helps to conceal your devices by focusing attention on *whether* you can achieve the promised result rather than on *how* you will achieve it. The formula also provides interesting conversation and permits you to test the mood of your audience before committing yourself. If you mention, say, fortune telling and no one shows an inclination to pursue the topic, you would be foolish to present *Horoscope*. On the other hand, if the spectators seize on the idea, *Horoscope* can become the climax of the conversation and may render it memorable.

Although the same principles apply to stage and club conjuring, practical difficulties arise. Conversation, the main atmosphere-builder in "impromptu" work, cannot be used. With rare exceptions, the style of presentation must be fantastic —which makes the suspension of disbelief more difficult. Finally, a formal act must maintain a faster pace. An expert comedian may talk for several minutes before he actually does anything, but he must be really expert.

Many performers are so conscious of these handicaps that they make no attempt to create atmosphere but start immediately with some trick. Without atmosphere, there can be no suspension of disbelief and hence no illusion. In a silent act, for example, the performer may enter in the black and white of evening dress. A cigarette suddenly appears in his right hand. As he places it between his lips, a gesture with his left hand provides a burning match. He lights his cigarette. When he waves the match to extinguish the flame, it becomes a white silk handkerchief. A touch transforms this into a rose, which he attaches to his lapel. He pushes the cigarette into his left fist leaving half of it in full view. He snaps his fingers and draws out the cigarette which has now become a black wand with white tips.

This is hardly baffling, but it is not intended to be. The very fact that it is not spectacular weakens and may even eliminate any suggestion of a challenge. At the same time, it establishes the performer as poised, competent, and polished. It also establishes him as a magician rather than a mere conjurer. He is not doing tricks for the audience. He is magically supplying his own wants by creating things from nothing or transforming them from something else.

This is the way audiences expect a magician to behave, and the way a "real" magician would be presented in a well-staged play like *The Charlatan*. By living up to the expectations of the spectators, the conjurer has caused them to suspend disbelief and has prepared them to accept the more important illusions which will constitute his main act. Finally, the appearance of the wand announces that the preliminaries are over and that the real show is about to begin.

The above opening is not everyone's meat. If you doubt your ability to be poised and polished, you will be wiser to establish your personality and your atmosphere with a brief, amusing talk. For example, you can bow and remark that you have the world's finest job: "Plenty of opportunities to travel, and it doesn't cost a cent. I do it all with my little magic wand."

Display the wand. Then take a road map from your pocket and open it. Say, "When I want to go anywhere, all I have to do is to spread a map on my trunk, find the town that I plan to visit, and place the tip of my wand on that spot." Start to touch the map by way of demonstration. Jerk back the wand

and exclaim, "Oops! Have to be careful though. If I'd touched the map that time, I'd have been in . . ." Peer at the map and add, "Montana!"

This takes twenty-five seconds. It presents you as a pleasant, amusing personality, creates an atmosphere of fantasy, and lulls the audience into a state of mind which suspends disbelief. Also, it is clearly marked as a prologue. As soon as you say "Montana!" the audience is prepared to have you offer some magic.

THE ETHICS OF CONJURING

Realistic illusions raise the question of ethics. Conjuring, like poker, has its own code; some deceptions are permissible, others are unforgivable. No one expects a poker player to tell the truth about the cards he holds. However, if you try to deceive by dealing from the bottom of the deck, you may get shot and you will certainly be shunned. A conjurer is allowed to lie about his methods but not to leave his audience with the belief that he really possesses supernatural powers. Men like John Scarne and Frank Garcia spend much of their time exposing dishonest gamblers, and the magical profession as a whole has done more to combat fake spiritualism than all other groups combined. The difference between a charlatan and a conjurer is comparable to that between a real-life faker and an actor who plays the role of a faker.

Even if ethics were not involved, you would be foolish to delude people about your powers. If you present *Horoscope* and leave your audience with the belief that you are a genuine astrologer, you get no credit for performing an illusion. Furthermore, some spectator will buttonhole you later and bombard you with questions that you cannot answer. When some trusting soul asks, "Is my husband true to me?" or "Should I make this investment?" you have no advice to give. But if you refuse to give any, your questioner is sure to think you lack the will to help him and cannot be convinced that you lack the power.

The conjurer needs both deception and conviction. Where does the deception cease to be legitimate and become both unethical and a source of future embarrassment? Fortunately, the answer is easy. We should deceive our audiences about our devices but merely convince them about the supernormal powers we imitate. The deception should be permanent; the conviction should never be more than temporary.

When you give a realistic presentation, by all means convince the spectators as thoroughly as possible. However, disillusion them at the end of the session. As you are about to leave, make some remark like "Don't tell anyone that my friend is a long-distance mind reader. They won't believe you. Besides, it was all done with mirrors." This eliminates any deceit, but it reveals nothing about how the effect was achieved. On the contrary, it creates a new mystery. You have amazed your friends by presenting a strange phenomenon. You now astonish them by divulging the fact that they cannot credit what they saw.

Another, and perhaps better, method is to end the evening with some simple trick which is unmistakably conjuring and which can delude no one into crediting the existence of supernatural powers. Then say, "I give you my word that this is just as much real magic as the telephone stunt was real telepathy.

Of course, illusion-breaking devices are unnecessary after fantastic routines which only a fool would believe or for cases like *The Strong Man's Secret* where you claim no exceptional power but give the illusion of doing one trick when you are actually performing another.

Chapter 3
THE MEASURE OF MEANING

The interest that an audience takes in any routine will depend largely on its *theme*. The value of any theme depends in turn on its interest for a particular audience. If a majority of the people present want their fortunes told and have at least a half-hearted belief in astrology, *Horoscope* has a powerful theme. But if you try to present it before a group of professional astronomers, who resent the whole idea of astrology, it will fail completely.

Most tricks have the same theme: "The performer does something that seems impossible." The nature of the impossibility is of secondary importance. What really counts is the lack of a rational explanation. This theme supplies interest but cannot make it rise very high, nor can such a theme sustain interest for more than a few minutes at most. No matter how breath-taking the climax may be, it comes at the end. Hence, it has no effect on the interest while the trick is going on. Furthermore, if any interest remains after the climax, it concerns only the. method used. The phenomenon itself is dismissed at once.

The situation in an illusion is entirely different. The theme involves freak-show secrets, telepathy, or astrology—something that is interesting in its own right. This interest is aroused immediately and can be sustained indefinitely if properly handled. It does not depend on the climax, except that a weak climax would be disappointing.

The themes of plays present difficult problems. The best minds in the theater disagree about the significance of *Hamlet*. Fortunately for us, the themes of illusions all follow the same simple pattern. Routines, such as *The Haunted Conjurer*, which provide surprise endings usually have two themes, but both of these take the stock form.

Every conjuring theme has four elements:

Who is involved? The *personalities.*

What is being exhibited? The *phenomenon.*

Why is the routine performed? The *purpose.*

How is the purpose achieved? The *proof.*

Let us analyze a few examples:

Dial Information. Personalities: the performer, his friend the telepath, the spectator who chooses the coin, the one who talks on the telephone, those described by the telepath, the other spectators. Phenomenon: telepathy. Purpose: experiment to test telepath's powers. Proof: telepath states value and date of coin, and describes two spectators.

The Strong Man's Secret. Personalities: the performer, two helpers, the audience. Phenomenon: stunt used by strong men in freak shows to display extraordinary strength. Purpose: demonstration. Proof: helpers are unable to pull pieces of string apart although performer merely nips them between a thumb and two fingers.

The Haunted Conjurer. This has two themes: (1) Personalities: a second-rate conjurer, his audience. Phenomenon: ability to perform a conventional trick. Purpose: demonstration. Proof (never given): performance of trick. (2) Personalities: a voodoo obeah man who has cursed the conjurer, the conjurer himself, his audience. Phenomenon: effect of obeah man's curse. Purpose: revenge. Proof: trick goes wrong in surprising but appropriate way.

As you read the illusions in this book, ask yourself: (1) who is involved, (2) what power is displayed, (3) why the display is made, and (4) how the power is proved. Do this for your own routines as well. Unless you are able to answer all four questions, you cannot hope to achieve the most interesting presentation.

THE PERSONALITIES

Robert-Houdin defined a conjurer as an actor playing the role of a magician. This supplies a valuable insight into the nature of conjuring, but it is too narrow. Although the conjurer must normally be an actor, he is by no means limited to the role of a magician. In "impromptu" work, he usually plays himself but pretends to possess some special ability, characteristic, or knowledge. Thus, in *Horoscope*, he poses as an astrologer. In *Dial Information*, he expresses his skepticism about the telepathic powers of his friend. In *The Strong Man's Secret*, he is not even an actor. He not only appears as himself, but his claim is literally true. He offers to demonstrate a method of faking exceptional strength and does exactly that.

A stage performer has a much wider range of roles. He can play a magician or a mind reader. He can demonstrate amazing devices from the world of tomorrow. In *The Haunted Conjurer*, he even impersonates a conjurer. However, that conjurer's personality differs sharply from the performer's own, his ability is decidedly inferior, and he is under a voodoo curse.

Many illusions permit a choice of roles. Thus, you can pose as a strong man yourself and use the method of *The Strong Man's Secret* to validate your claim. Again, in *Dial Information*, you can pretend to be psychic and transmit a message to your friend. Although these roles are less promising than those described with the routines, special circumstances may make them ideal. For example, if your muscles bulge and you already do a series of strong-man stunts, you may present the string demonstration as a feat of strength and not as a trick.

Such variations are important. Do not jump at the first role which suggests itself. Explore the possibilities and select the one that is best adapted to your own personality, your audience, and the conditions under which you perform.

Although the most important personality is the one portrayed by the conjurer himself, the others must not be overlooked. The obeah man in *The Haunted Conjurer* and any freak-show performers mentioned in *The Strong Man's Secret* should be made to seem as real as good actors make offstage characters seem in a play. If you have assistants, they must also be given roles. Failure to do this explains why so many assistants are more of a distraction than an asset. Lastly, the roles of the spectators deserve consideration. In *The Strong Man's Secret*, they are onlookers observing a supposedly serious demonstration. In *The Haunted Conjurer*, they form an audience which has gathered to watch an exhibition of conjuring, but which is lucky enough to see some genuine voodoo magic instead. In *Horoscope*, they are "sitters" listening to each other's fortunes. Each of these roles calls for an entirely different attitude on the part of the audience.

The Phenomenon

Many routines also permit a choice of phenomena. The basic plan of *Horoscope*, for example, can be used for any phenomenon which depends on connecting each spectator with a particular object, date, or number. These include:

Graphology. Read characters from handwriting.

Doodleology. Read characters from doodles.

Psychometry. Read characters by touching small objects belonging to individuals. Objects are first hidden by being wrapped in coded sheets from your notebook.

Taste Profiles. Have spectators list their favorite colors, flowers, film stars, and so on. Pretend to base your analysis of each person's character on his choices. Somewhat similar "profiles" are widely used in industrial psychology. Hence, this can be made to seem highly scientific and will impress people who would laugh at astrology.

These are only samples, but they demonstrate the folly of building your routine around the first phenomenon that occurs to you. Whenever you work out a routine, list every phenomenon that you can find. Try out the most promising ones on audiences and note which theme arouses the most interest. The result may surprise you. Any relationship between the illusions you like to present and those that your audiences like to watch is purely coincidental.

Remember also that audiences differ. The best theme on earth can fall flat if you use it on the wrong audience. The most successful play I ever staged bored two audiences so badly that they walked out before the third act. There was nothing wrong either with the performances or the audiences; they simply did not suit each other.

The fact that every basic routine offers a choice of themes permits you to adopt your presentation to your audience. If you use *Horoscope* before most adult audiences, you might switch to *Taste Profiles* for an audience of business and professional men who pride themselves on being hardheaded. For children, *Doodleology* would be a wiser selection.

The Purpose

Except in cases like *The Haunted Conjurer*, which have two themes, the purpose is always the pretended purpose for presenting the routine. The performer's real motive may be a desire to entertain or simply a wish to show off. This does not, or at least should not, affect the theme-purpose, which is invariably false.

Probably 95 per cent of all professional routines and 75 per cent of *all* routines are demonstrations. Most of the rest are experiments. Do not confuse the two. The man who gives a demonstration knows, or believes that he knows, exactly what the result will be. The experimenter is trying to learn what will happen. He may feel confident of the result, but cannot be sure until he tries the experiment. He may even turn out to be wrong. Thus, in *Dial Information,* you propose an experiment which you claim will prove the telepath to be a fake. Much to your "surprise," he passes the test with flying colors.

Experiments are more entertaining than demonstrations. They give the spectators a sense of participation. They introduce an element of uncertainty, which is inherently dramatic. An experiment that fails may still be interesting; a demonstration that fails simply falls flat. Experiments are also more convincing. They permit much greater use of suggestion, and they weaken the idea that the performer is merely doing tricks.

Unfortunately, experiments are largely confined to "impromptu" work. The stage or floor-show performer is expected to know exactly what he is about and not to take up time with untried experiments. Furthermore, experiments normally require detailed explanations. These can be highly interesting when time permits, but the professional must make every second of his act count.

Mentalists usually combine demonstrations and experiments. They claim supernatural gifts but admit that these are not under control. The act as a whole demonstrates the powers of the performer. However, each individual "test" is an experiment; will the power work this time or will it fail?

Make sure that the audience knows whether you are offering a demonstration or conducting an experiment. You need not always use the actual words, but never leave any doubt as to your purpose.

Other purposes occur, but they are rare. This does not mean that we can afford to overlook them. On the contrary, their very rarity gives them a freshness that can be attained in no other way.

One purpose, which should be much more common, is that of putting magic to some practical use—such as providing you with a match and a cigarette. As this is the sort of thing that a real sorcerer would do, it helps to build atmosphere. The silent opening on p. 33 has already provided an example. Such *applied magic* can be used at any point in a routine.

Another, and somewhat more common, purpose is the lesson. Lessons in magic usually prove popular with both children and adults. Here is one example:

THE EXPANDING RABBIT

When a layman thinks of conjuring, he thinks of taking a rabbit out of a hat. Curiously enough, this illusion is rarely performed. It is sometimes imitated by taking silk handkerchiefs from the hat and then lifting a rabbit from the silks. However, you can spend a lifetime among conjurers without seeing anyone display an empty hat, pull out a rabbit, and then show the hat still empty. Our example does exactly that. The basic principle was suggested to me by Ed Mishell and the late Sabar.

After a boy has helped with a routine, thank him and declare that he appears to have talent for magic. All he needs is a few lessons. Would he like to learn how to take a rabbit out of an empty hat?

THE EXPANDING RABBIT

21. STUFFED BABY "RABBIT"

The baby is made of rabbit's fur stuffed with sponge rubber. The pull goes up your sleeve. Get the baby in your hand before you start the routine. Let it fly up your sleeve when you put your hand into the hat.

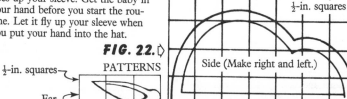

FIG. 22.

Hand him a high hat. Explain that the first step is to make sure that the hat is really empty. Let him look into the hat. Take the hat back and place it on your table. Confess that a magician cannot really pull a rabbit from a completely empty hat. You must first put the rabbit into the hat. The difficulty is to get the rabbit in without letting anyone see you do it. You accomplish this by using a very small rabbit—one small enough to hold in your hand without being detected.

Open your left hand and display a baby rabbit. As you do this, take the hat from the table with your right hand.

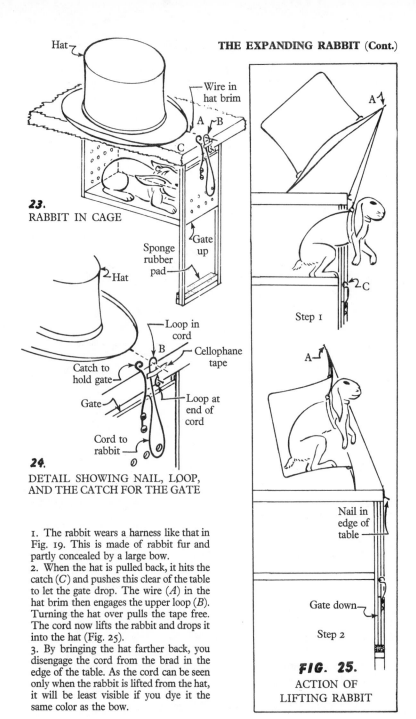

23.
RABBIT IN CAGE

24.
DETAIL SHOWING NAIL, LOOP,
AND THE CATCH FOR THE GATE

Step 1

FIG. 25.
ACTION OF
LIFTING RABBIT

1. The rabbit wears a harness like that in Fig. 19. This is made of rabbit fur and partly concealed by a large bow.

2. When the hat is pulled back, it hits the catch (*C*) and pushes this clear of the table to let the gate drop. The wire (*A*) in the hat brim then engages the upper loop (*B*). Turning the hat over pulls the tape free. The cord now lifts the rabbit and drops it into the hat (Fig. 25).

3. By bringing the hat farther back, you disengage the cord from the brad in the edge of the table. As the cord can be seen only when the rabbit is lifted from the hat, it will be least visible if you dye it the same color as the bow.

"Now, then," you say, "I hold the little rabbit so that it is completely hidden and put it into the hat." Do so and add, "Here's where the magic comes in. I pronounce the ancient Egyptian name of power, 'Ulapaga Karkhenmu Mamuremukahabu!' The rabbit grows, and grows, and grows—and behold!" Lift the rabbit from the hat and hand the hat to the boy. *Never hold a rabbit by the ears; they are delicate and tender.* Put your hand under his body.

When you use livestock always treat each animal as a cherished pet. Even if you are not guided by humanitarian motives, this is good showmanship. A large percentage of your audience is made up of animal lovers. They enjoy seeing animals petted and bitterly resent even a suggestion that they are not handled gently. Consideration for your livestock may slow up your act and decrease its *flash*, but kindness to animals has its own sentimental appeal. Also, no one will rehire you for roughness, but many spectators will condemn you for it and will refuse to recommend you even though they were delighted with the rest of your act.

Figs. 21 and 22 explain the baby rabbit, and Figs. 23–25 show how the live rabbit gets into the hat. If you like this routine, I recommend beginning with some version which omits both the toy rabbit and the boy. Simply take a real rabbit from the hat. That will let you use both hands for *loading* the rabbit into the hat. When you can accomplish this smoothly, you will be ready to attempt the one-hand manipulation required by *The Expanding Rabbit*.

A few illusions may be represented as *contests*. This adds a sporting element which has a strong appeal for most audiences, even though they feel sure that the performer will win. Here is a *quickie* that you can use to squelch some boy who shows signs of becoming a nuisance:

THE BEST BET

Get the boy up on the stage and say, "My next demonstration requires a rope with three knots in it. Can you tie a knot?" When he says, "Sure," give him a rope and let him prove it. Have him tie a second knot.

Display another rope and ask, "Are you a sport?" He will almost certainly claim to be one. Offer to bet that you can tie three knots in your rope before he can put one more knot in his. If he wins, you will teach him how to pull a rabbit out of a hat. If you win, he must keep quiet for the rest of the show.

The boy will take some time to tie his knot. You tie three knots by simply tossing one end of the rope away from you. Figs. 26–28 explain the method. Face the audience and remark, "Useful thing, magic."

THE PROOF

The effect of your illusion should be proof or at least strong evidence that the power you claim is genuine. Conjurers often claim powers that they cannot prove. For example, a glance

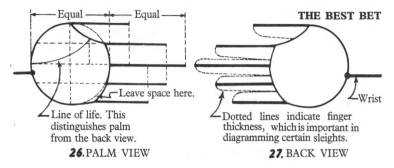

— Equal — — Equal —

⌐Leave space here.

⌐Line of life. This
distinguishes palm
from the back view.

26. PALM VIEW

THE BEST BET

⌐Wrist

⌐Dotted lines indicate finger
thickness, which is important in
diagramming certain sleights.

27. BACK VIEW

Diagrammatic Hands for Use in Making Notes

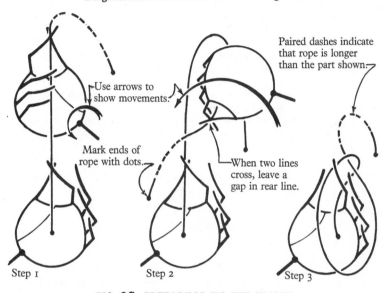

⌐Use arrows to
show movements.

Mark ends of
rope with dots.⌐

Paired dashes indicate
that rope is longer
than the part shown.⌐

⌐When two lines
cross, leave a
gap in rear line.

Step 1   Step 2   Step 3

FIG. 28. PREPARING TO TIE KNOTS

As you gather the rope into your hands,   shown. Take End *A* in your right hand.
casually make three loops like the one   Drop the rest. Three knots will form.

through any dealer's catalogue will reveal a number of *divination* tricks. The performer announces that he can read minds or
perceive hidden objects. To justify this, he displays a set of
special dinguses which have obviously been turned out by a
manufacturer of conjuring apparatus, and which look like
nothing else on earth. A spectator selects one. They are hidden
in some way. The performer then triumphantly names the one
selected. This is supposed to be proof that he is psychic.
Actually, the audience regards it merely as proof that he has
bought a trick from a dealer.

The popularity of such tricks with performers suggests that the idea behind them may be fundamentally sound. Let us see what we can do with one.

Our illusion will certainly be more convincing if we confine ourselves to commonplace objects. Ordinary lead pencils will do if they are just alike except for the colors of the enamel. You can buy hexagonal pencils enameled in red, yellow, brown, green, and blue. They may or may not have erasers, and they need not all be the same length. However, they should all be sharpened in the same sharpener to make their points identical. Hold your hands behind your back. Have a spectator choose a pencil and let you feel the enamel near the point. You then name the color.

The second weakness in commercial divination tricks is that the performer claims to have general extrasensory perception but is able to demonstrate it only in one specialized case. His claim is too broad for his proof. The illusion will be much stronger if we conserve by weakening the claim until it matches the proof. You can do this in the present example by dropping any claim to psychic powers but insisting that you can recognize color by touch.

We are now ready to work these ideas into a routine.

CHROMAVOYANCE

Have your lead pencils ready in your home or office. If you carry a set of pencils in your pocket, you will arouse suspicion. Begin by remarking that the eye is not the only organ of light; the whole skin is light-sensitive as well. This will start an argument. Defend your position by pointing out that the skin can feel heat radiation, which is nothing but infra-red light. As this is undoubtedly true, it creates a suspension of disbelief.

Say, "You can do it with other colors, too. Didn't you ever touch something and know that it was red or yellow?" Show surprise when the spectators admit that they have never felt a color.

Speak half to yourself as though you were trying to find an explanation for this strange lack of ability in your friends. "Of course, it doesn't work in the dark. You can't feel color without light any more than you can see it without light. And when there is light, you know what color a thing is before you touch it. If you don't use a sense, it grows weaker. Besides, you can't get much of a color sensation except from shiny objects, and most objects are dull."

It now occurs to you that you may prove your point by letting your friends feel the colors of some shiny objects. What is handiest? Oh yes, pencils. You "manage" to find four or five.

"Anyone," you declare, "can tell red from blue. Red gives a much stronger sensation because it is closer to infra-red in the spectrum."

Have someone shut his eyes and try the test. When he fails, let the others experiment in turn. If you do this seriously, you will have your audience torn between the idea that you are indulging in an elaborate joke and the belief that they could distinguish color by feel if their sense of touch were not deficient.

While you are "experimenting" on the audience, someone will probably challenge you to give a demonstration yourself. If no one does challenge you, offer to prove your color-sensing ability. Turn your back. Put your hands behind you. Have someone let you feel a pencil near the point. If it is red, announce it quickly. If it is blue, say, "I don't get any sensation at all from this. Did you sneak in a black pencil on me? No? Then it must be blue or purple."

The secret is simple. Pencils with water-soluble colored "leads" are available at art stores in almost every conceivable hue. Get those with "leads" that match the enamels on your lead pencils. Wet the colored "leads" and rub some of the color off on the sides of the corresponding lead pencil near the point. When you make your test, moisten a finger slightly, rub it on the chosen pencil, and bring that hand where you can see it while you continue to feel the pencil with the other hand. As soon as you see the stain on your finger, you are prepared to announce the color of the pencil.

This is a splendid example of how the magic of drama can turn a weak two-minute trick into ten minutes or more of absorbing entertainment and leave half your audience convinced that you really do have a sense of color touch. It does require some acting ability, but so does every kind of drama.

Although weak claims are best when the proof is weak, you should always look for stronger proof—even though it means inventing a new effect and a new device. Routines like *Chroma-voyance* fall into the same general class as telepathy and clair-voyance. If you like this sort of thing, say to yourself, "Suppose I really had clairvoyant power. What is the strongest proof I could offer?" A reasonable answer would be, "Have a spectator make a drawing. If I reproduce that without seeing it, no one can ask for more conclusive evidence." Is this an impossible requirement? By no means. Here is one way to meet it:

MENTAL TELEVISION

Announce that you are about to perform an experiment in mental television. Hand someone a ball-point pen, a sheet of paper, and a paperback book to serve as a drawing board. Tell him that he is to sketch a simple diagram or picture. You will then endeavour to reproduce it.

Explain that this is done by clairvoyance, not by telepathy. You cannot read his mind; you visualize the actual drawing itself. He must, therefore, restrict it to a few lines in order to keep your vision from becoming confused. Also, he must make the lines good and strong. Otherwise, you will have difficulty. Your vision is dim at best. You can liken it only to a television picture that is slightly out of focus and covered with "snow."

As soon as he has completed his drawing, tell him to fold it and put it into his pocket. Take the pen and book from him and place another sheet of paper on the book. Concentrate intensely and reproduce his drawing on your sheet of paper. Hand your drawing to a second spectator. Then tell the first one to open the original and give it to the person holding yours. After this person has compared the two, instruct him to pass them around so that everyone can see how closely they resemble each other.

MENTAL TELEVISION

29.
SPECTATOR'S DRAWING

30.
MENTALIST'S "COPY"

When anyone makes firm lines with a ball-point pen on a piece of paper placed over a paperback book with a shiny cover, the design is impressed on the cover. This can be seen only while the book is held at exactly the correct angle to the light. Before performing at home, experiment with your lights so that you can quickly tilt the book at the correct angle and take in the sketch with one glance. When working away from home, begin by placing a piece of paper on the back cover of the book and making a few notes. Hold the book at different angles until you can read your notes. Do this before you even mention clairvoyance. Otherwise, you may discover that the lighting arrangements are impossible or that you have picked up an unsuitable book. Have the spectator use the front cover as his drawing board.

In making your own drawing, never copy exactly. If you do, someone may suspect that you have a secret source of information. Here is another case where conservation pays; reproduce the general outline, but interpret it differently. Thus, the crude drawing of a girl in Fig. 29 may be copied as an even cruder sketch of a tree (Fig. 30). This type of copy often crops up during serious experiments in clairvoyance. It therefore makes a strong impression on anyone familiar with the literature on the subject.

Mental routines like this can provide "proof" which comes close to being ideal. In most other types of illusions, however, the proof is normally less than perfect. After you have found the best available proof, ask yourself whether it is adequate to convince the average spectator temporarily. If it fails to reach this level, weaken your claim or abandon the routine.

Although you should always look for ways to prove the strongest possible claim, this does not mean that a strong claim is necessarily better than a weak one. *Chromavoyance* may well be more entertaining than *Mental Television*. Its fresh theme makes it especially interesting and keeps spectators from automatically classifying it as a conventional mind-reading trick. Moreover, it permits a presentation which gives the impression of being reasonable and as nearly scientific as circumstances permit. *Mental Television* might seem suspect even if it were genuine; *Chromavoyance* looks genuine even though it is actually faked.

TREATMENT

Some themes permit only one *treatment*. *The Haunted Conjurer* requires a light touch. Both *Chromavoyance* and *Mental Television*, on the other hand, will fall flat if they are not presented with the utmost seriousness.

Other illusions offer a wide range of treatments. *Horoscope* can be presented in deadly earnest; the conjurer poses as a fanatic whose mission in life is to convince the world that astrology is a valid and exact science. At the opposite extreme, he may pretend to make fun of the whole thing by introducing a cheap, paperback book on astrology and jesting about "all those heavenly rams, bulls, and virgins." He then goes into a burlesque of the routine on p. 25, pretending to take his character readings from the book. However, the spectators soon notice that although his readings may be funny, they are also remarkably accurate. Given the right audience and a skilful presentation, this can create an even stronger impression than a serious treatment would make.

Treatment applies to both the theme and the presentation. They are usually handled alike, but you may treat the theme seriously and the presentation lightly or vice versa without seeming to contradict yourself. In *Horoscope*, for example, you might pretend to be on such intimate terms with astrology that you can afford to joke about it. Introduce the subject in all earnestness and then make your readings amusing by giving them a comic twist. Conversely, you can joke about astrology and then say, "But the really funny thing is that the darn thing works. I'll show you." Then proceed to offer serious readings.

The treatment of a routine deserves all the thought you can give it. A well-chosen treatment may turn a silly trick into a near miracle.

The conjurer who appears before audiences of different types should vary his treatment to suit each audience. When he presents a routine for his fellow conjurers, he can offer it simply as a puzzle. When he entertains children, a fantastic treatment will be appropriate. When he performs for adults, he may adopt a serious attitude.

Chapter 4
WHO ?

Themes are so important that we could give only a bare out-line in the previous chapter. We are now prepared to examine them in detail and consider some of the more interesting varia-tions. The number of purposes is limited, and we have already covered all the common ones. However, each of the other theme elements offers a wide range of possibilities. Many of these are almost never exploited by conjurers. They therefore offer welcome opportunities to the performer who wants something different. This chapter deals with the personalities who should be considered when planning a routine.

THE CONJURER'S ROLE

We have seen that the conjurer is not limited to imperson-ating a magician. Actually, except when performing for chil-dren, the role of a magician has little to offer. It is obvious, hackneyed, and implausible. Furthermore, audiences expect "real" magic to have a purpose, but it is difficult to find any plausible purpose for most routines—even when a fantastic atmosphere has been firmly established. Why should a magician make a bird cage disappear, saw a woman in half, or take a rabbit from an empty hat ? Even the most credulous observer finds trouble in believing that the possessor of mysterious powers would waste them on such meaningless trifles.

Spectators at an "impromptu" performance are even less likely to credit the conjurer with magical powers—especially when some of them know him personally. Under these con-ditions, the shallow and momentary conviction of a routine like *The Singular Singletons* is the most you can expect when you pretend to be a magician.

You can make your task much simpler by limiting your claim to something more plausible than magic. Thus, in

Horoscope, you profess to have studied astrology, and in *Chromavoyance*, you demonstrate your extraordinary sense of color touch. As such things are compatible with your everyday personality, audiences find them easy to credit.

These considerations virtually restrict the "impromptu" performer to one role, Himself. However, even Himself is a role. No good performer is ever completely natural, he just seems that way. He tries to conceal his faults and make the most of his assets. He stresses characteristics which make his presentation more vivid and minimizes those which tell against it. Thus, the Mentalist of *Mental Television* should seem more "psychic" and less earthy while exhibiting his clairvoyant powers than he did while talking politics earlier in the evening.

When you present an "impromptu," think of Yourself as a glorified version of yourself, and add subtle hints that suggest the type of person who might actually possess the powers you claim. At the same time, you must be doubly careful not to overdo your characterization. If the audience becomes consciously aware that you are not literally being yourself, all hope of conviction is lost.

Stage and club work permits a much wider range of roles than does "impromptu" conjuring. Plays like *The Tempest* and *The Charlatan* prove that audiences will suspend disbelief toward magicians if the treatment and the performer's characterization combine to create an appropriate atmosphere. But even here, more plausible roles offer better prospects. They are both fresher and easier to handle.

Thus, you might pose as a Highbrow Lecturer who has been asked to give a popular talk on some profound subject and to include a few simple demonstrations. Shortly after you have received a serious introduction from The Master of Ceremonies, you discover that something is wrong with your apparatus. While you are struggling with it, a curvaceous young woman in tights wanders on from the wings. After watching your misadventures for a few moments, she informs you that you have inadvertently borrowed the apparatus, or *props*, of Marvello the Magician. She, it appears, is Marvello's Assistant. Marvello himself has just stepped around the corner for a quick one. You become interested in the props. The Assistant offers to explain. Her understanding of the mechanism proves less than adequate. More and more things go wrong in improbable ways until the act ends in some major, but comic, catastrophe. If this is worked out in detail so that the effects seem like genuine accidents, and if both performers stay resolutley in character, the result can be hilarious. It would make an especially good act for banquets where the audience is resigned to serious talks but where a comedy-conjuring act would be a welcome surprise.

In the preceding paragraphs, I have capitalized the names of the various characters as they would appear in the script of a play. I shall continue to do so throughout the rest of this book to distinguish the role a person plays from the person himself. Thus, in *The Haunted Conjurer*, "the conjurer" refers to the real and (I trust) highly competent performer, but "The Conjurer" indicates the nervous, thumb-fingered zany he impersonates.

Other promising character roles include:

An Absent-Minded Professor who lectures on chemistry or physics only to have his demonstrations go wrong.

A Psychologist who claims no extrasensory powers but who reads people's minds by observing subconscious subtleties in their behavior.

A Master of Ceremonies substituting for a conjurer who has gotten drunk but claims that any fool can work his tricks by following the directions in "this little book."

GROWING HAIR ON A BILLIARD BALL

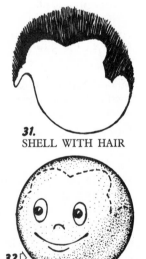

Grease the ball. Paste layers of tissue paper on it with white glue. Paste about three layers and let them dry before applying the next batch. When complete, cut to shape shown and remove from ball. Most large drugstores carry crepe hair. Unravel two or three inches. Wet and iron until straight. Glue to shell end-on. Draw the features on the ball with a magic marker or get an artist friend to do it. Have the bare side of the ball toward the audience. Conceal the shell in your left hand. Slip this on the ball as you pick it up and pretend to draw the features. Sprinkle the ball with Swamp-Root Remedy. Finally, turn it around and uncover it to reveal the face and hair.

31.
SHELL WITH HAIR

32.
BILLIARD BALL

A Pitchman who attempts to sell something, such as "Dr. Simpson's Sympathetic Swamp-Root Syrup—cures dandruff, glanders, leprosy, and housemaid's knee. Can also be used as a sheep dip, and—when mixed with three parts of water—it makes a refreshing, nonalcoholic beverage." Comedy acts of this nature offer many opportunities to introduce conjuring while demonstrating the marvels of the product. Thus, you could guarantee that Dr. Simpson's Sympathetic Swamp-Root Syrup will grow hair on a billiard ball, and then prove it by using the paper-mâché shell shown in Figs. 31 and 32.

A whole series of roles may be found among people who have developed some ordinary faculty to an extraordinary degree. Strong men, jugglers, pickpockets, and card sharps come under this head. So do memory experts and lightning calculators. As people with these talents actually exist, the routines disarm any suspicion of trickery when presented realistically. These roles permit so much variety that routines based on any one of them can be combined in a unified act. Here is an easy example:

NUMBER PLEASE

If you can borrow a desk calculator and secure the assistance of a friend, this provides a real novelty for an amateur vaudeville show. You will also need a large pad of newsprint like those used in chalk talks, an easel, and a black crayon.

Remark that modern bookkeepers use machines and have lost the power to do mental arithmetic. You belong to the old school as you propose to prove. Ask each spectator in the front row to think of a number with from one to seven digits. Each person is to announce his number as you point at him. Speed is important. Point to the first spectator. Write his number with your crayon, repeating it aloud as you do so. Immediately point to the second spectator. Write his number. Draw a line and write the total from left to right.

Your friend in the wings does the actual adding on his machine. As soon as he has the total, he writes it on a sheet of cardboard where you can see it. Multiplying and dividing large numbers is equally easy and equally effective. Give your concealed assistant a table showing squares, cubes, and square- and cube-roots. He must practice using these rapidly, but the ability to extract the cube root of, say, $79,507$ (43^3) almost instantly makes a tremendous impression on people who have trouble balancing a checkbook.

Look for ways to add showmanship. For example, have a series of numbers called out as in the adding demonstration, but let each Caller decide whether it is to be added or subtracted. Another good stunt is to have one or two secret friends in the audience propose difficult problems to which you already know the answers.

CASTING YOURSELF

Young conjurers often pick some famous performer and then imitate him in every possible way. This is a sure road to failure. Slydini's act is built around his off-beat personality and his accent. If you could duplicate each word and move precisely, you would not get Slydini's results. If Mark Wilson coached you as his understudy, you would still not be Mark Wilson.

Every competent performer tailors his act to capitalize on his virtues and conceal his faults. You have a different set. Dr. Faust's beard goes well with his commanding figure. Even if a thinner man could grow an equally heavy beard, it would make him look like a poet or a beatnik and not like Dr. Faust.

The imitator's failure is not due to lack of ability but to the fact that he has attempted the impossible. Neither Dr. Faust nor Mark Wilson could imitate Slydini, and neither would be foolish enough to try. Why should you rush in where they would not dream of treading?

Even when a beginner avoids copying a particular idol, he often chooses a role because it flatters his ego instead of asking whether it suits his personality. Actors frequently display the same mania, but producers usually prevent Elvis Presley from playing Hamlet or Jackie Gleason from appearing as Romeo. Conjurers have no such safeguard. One of the most ardent young conjurers I know fancies himself as a suave, sophisticated, society entertainer. His top hat and tails fit his body, but they make his personality look silly. The sad thing is that he was designed by nature to portray the type of wistful bungler that made stars of Harold Lloyd and Jerry Lewis. If he cast himself in such a role, he could be a hit, perhaps a big hit. As long as he attempts to impersonate a man of the world, he is foredoomed to failure.

Casting is never easy, and casting yourself is doubly difficult. Few of us, even in our most candid moments, have the power to see ourselves as others see us. Your wisest plan is to take several roles, big or little, in amateur plays under a competent professional director. After he has seen what you can do and how audiences react to you, ask his advice. He may not be able to select your best characterization, but he can probably keep you from picking one which is hopeless. Unfortunately, this procedure is necessarily slow and not always practical. The next best plan is to ask a number of people, including some who are not close friends, to name several roles in current films or television programs that they believe you could fit. Write the answers down; you might forget those which fail to flatter you, and these are the very ones which are most likely to prove useful. When you have collected several dozen suggestions, try to classify them. Are the roles comic or serious? Lowbrow or highbrow? Light or heavy? Warm or cold? Are they character roles or *straight* parts? If they are character roles, what type or types predominate?

I am not advising you to count votes and adopt the role that most people seem to favor. Your best friends may be wrong, and a seemingly freak suggestion by a near stranger may be just what you need. Nevertheless, the recommendations from other people will give you at least some help in viewing yourself objectively. If no one considers you a comedian, your chance of succeeding as a purveyor of Dr. Simpson's Sympathetic Swamp-Root Syrup will not be good.

Ordinarily, you should make your role *sympathetic*. The audience should like you and see the routine from the stand-point of your character. However, there are exceptions to this rule. In *Dial Information*, for instance, you pose as a man who wants to lure his Telepathic Friend into a trap. This is a dirty trick, and you should make the audience aware of the fact. That will make them sympathize with The Telepath and let them rejoice when he triumphs in the end.

Although you should normally create a sympathetic characterization, there is no advantage in making it admirable. An audience does not need to admire a role in order to admire the performer. Jack Benny lost nothing by portraying a tightwad, and Bob Hope has done nicely while impersonating a long series of featherbrained cowards. If you try to make The Conjurer of *The Haunted Conjurer* strong and able, you will fail unless you turn the act into a dramatic struggle between The Conjurer and The Obeah Man. That would be an almost impossible task. However, if you are a wise enough showman to make The Conjurer comically incompetent, he can be highly amusing.

At the same time, remember Aristotle's warning and "never make a character unnecessarily bad." Your Conjurer should be weak, frightened, and a little awkward because those qualities make him funny. However, nothing is gained and much is lost by making him sloppy, stupid, or vulgar.

To sum up: create a character that the audience will enjoy watching in the routines you perform. Avoid qualities which merely flatter your own vanity or provide excuses for laziness. Give him any faults that will make the routine more effective, but eliminate every undesirable characteristic which does not clearly add drama or comedy to your act.

Casting Your Audience

Like the individual performer, each audience is limited to a comparatively small number of roles. An audience of believers in extrasensory perception will play its part in a test of telepathy, whereas one composed of skeptics may never get into character. Just as you must select a role for yourself that fits your personality, you must select a role that fits the makeup of your audience. People who do not play bridge cannot appreciate *The Singular Singletons* but may perform their parts perfectly during *Chromavoyance*.

Even when the spectators are well cast, you must put them in character by creating and maintaining the proper atmosphere. Everything that occurs during the session affects this atmosphere. If someone in a social gathering has done a series of card tricks, your chance of succeeding with *Mental Television* is negligible. If you start a stage act with impressive mental effects, the *Expanding Rabbit* or *The Haunted Conjurer* will strike a sour note and throw your audience completely out of character.

Audience roles cannot be characterized explicitly. You should, however, be able to cast your audiences in one of a half dozen broad categories:

Onlookers for exhibitions like *The Haunted Conjurer* or a contest along the lines of *The Best Bet*. Onlookers are not expected to do anything but suspend disbelief and enjoy themselves.

Witnesses to a demonstration such as *Number Please* or an experiment like *Mental Television*. In theory, at least, these are supposed to reach independent conclusions just as though they were watching a demonstration of some new household appliance or a genuine scientific experiment.

Participants in an experiment. In *Dial Information*, for example, the whole audience is asked to concentrate on the date of the coin because collective thoughts are more apt to be transmitted than those of an individual.

Prospects to whom the performer pretends to sell something.

Pupils whom the conjurer tries to teach how a trick is worked so that they can use it to fool their friends. *The Expanding Rabbit* is one example. This role normally stresses trickery. Hence, it must be handled with caution or it will make conviction impossible. Either teach something that is not supposed to be a trick or make the trick secondary, as it is in the case of *The Haunted Conjurer.*

Finally, the audience as a whole may be cast as *Victims of Mass Hypnosis.* Many conjurers use this idea, but they do so halfheartedly. That is dull without being convincing. The two illusions which follow treat mass hypnosis with the seriousness which it deserves.

Begin by stating that many of the feats attributed to Eastern magicians are probably nothing more than demonstrations of mass hypnosis. Travelers have taken pictures of magicians' tricks, but when the print was made, it did not show the marvel that the photographer was sure he had seen. Only the lightest stage of hypnosis is needed for this sort of effect.

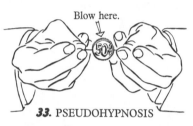

Blow here.

33. PSEUDOHYPNOSIS

The magician can bring the spectators to this stage merely by having them watch a bright object for a short time. Offer to demonstrate. Arrange the light so that it falls on you. Pick up a half dollar between two pins and blow on it (Fig. 33). It will spin merrily. Tell the spectators to watch the coin. When it stops spinning, assure them that they are now in a mild hypnotic trance.

SNIFF-SNIFF

Have someone draw a glass of water and ask him to smell it. He does so and reports that it smells like any other water. Smile and ask what he expected. Then say, "Just put it on the table." Ask another spectator if he has a good sense of smell. Do not use him unless he says, "Yes," or the illusion may fail. If he claims that his sense of smell is good, assure him that the liquid in the glass is whiskey. Prove it by holding the glass under his nose and letting him sniff. Repeat this with the third spectator but inform him that the glass contains ammonia. Hold it under his nose, and he will admit that it certainly smells like ammonia.

The illusion is created by rubbing a little whiskey on your right forefinger and a little ammonia on your left. Hold the glass in your right hand to give the scent of the whiskey and in your left to provide the smell of ammonia. Of course, any two sharply distinct odors can be used.

Before anyone asks you to make him smell roses or garlic, start another routine with a hypnotic theme. The next example will do nicely.

THE SINGING GLASS

Have someone choose a card and show it to the other spectators. Make sure that everyone sees and remembers it. Tell the person who chose the card to replace it. Shuffle the deck, and spread it face up on the table. While this is being done, drink the water and prepare the glass as illustrated in Fig. 34. Point out that it is obviously impossible for the glass to recognize the chosen card or to do anything about it if it did. However, as the spectators are now hypnotized, they will all be convinced that the glass sings when it passes over the card. Assure them that the sound will be entirely imaginary.

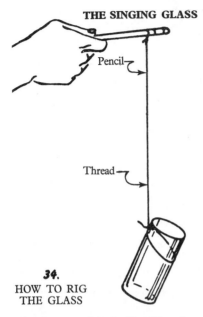

THE SINGING GLASS

Pencil

Thread

34.
HOW TO RIG
THE GLASS

Move the glass along the row of face-up cards. Sure enough, when it reaches a point above the chosen card, everyone receives the distinct impression of hearing a musical note.

Learn what cards are on the face and back of the deck. Have the chosen card replaced on top and the deck cut. You, or a spectator, can give it one quick shuffle. The chosen card will still be between the two noted cards. Other cards may also be there. However, as the glass is not an accurate pointer, it can be two or three cards off and still seem correct.

Make the glass sing by twisting the pencil slightly. This causes the thread to vibrate, and the glass acts as a resonator.

When casting your audience, try to give it the most active role that the situation permits. Thus, in most divination tricks, one spectator chooses an object and the mentalist divines it while the rest of the audience merely watches. In *Chromavoyance*, on the other hand, each spectator is offered a chance to detect hue by touch.

As soon as you decide to perform on some particular occasion, ask yourself what role or roles you can most readily induce your audience to adopt. The simplest procedure is to analyze your probable public by mentally filling out the following questionnaire:

How many people?
Male, female, both?

Average age ? Mixed ages ?
Highbrow or lowbrow ?
Type of occasion: light or serious ?
Previous preferences (if any) indicated by people whom you expect to be present ?
Approximate total time that you can take up and still "send them away wanting more" ?

Your answers will reveal a clear picture of your probable audience. You can then use this as a basis for selecting suitable roles. Once you have determined the roles, choose routines and treatments to match.

That may seem like too much trouble at first, but experience soon makes it quick and easy. In any case, it is well worth while. It improves your chance of convincing the spectators and greatly increases your chance of entertaining them. Above all, it provides invaluable training in the vital art of seeing your performance through the eyes of the audience.

After you decide on the best role for your audience, you must lead it to adopt that role unconsciously. This requires doing two things simultaneously. First, create the appropriate atmosphere. If you fail to convince spectators that *Dial Information* is a serious test of The Telepath's powers, you must not expect them to think and act like Participants. Second, treat the spectators as if their roles were genuine even when the routine is fantastic. The spectators for *Sniff-Sniff* and *The Singing Glass* are cast as Hypnotic Subjects. You cannot hope to make them believe that they are actually hypnotized, but you can persuade them to suspend disbelief if you behave toward them exactly as you would if you had really hypnotized them.

CASTING VOLUNTEERS

When you need a spectator to assist you, it is normally wise to ask for *volunteers*. This does not prevent you from having a free choice. In most cases, you will either get many applicants or none at all. Whatever happens, smile at the one you want and say, "You, sir, will you be kind enough to help me?" Even if he has not volunteered and many others have done so, there is nothing suspicious in this. The spectators know that if you had *planted* an assistant among them, you would have instructed him to volunteer. Hence, they will not accuse you of trickery when you pick a person who has not volunteered.

The reason for requesting volunteers instead of simply drafting someone is that you should give the impression of being willing to accept any member of the audience as a temporary assistant. Unfortunately, many conjurers really do accept anyone. They overlook the fact that in taking volunteers they are casting roles in their acts. Such random casting is enough to make a stage director shudder. Experienced conjurers attempt to secure volunteers who will be cooperative and who will not try to show off, but few performers ever go further than this.

Actually, it is only the beginning. There are no universal rules for selecting "volunteers"—even a show-off may be an asset in some situations. Nevertheless, the following suggestions are usually valid:

In the great majority of routines, try to choose someone who will interest the audience at sight. No performer would paint a piece of apparatus gray. He knows that it would make the act seem dull. Then why should he use a drab spectator?

Pick a pretty girl in a bright dress. However, do not use a real beauty, or the audience will watch her rather than you. A man should be odd in some way that will not suggest either pity or embarrassment. A fat man, or one who is tall and thin, is a good bet. A boy with red hair, freckles, and protruding ears is ideal.

Form the habit of scanning the audience for prospective volunteers as soon as possible. You can do this almost subconsciously. The spectator who catches your eye will also catch the eyes of your audience. Show-offs catch the eye, but they are usually easy to distinguish from people who will be helpful. They may wear loud clothing. They rarely pay close attention to the performer. They may even talk to their neighbors during your act. When you observe any of these symptoms in a spectator, choose someone else.

As soon as you have located the most colorful prospects, mentally assign them to their future roles. Thus, if you have a comedy illusion that calls for two helpers, you might pick a tall thin man and a short fat one. This will automatically make the routine funnier than if both men were of average size.

The variety of minor roles in conjuring routines is limited. The following checklist covers most of those that you will be called upon to cast.

Helpers perform routine services, such as pulling on the string(s) in *The Strong Man's Secret*. They may be chosen merely for convenience. However, even for close-up work it is better to select people whose appearance or personalities will contribute to the interest or amusement of the rest.

A *Subject* draws a card, has his mind read, or has some other direct connection with the supernormal aspect of the routine. Thus, the person who deals the cards in *The Singular Singleton* is A Subject. Credulous people make the best Subjects. Their willingness to believe will influence the rest of the audience in serious illusions like *Mental Television*, and it serves as a source of amusement in fantastic routines like *Sniff-Sniff*. In *The Singing Glass*, all of the spectators act as Subjects. When a number of individual readings are given, as in *Horoscope*, those whose personalities are read or who receive "spirit messages" should be referred to as "sitters." However, there is no real distinction between subjects and sitters.

A *Lender* provides some key article, such as a handkerchief or a dollar bill. His function is to guarantee that the item is genuine and is not prepared in any way. Often, he must also testify that the article returned to him is the same as the one he lent. Lenders should be chosen for their apparent integrity. Prefer those who are strangers to you.

If the audience is apt to suspect that your apparatus is faked, one or more *Inspectors* may be appointed to examine it and pronounce it above suspicion. Inspectors, like Lenders, should be people who will convince the other spectators that they are both trustworthy and hard to fool. An obviously stupid or spineless Inspector will not be accepted as a guarantee of your innocence but will be interpreted as evidence of your trickery. Howard Thurston never grasped this point. He would invite a manifestly weak-willed spectator to come onto the stage and ask him to make "a full and complete examination." Thurston then seized his victim by the nape of his neck and rushed him past the danger spot without giving him a chance to inspect anything. This maneuver simply called attention to the weakness of the illusion. If An Inspector will not be convincing, you are better off without him.

In some cases, an inspection must be more or less "official." Houdini's version of *The Needle Trick* would have been weakened if he had not let a committee inspect the needles and thread, and if he had not asked a dentist to examine his mouth. However, except where suspicion is inevitable, inspection is more likely to arouse skepticism than to allay it. When an object looks commonplace, most people will accept it at face value. But if you give the least hint that its innocence is open to question, they assume that it must be fraudulent. Fortunately, you can normally silence doubts by a kind of unofficial inspection. Simply let a volunteer hold the prop while you proceed with another phase of the routine. By audience logic, the fact that the volunteer is free to examine the article proves that there is no fakery for him to find.

When a routine like *The Expanding Rabbit* professes to teach magic, the volunteer is cast as *A Pupil*. In contest illusions, such as *The Best Bet*, the volunteer is *A Contestant*.

Whenever a routine calls for a "volunteer," form a clear idea of his role while you plan your presentation. Try to decide what qualities you would like him to have. Then search for satisfactory candidates as soon as you have an opportunity to look over your audience. You cannot expect to find "volunteers" who match your specifications perfectly. Nevertheless, those whom you choose deliberately will fit their parts much better than would the best ones you could hope for if you ignored the problem of casting and took the first spectator who offered to help.

Once you have your "volunteer," keep him in character by treating him as if his role were genuine. You will do this almost automatically with Helpers or Lenders, but you can easily overlook it when working with Pupils or Contestants.

Chapter 5
MAKING THE MOST OF
ASSISTANTS

No aspect of conjuring has been so neglected as the use of assistants. The theory prevails that an assistant is a sort of animated prop. The Great Man may be compelled to grant her a brief moment of glory while he causes her to float on air or saws her in half. But apart from this, her sole purpose is to wait on him. When not engaged in such menial service, she is supposed to stay out of the way and remain as inconspicuous as possible.

This is poor showmanship. As soon as your assistant appears, the audience notices her and thinks about her. If she does not add to your presentation, she will surely detract from it; there is no middle ground. Unless you give your assistant a role that makes her an integral part of the act, you are better off without her.

Several misconceptions are responsible for the almost universal failure to get full value from the use of assistants.

An assistant cannot function effectively without ample rehearsal. A conjurer often has trouble persuading a girl to assist him at all. If he insists on adequate rehearsals, she balks and threatens to quit. This forces him to reduce her participation to the bare essentials—actions that she can perform without rehearsal.

Something is wrong here. All over the country, girls fight for even the smallest parts in amateur plays. If they are selected, they spend many hours at rehearsal waiting to go through their brief scenes. Why do they find a play so much more appealing than a conjuring act? The answer is that the play offers them genuine roles. These may be small, but they are essential elements of the total effect.

The ordinary conjuring act, on the other hand, uses the assistant as a mere convenience. A girl may rehearse the part of A Waitress in a play, but nothing will persuade her that she needs to rehearse the job of actually being a waitress. The solution does not lie in cutting the assistant's role to a point where she can do without rehearsal. On the contrary, it should be increased to the point where she wants to rehearse.

An exception needs to be noted here. Mental acts that involve assistants often use elaborate codes which must be memorized. For some reason, women object strenuously to this. Few of them will learn a code even when it means the chance of obtaining a leading role.

A second excuse for neglecting assistants is that the conjurer, quite properly, regards himself as the star. He then jumps to the conclusion that he can add to his prominence by suppressing his assistant. This does not work. Instead, he must focus some attention on the girl in order to gain still more attention himself.

No audience can concentrate on one thing for long, and no spectator will even make the attempt. His mind is sure to wander. You can control this wandering by constantly providing some new object for attention. Thus, you may shift the interest of your audience from your face to your hands, from your hands to your words, and from your words to some prop. This is fairly easy when you are alone on stage because there is nothing to compete with the things you do, say, and handle. But when you use an assistant, the case is altered. You cannot prevent her from attracting some attention no matter how inconspicuous she may be.

Actually, an unrehearsed assistant is anything but inconspicuous. She fidgets. She falls into positions which may not be awkward, but which are certainly not graceful. If she pretends amazement at your miracles, the pretense is obvious. If she fails to react, her indifference communicates itself to the audience.

Although you cannot keep your assistant from receiving attention, you can control both its timing and its strength. Throw attention to her briefly but at carefully chosen moments. Give her something to do which deserves that attention. Then have her direct the attention back to you. This is the technique used by star actors. They know that no audience will watch them constantly. A momentary switch to another actor provides relief and gives the star a fresh start.

Intermittent attention of this sort has another advantage. Stars shine by contrast. Audiences realize that you deserve no credit for outshining a waitress-assistant. The stronger the girl is, the more credit you get for remaining the star. Jack Benny summed this up in a sentence. Someone asked why he let Rochester steal his scenes. Benny replied, "I'd much rather have him steal my scenes than have him steal somebody else's." Benny knew that letting Rochester steal a few scenes helps the show. He also knows that he can afford it because he takes five or six scenes to every one that Rochester can steal.

As long as a performer stays well ahead of his support, he is the star. This is easy for a conjurer; he takes most of the attention, he takes it at every important moment, and he appears to do all the magic—or at least all that matters. The man who has those advantages and cannot outtop any assistant on earth had better work alone.

Perhaps the most common, and certainly the most serious, reason for not making full use of assistants is the lack of suitable material. Except for mental routines, where she acts as A Mind Reader, I do not know of a single trick on the market today which gives the assistant a real role. At most, she is mere livestock and differs from a dove or a rabbit only in being larger.

My own ideas on roles for assistants tend to be highly specialized. They are based on the personalities of individual performers and have little value for anyone else. The suggestions that follow originated in the fertile brain of my friend Robert Tilford of Baltimore.

APPLIED MAGIC

Working with an assistant offers many opportunities for quickies in which magic takes care of routine chores. For example, you put a cigarette between your lips and your assistant lights it by striking a match on the other side of the stage. Self-lighting cigarettes are available from dealers, but the use of an assistant is not mentioned in the instructions.

Quickies like this one have many advantages. They are good showmanship in their own right. They give your assistant brief prominence but leave no doubt that you are the star. They enrich the act by adding more magic per minute without turning your performance into a meaningless collection of small tricks. The interchange between yourself and your assistant introduces human interest, which most conjuring sorely lacks. Above all, applied magic is the sort of thing that a "genuine" magician would do. It therefore helps to convince the audience that you really are a magician. If you can establish this conviction, and the atmosphere of fantasy that goes with it, adding a little more showmanship will enable you to offer conventional tricks as demonstrations of magic.

SHARED EFFECTS

There are a number of pretty tricks in which The Magician and His Assistant can share. For example:

FAN-TASTIC

The standard *Dye-Tube* routine may be presented in connection with the *Color-Changing Fan*. Both items are available at most dealers. The Magician displays a sheet of paper. He rolls this into a tube and hands it to The Assistant, who gives him her closed fan in exchange. She pushes a white silk handkerchief into one end of the paper tube. The Magician flicks the fan open. It is green. He waves it at the tube. When the handkerchief emerges at the far end of the tube, it also is green. Presumably, it has been dyed magically by association with the green fan. The Assistant inserts another white handkerchief into the tube. The Magician snaps the fan shut. When he opens it again, it has turned yellow. He waves it a second time, and a yellow-dyed handkerchief appears at the end of the tube. This action is repeated once more. The fan turns red, and the third handkerchief is dyed the same color. The handkerchiefs should match the fan as closely as possible. This will probably require both hunting for suitable handkerchiefs and repainting the fan.

THE CARELESS ASSISTANT

Tricks in which The Magician supposedly makes a mistake are more impressive when his Assistant commits the blunder. A good example is *The Mismade Flag*, which is really another dye-tube trick. The Magician rolls paper into a tube. He calls attention to the fact that The Assistant holds a red, a white, and a blue silk handkerchief. She pushes these into the tube. However, neither of them notices that the blue handkerchief has not been thrust home. It slips out and falls to the floor. The Magician turns the handkerchiefs into an American flag, but as the blue silk was missing, the canton of the flag remains white. The blue silk is picked up. It and the mismade flag are placed in the tube. This time, the flag emerges properly colored.

THE SORCERER'S APPRENTICE

Every character in a play is there for a reason. What is your reason for using an assistant? If she is just a glorified hired girl, her connection with magic is slim at best. Why not introduce her as your Apprentice? Remark that she must study for another five years before she becomes a witch and ten more to be a full-fledged sorceress. In the meanwhile, she earns her keep by doing odd jobs.

Near the middle of the act, you can announce that although your Apprentice is not yet qualified to mix a love philter or put the evil eye on anyone, she has developed some skill with amusing trifles and would like to show what she can do. Our example is a slightly altered version of *The Mismade Flag*, but any convenient trick that appears to go wrong the first time will fit here.

The Apprentice puts the red, white, and blue handkerchiefs into the paper tube and chants, "Aba, athai, abatroy, agera, prosha!"

When she reaches the syllable "-ge-" you wince and remark, "My dear girl. How often must I tell you to pronounce that 'a-gay-rah' not 'a-gee-rah'?" She pouts and insists that she did say "a-gay-rah." You reply, "Very well, continue and see what happens."

She pats the tube, a flag with a white canton and a blue handkerchief come out. Shake your head sadly. Take the tube, put the flag and the handkerchief back in. Pronounce the spell properly and bring out the completed flag.

This is done with the apparatus sold by your dealer, but you will need a duplicate blue handkerchief.

ONE TOUCH OF VENUS

You cannot exploit your assistant's sex appeal unless she has it. But if she does, it can be a great asset. Unfortunately, capitalizing on it without vulgarity requires a good deal of imagination. The following routine will fit many acts. It is also a fine example of how Bob Tilford breathes new life into worn-out tricks. His version is a full-fledged illusion that will fit neatly into a haunted-conjurer act.

TWENTIETH-CENTURY NYLON

Display two green scarves. Tie them together. Give them to your Assistant who puts them in the bosom of her dress but leaves 6 or 8 inches of one hanging out. Pick up a red scarf. Wad it into a ball in your right hand. Announce that you will cause it to fly through the air invisibly and knot itself between the two green ones. When you toss it toward the girl, it has disappeared.

Confidently, take the end of the green scarf and pull. When it clears the girl's bodice, you observe with chagrin that instead of being tied to the red scarf, it is attached to something long and thin. When this clears the bodice, you realize what it is and exclaim, "It's your stocking!"

The Assistant lifts her skirt to see if this can be true and discovers to her consternation that one stocking is indeed missing and that the red scarf is tied around her leg like a garter.

One of the Assistant's legs is bare from the beginning. A duplicate red scarf is tied around this leg. The stocking on the other leg is supported by a girdle or a garter belt. If the girl's skirt comes to the floor, the stockings should contrast with her skin. If the skirt is shorter, the stockings should be almost—but not quite—flesh color. Then, the fact that one leg is bare will not be noticed until attention is called to it by lifting the skirt.

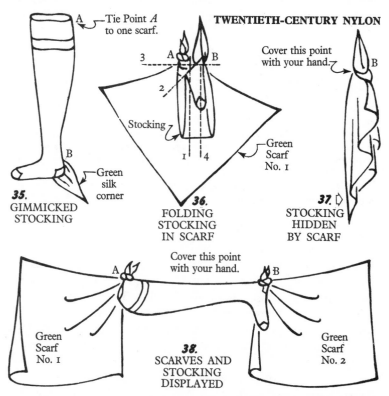

35. GIMMICKED STOCKING

36. FOLDING STOCKING IN SCARF

37. STOCKING HIDDEN BY SCARF

38. SCARVES AND STOCKING DISPLAYED

Cut off one corner of a green handkerchief and sew it to the heel of a stocking (*B*, Fig. 35). Tie Point *A* to Green scarf No. 1. Take several stitches in this knot to keep it from becoming untied. Spread Scarf No. 1. Make Folds 1-5, Fig. 36.

Drape scarf around stocking (Fig. 37). When you perform, knot the unprepared green scarf (No. 2) to the green silk on the heel at *B*. Give both the scarves to your assistant who proceeds to tuck them into her bodice.

Your dealer can sell you a *pull* that will enable you to get rid of the first red scarf. Figs. 35–38 show how to make the stocking appear between the two green scarves.

THE ANTIGRAVITY HAT

Sweatband
Baffle
Water

39 HAT ON TABLE

Rip away a few stitches at the back of the sweatband to let the water out when you empty the hat. Otherwise, some of the water will stay under the band.

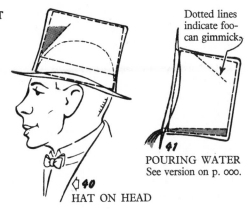

Dotted lines indicate foo-can gimmick,

41

POURING WATER
See version on p. ooo.

40
HAT ON HEAD

THE UNHELPFUL HELPER

A conjurer with a teen-age son soon learns that the boy is not of much value as an assistant. He has little to do, and that little rarely requires his full attention. His mind wanders. He makes aimless movements which distract the audience. As a result, he does far more harm than good.

This can be corrected by giving the boy a real part in the act. I have found only one role which meets the requirements. However, it has decided advantages both from the standpoint of comedy and from that of deception.

The boy poses as A Member of the Audience. He is the first to respond when The Magician calls for a volunteer. Once on stage, he examines the apparatus whenever the conjurer turns his back. By doing so, the boy acts as an unofficial inspector. As he can find nothing wrong, he convinces the audience that the equipment is innocent.

Soon, the boy decides to show off. At this point, a suggestion of Annemann's fits perfectly. He printed this in his magazine *The Jinx*, but as far as I know, it has never been used.

THE ANTIGRAVITY HAT

The Magician's hat is upside down on a table. Near it stands a glass or bottle of some liquid. The Boy yields to temptation. He pours a cupful of the liquid into the hat. This should be timed so that The Magician almost catches him at it. The Magician now does a number in which he wears his hat. But when he puts it on, The Boy is disappointed—no water runs out. The apparatus for this, known as a *foo can*, is shown in Figs. 39–41.

Undaunted by the failure of his joke, The Boy picks up something else, say, a cane, and swaggers about the stage. This time The Magician does catch him. He waves his wand and says, "Betu, Baroch, Maaroth!" The cane disappears. That frightens The Boy so badly that he jumps off the stage, runs down the aisle, and dashes out the door of the auditorium.

Both the conjurer and his son will be tempted to overdo this. It is fatally easy to invent actions which are funny but which give the game away. The act can be amusing if the audience realizes that The Boy is a plant, but it will be more hilarious —and infinitely more convincing—if the spectators believe he is a stranger.

The boy's part should come near the end; just before the final illusion is ideal. The act must be thoroughly rehearsed, and much depends upon the boy's temperament and acting ability. However, under favorable circumstances, this father-and-son act offers a real opportunity.

PAPA'S LITTLE GIRL

A conjurer's young daughters are not well suited to comedy, but they can play a wide range of attractive roles in serious presentations. Here is one possibility for a girl about ten years old.

THE UNBEATABLE DRUM

After the act gets well under way, The Magician announces that he will introduce his Assistant. The child enters dressed as a drum-majorette but has a toy drum instead of a baton. She faces the audience and prepares to beat her drum. On a signal from her father, she strikes the drum with all her force—and the head breaks. As she is on the verge of tears, her father turns the drum over and encourages her to try again. This time she breaks the other head and really does cry. He takes the drum to his table, holding it so that the audience can see through it. The Magician replaces the drumheads with sheets of paper. He returns it to the girl, saying, "Be careful; the new heads are only paper. Don't . . ." But before he can finish, she breaks the head once more. When she starts to bawl, he reaches into the drum and pulls out one toy after another until she has more than she can hold.

The technical details are given in Figs. 42–44. Articles used in loads of this sort must either nest or be compressible. Thus, if you make dolls which consist of silk dresses and thin plastic faces, you can pack one inside the other so that half-a-dozen of them will occupy much less space than a single regular doll. Nevertheless, they will look like ordinary dolls to your audience if you handle them properly and display only one at a time—especially when their costumes are so different that the dolls do not look like a set.

Rubber goods also make excellent production items. These are either hollow shells of latex or are modeled from some highly compressible sponge plastic. Those on the market usually simulate fruit or other

THE UNBEATABLE DRUM

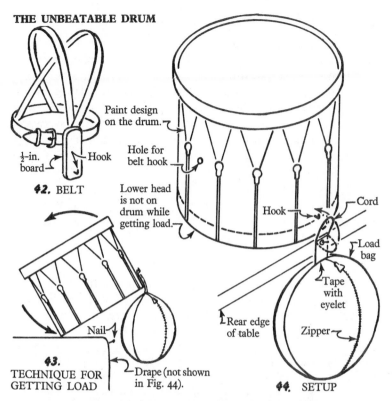

42. BELT

½-in. board

Hook

Paint design on the drum.

Hole for belt hook

Lower head is not on drum while getting load.

Hook

Cord

Load bag

Tape with eyelet

Zipper

Rear edge of table

Nail

43. TECHNIQUE FOR GETTING LOAD

Drape (not shown in Fig. 44).

44. SETUP

The hook on the girl's belt makes it easy to reverse, remove, and replace the drum. The drumheads are paper.

The load is obtained by the method used in *The Expanding Rabbit*, but the procedure is simpler.

edible objects. However, it is easy to cast toys from liquid latex. You will need models. These may be real toys, or you can mold them from plasticine. The only other requirements are latex, latex paint, and plaster of Paris. Most hobby shops carry these, and the clerks can teach you how to use them.

The Assistant as Conjurer

Almost every conjurer has read how the illusions in *The Charlatan* baffled Dr. Tarbell and his friends, but few of them have put their lessons to use. At least half of the material in the average stage act uses mechanical devices which anyone who knows the secret can operate. The best person to do this is the assistant. No one suspects him or her, and most of the time all eyes are focused on the conjurer. The Boy in *The Unhelpful Helper* is an obvious example. The principle is equally applicable to conventional acts. Thus, loading the rabbit of *The*

Expanding Rabbit into the hat is a delicate operation—when the conjurer does it. If the animal squirms violently at the wrong moment, there will be a flash of white fur and the secret is revealed. But if the assistant loads the hat, the danger is nil. The Magician shows the hat empty and gives it to the girl who lays it casually on the table. They both turn to the boy while The Magician displays the toy rabbit saying that it is a baby. No spectator is going to miss this bit. While attention is fixed on the toy, the assistant casually takes the hat from the table, loading the rabbit as she does so. When she hands the hat to The Magician, the hard part is over. The Magician never went near the table, and most of the audience will swear that he held the hat the whole time.

Casting Assistants

The assistant's characterization is as important as the conjurer's own. In fact, the conjurer cannot hope to stay in his character unless the assistant maintains hers. The two roles must be consistent with each other. An Absent-Minded Professor cannot plausibly introduce an eye-filling assistant in tights. However, such a combination is completely believable if she poses as The Assistant to Marvello the Magician.

Do not stop with your first idea for your assistant's characterization. Try to find several different types. Your first thought may not be the best, or it may require a type of girl who is not available. If you want to impersonate An Absent-Minded Professor and cannot persuade any whistle-worthy lass to assist you, do not despair. You can get as much comedy if your Professor is aided by his Middle-Aged Wife or Teen-Age Niece, who does not quite understand what she is supposed to do—and who balls up the Professor's demonstrations even more than he does himself.

Any change in the characterization of your assistant will mean a change in your act. Thus, if you work with Marvello's Assistant, you will need Marvello's props. If you use The Professor's Niece, your props must seem to be things that The Professor might plan to employ for his own "scientific" demonstrations. This means that you must determine both your own characterization and that of your assistant before you plan your act. If you work out the act first, fitting characters to it is a hopeless task.

Even when the girl portrays A Typical Conjurer's Assistant, she must be given a definite characterization. She may be beautiful-but-dumb. This is especially good when she does much of the conjuring; no one will dream of suspecting her. She may be highly efficient, always ready when needed, unobtrusive but alert when idle. She may be a personification of wide-eyed wonder; no matter how often she sees the illusions, she never quite believes that they are really happening.

The role must fit the girl. Do not choose a characterization because you like it or because your assistant likes it. A girl who is completely believable as An Efficient Assistant will convince no one if she tries to portray wide-eyed wonder. This is vital. Unless both you and your assistant feel that her characterization is absolutely right, try something else.

An assistant must react in character to what goes on, but she should never overact. As she has presumably seen the routines many times, surprise on her part is out of place except in illusions where something "goes wrong." This is true even for the wide-eyed wonder type; she can be continually amazed but not continually surprised. When an assistant is placed in peril, as in *Sawing a Woman in Half*, coach her to seem nervous and apprehensive. Her attitude should be, "This magic has always worked before, but my good luck can't last forever." When the danger is passed, have her reveal her relief. In short, whatever role the girl plays tell her to behave just as she actually would if everything that you claim or imply were true.

The assistant who acts as a medium or takes a character role must look and dress the part. This permits a wide range of choices because you can arrange the role to fit the assistant you get. However, if she is to play The Typical Magician's Assistant, she must be decorative and graceful. Your wife, your girl friend, or your maiden aunt may be charming and useful, but unless they look well on stage, they will spoil your act. Youth is desirable but not essential. What counts most is the figure. A slim, white-haired woman of forty is a better choice than a chubby girl of twenty.

SECRET ASSISTANTS

A *confederate* is an assistant who poses as an innocent Member of the Audience. Many conjurers disapprove of using confederates on the ground that it is unfair! This is nonsense. What counts is the illusion. If you can create a better illusion by using a confederate than you can without one, by all means use him.

The real objection to confederates is that they are likely to be suspected. If they are, the illusion is destroyed. On the other hand, when the confederate is not suspected, the illusion can be overwhelming.

In "impromptu" performances, try to avoid employing your wife or best friend as a confederate. When you must use such a person, cast him in a role which makes him seem to be playing a trick at your expense. This is the scheme adopted by Frederic Tilden in *The Charlatan* to convince the audience that his lawyer-assistant was really his enemy. Here is an illusion which depends entirely on this principle.

BOOBY TRAP

After you have performed *Chromavoyance*, your confederate remains unconvinced. You were the one who suggested using pencils in the test, and he suspects that the pencils were faked in some way. You claimed that you could detect the color of any shiny object. He, therefore, challenges you to let him select the object while you are out of the room.

Hesitate, complain that the demonstration requires great concentration and is very tiring, but finally give in.

When you are gone, your confederate says, "I still think he's been tricking us. Let's turn the tables. He'll make a guess and hope to be lucky, but he's bound to name a color. I'm going to cross him up by handing him something white." The confederate "finds" some shiny white object, warns the others not to spoil the game, and calls you back into the room.

You dutifully turn your face away, and he lets you touch the object. Appear puzzled. Take your time and speak half to yourself. "It can't be black or blue or purple because I get a strong sensation. It's strong, but it isn't definite. Red, pink, orange, yellow, brown, green—it feels a little like all of them. But that's impossi. . . . Wait a minute! A mixture of all colors makes white or gray. The sensation's too strong for gray, so it must be white."

This is extremely convincing. It also chokes off anyone else who might want to suggest a test of his own.

An *accomplice* is a concealed assistant—a secret helper who hides in the wings, under the stage, or in a piece of apparatus. the effectiveness of an accomplice depends on the fact that the audience does not even suspect his existence. Hence, a regular assistant cannot become an accomplice merely by walking off stage. In fact, when an accomplice is working, your other assistant(s) should be clearly visible in order to avoid any suggestion that a device is being operated by an unseen member of your troupe. The assistant who operates the computing machine in *Number Please* is a typical accomplice.

Chapter 6

CASTING THE SPELL

Strictly speaking, the term "magic" applies only to phenomena connected with sorcery, alchemy, witchcraft, fairies, superstitions, and kindred fantasies. Although conjuring is by no means restricted to magical themes, these are by far the most common.

Writers of fairy tales or fantastic stories adopt an attitude toward magic which differs sharply from that assumed by the average conjurer. Writers make conviction their first goal; conjurers tend to assume that because no one can be expected to take magic seriously, conviction is impossible and any attempt at it will be futile. Writers know that the over-all impression made by their work depends more on their ability to create an atmosphere of fantasy before they get to the magic than it does on the magic they describe; conjurers normally ignore atmosphere entirely and almost never give it more than a passing thought. The magic in a story always makes sense; a character may change straw into gold from greed or transform a prince into a frog from spite, but story-book magicians never present effects merely to show off. In the whole history of thaumaturgy, no wizard ever did a conventional card trick, made a silk handkerchief disappear, or turned a bottle into a wineglass.

If you have seen many conjurers perform, you know the art has fallen into a rut. I suggest that the writer's approach to magic offers a possible way out.

MAGIC LORE

When a careful author decides to deal with a magical theme, he begins by reading books on witchcraft, voodoo, necromancy, or whatever branch of the subject he intends to treat in his story or play. A hack writer may neglect this approach, but even he bases his ideas on his memory of fairy tales and any scraps of magic lore that may have come his way.

The lore of magic is scientifically false but psychologically sound. Superstitions and magical concepts have survived through the ages because *they are the kind of ideas that people find easy to accept*. Writers go on the theory that the royal road to conviction follows the natural beliefs (and prejudices) of the human race. They imitate "real" magic because it is the sort of material readers are most apt to swallow. The conjurer who ignores "real" magic as a source of clues to credulity will encounter heavy going on an uphill path. He must expect to find conviction difficult.

A study of magic lore can do a great deal for any conjurer. It will give him the *feel* of "real" magic. "Feel" is difficult to define, but every actor knows that it is just as genuine and just as important as the boards of the stage on which he walks.

Esoteric knowledge always impresses people. If you can talk with authority on cantrips and pentacles, rituals and amulets, you can lull almost any audience into a suspension of disbelief in your magic power.

This sort of knowledge cannot be faked. The fact that the spectators are completely ignorant on the subject does not mean that a smattering of information about magical beliefs and practices will fool them. Without real knowledge, mistakes are inevitable; the audience may not detect specific blunders, but the performer's awareness that he is faking plus something in his attitude gives him away. Conversely, when he does know his subject, his self-confidence makes the strongest possible impression on his public.

THE METHODS OF MAGIC

You cannot read much about magic without learning that it has its own strict logic. Except in the cheapest fairy stories, the power is not in the magician but in something that he does, says, or owns. Furthermore, each power has its limitations; before a magician casts a spell, he must know exactly what spell to cast. A spell that can transform a pumpkin into a coach should not be expected to transform lead into gold or even into pewter.

Conjurers usually claim powers themselves. They may eke this out with a flick of a wand or a few "magic words," but I never saw one who made a serious attempt to act like a magician.

The implements favored by "real" magicians varied enormously in detail. Nevertheless, they were strictly limited to a few types. Most of these are easily imitated by the conjurer. As they are excellent devices for creating atmosphere and present almost no drawbacks, I strongly recommend their use as standard practice.

Perhaps the most typical magic item is the "self-working object." A magic carpet is one example. Here is another.

THE SYMPATHETIC PENDULUM

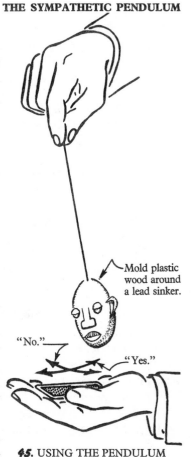

THE SYMPATHETIC PENDULUM

Mold plastic wood around a lead sinker.

"No."

"Yes."

45. USING THE PENDULUM

Display a small but heavy and strangely designed pendulum attached to eighteen inches of cord (Fig. 45). Explain that African witch doctors make these and use them for divining. You have no idea of how they operate, but they certainly work. You do not even have to hold it yourself. Offer to demonstrate.

Let someone draw a card, look at it, and place it face down in his left hand. Have him hold the pendulum over it. Explain that the pendulum answers questions by swinging. It swings lengthwise over the card for Yes" and from "side to side for "No."

Ask if the card is red. If it is actually the King of Spades, the pendulum will swing from side to side. When you inquire whether the card is a Spade, the pendulum swings lengthwise. Continue to ask questions and receive answers until you learn the name of the card. You can always do this in six questions if you ask the right ones. These are worth memorizing as they can be used in many routines.

1. "Is the card red?"
2. If the answer is "Yes," ask "Is it a Heart?" If no, ask "Is it a Spade?"
3. "Is it seven or less, counting Ace as low?"

4. "Is it an odd-numbered card, counting Ace, Jack, and King as odd?"
5. If higher than seven, ask, "Is it a face card?" If the answer is "Yes" and the card is even, it must be the Queen. If the answer is "No" and the card is odd, it must be the nine.

   If seven or less and even, ask, "Is it the deuce or the four?" If the answer is "No," it must be the six.

   If seven or less and odd, ask, "Is it the Ace or the trey?"
6. If the card has not yet been determined, it must belong to one of the following pairs: Ace or three, two or four, five or seven, eight or ten, Jack or King. As you already know which pair, you have only to name one card of the pair. The answer will determine whether it is the one you name or its mate.

The Subject actually swings the pendulum by minute, unconscious movements of his hand. If some spectator suggests this, reply boldly, "Oh no. The pendulum is self-working. I'll prove it."

Have another person draw a card. This time you hold the pendulum. In spite of the fact that you have not been allowed to see the card, the pendulum answers every question correctly.

The simplest way to work this is to use a confederate. I have The Subject show the card to the Witnesses. My confederate then signals the card by the simple code illustrated in Figs. 46–50. I cannot recommend this code too highly. An unlimited number of dramatic illusions can be performed with its aid.

A "magic implement" produces magical results in other objects. Aladdin's lamp is typical, and so is every magician's wand. Conjurers tend to overlook the psychological value of a wand. Many of them never pick up a wand except when they need an excuse for keeping something concealed in the hand that holds the wand. This is poor showmanship. The use of a wand creates atmosphere. Every layman's mental picture of a magician includes a wand; when the wand is omitted, something is missing. Furthermore, most presentations become more dramatic when the audience is informed of the exact moment when the marvel takes place. Thus, at the climax of *The Expanding Rabbit*, you might say, "When I tap the hat with my magic wand, the little rabbit will grow, and grow, and grow—until he fills the whole hat. Watch!" Tap. Peer into the hat. "Yes, he's getting larger and larger. Look." Hold the hat under the boy's nose too close for him to see clearly. "There. He's full-grown now." Lower the hat so that the boy can get a good view. Then lift the rabbit from the hat.

The fan used with the dye-tube routine on p. 66 is a specialized magic implement. Furthermore, it works by sound magical logic. As the fan changes color it "naturally" changes the color of anything at which it is waved. The fan makes the illusion much more convincing than it would be if the dye tube were used alone. When waved with appropriate showmanship, the fan wafts the spectators into a frame of mind where magical logic seems altogether reasonable.

A "talisman" resembles a magical implement but confers its powers on the possessor instead of working them directly.

HAND SIGNALS

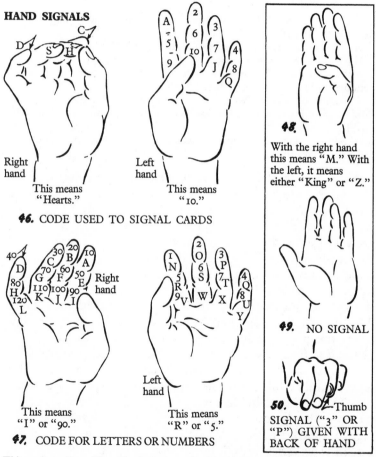

Right hand
This means "Hearts."

Left hand
This means "10."

46. CODE USED TO SIGNAL CARDS

48. With the right hand this means "M." With the left, it means either "King" or "Z."

Right hand
This means "I" or "90."

Left hand
This means "R" or "5."

47. CODE FOR LETTERS OR NUMBERS

49. NO SIGNAL

50. Thumb SIGNAL ("3" OR "P") GIVEN WITH BACK OF HAND

This code works with cards, letters, or numbers. Use initials to designate particular spectators. Note that the codes on both hands read outward from the thumbs. Fig. 50 shows that signals can be read from the back of the hand.

A toad stone is a typical talisman. You can use one to create atmosphere in many illusions beside *The Singular Singletons.*

Sorcerers set great store by spells. Here are a few "genuine" spells copied from old books. If you take the trouble to memorize some of them, you will find that they are unsurpassed for creating atmosphere with magical themes.

Abac Aldal Iat Hibac Guthac Guthor Gomeh Tistator Paliel Tzaphniel Matmoniel.

Heloy Tau Varaf Panthon Homnorcum Elemiath Serugeath Agla On Tetragrammaton Casily.

Dalmaley Lameck Cadat Pancia Velous Merroe Lamideck Caldurech Anereton Mitraton.

Helon Taul Varf Pan Heon Homonoreum Clemialh Serugeath Agla Tetrogrammaton Casoly.

Beelzebuth Lucifer Madilon Solymo Saroy Theu Ameclo Segrael Praredun Adricanorom Martino Timo Cameron Phorsy Metosite Prumosy Dumaso Elivisa Alphrois Fubentroty, Venite.

The difficulties of pronunciation were intentional. If a spell proved ineffective, failure could always be explained by mispronunciation. Furthermore, a layman who happened to read a sorcerer's textbook, or *grimoire,* would not dare to use a spell because even the smallest error might prove disastrous. The Apprentice's failure with *The Mismade Flag* is dramatized by ascribing it to her mispronunciation of a single vowel.

If you pretend to achieve your effects by spells, you can capitalize on this need for precision when something really does go wrong. Apologize saying, "These spells are tricky. Make a mistake in one syllable and . . . , 'Poof!' I must have lisped on 'Serugeath.' It's lucky I didn't use a soft 'g.' That *would* have been serious." The audience will regard this as byplay and will fail to realize that you are covering a blunder.

One pronunciation is as good as another for conjuring purposes, but get yours down pat before using a spell in public. Chant the words or mumble them under your breath. In either case, give the spell your whole attention. If it were genuine, you would not dare to slight it; the spell would work the magic and it would be more dangerous than a live bomb. When you do not treat a spell seriously, you cannot expect your audience to do so.

In a lighter vein, you may prefer the magic words used by conjurers in different countries. Most performers treat these casually, but that is a grave mistake. The words themselves are not very magical. The only way to lend them any effect at all is to pronounce them in a loud voice with the utmost solemnity. A few examples follow:

CHINESE: Tien ling ling. Dee ling ling. Bien!

EGYPTIAN: Galli, Galli, Galli. . . . [*Said many times very rapidly.*]

FARSEE (spoken in Persia or Iran): Yardegar!

GERMAN: Simsalabim-salabam-salabim.

HUNGARIAN: Cheereeboo! Cheereebah! Cheereebee!

KOREAN: Yobo Sao.

Houdini invented a "magic word" which has an authentic ring, "Anthropropolagos."

When you use a spell, remember that the spell does the work. Either time the effect to occur on the last syllable of the spell, or recite the spell and then set off the effect with a flourish of your wand.

Wizards had deep faith in magic chemicals. Greasy messes called "ointments" were prepared and rubbed onto parts of the body. These hardly suit modern conjuring, but magic powders and fluids known as "witch's brews," "magic potions," or "elixirs," can be impressive if they are properly handled.

Conjurers who perform illusions like *Levitation* and *Sawing a Woman in Half* usually "hypnotize" their assistants. This is rather silly. The effects of hypnosis are well known and do not include either levitation or the ability to withstand bodily injury. Nevertheless, some preparation is clearly needed to create an impressive atmosphere. I suggest that three sips of a poisonous-looking elixir would be just the thing. The assistant's expression should convey the idea that she dislikes the taste but needs to drink the vile stuff because it is the only thing that will help her through her fearful ordeal.

Powders are more useful than elixirs. They can supply the magic for many effects. Unfortunately, most conjurers use them merely as an excuse for putting one hand into a pocket to pick up or dispose of some secret fakery. The powder is called by the ridiculous name of "woofle dust." It is frankly imaginary, and is apparently carried loose in a pocket. When handled in this way, powder is such a lame excuse for reaching into the pocket that it draws attention to the move instead of disguising it.

The real value of magic powder lies in its ability to create an atmosphere of sorcery. Give yours a mysterious title such as "The Powder of Annihilation," or "The Dust of Khufu." Use actual powder. You need something that will not soil a rug; ground spices, such as nutmeg or marjoram, do nicely. Store the powder in a small, ornate bottle or vial of the type in which perfume samples are sold. Keep the vial in the pocket that you would use to hold your most priceless possession. When you take it out, treat it reverently. There is no harm in employing it to cover a secret move, but that is secondary. Make it pay its way as atmosphere. Any value it may have as a disguise should be a bonus.

Medieval necromancers usually practiced their art within the borders of a design drawn on the floor. Such designs, known as "pentacles" have no value for the conjurer, but smaller versions inscribed on paper and called "sigils" (pronounced sid-jils) can be put to good use.

THE SIGIL OF SOLOMON

Discuss pentacles and their uses. Explain that smaller replicas, technically termed sigils, are quite handy for such mantic operations as answering questions and discovering secrets.

Take a piece of paper measuring about 3 by 4 inches. Draw the sigil on it (Fig. 51) while you mumble one of the incantations on pp. 81 or 82. Explain that every detail of the ritual must be strictly observed. Thus, the triangles must be drawn counterclockwise, and all writing must be in capitals because the ritual was worked out long before small letters or "minuscules" were invented. Hand the paper to a spectator. Tell him to turn it so that the letters E H Y H are erect and print the name of some dead person unknown

THE SIGIL OF SOLOMON

51. DIAGRAM WITH NAME PRINTED IN CENTER

to you within the sigil. Remind him that no sorcery can succeed unless he conforms to even the most minute details of the arcane ritual.

All this should be treated with the utmost solemnity, as though you were taking a serious risk in demonstrating the secrets of sorcery before

52. CENTER-TEAR PRINCIPLE

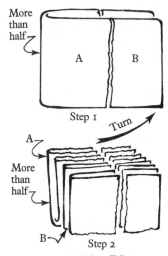

More than half

A | B

Step 1

Turn

A

More than half

B

Step 2

FIG. 53.
METHOD OF TEARING

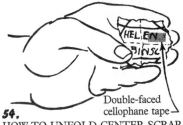

Double-faced cellophane tape
54.
HOW TO UNFOLD CENTER SCRAP

When the paper is folded once each way tearing it twice as shown will leave you with the whole center in your left hand. Have a half-inch square of two-sided cellophane tape wrapped in a scrap of cellophane from a pack of gum or cigarettes. Keep this in your pocket. When you are ready to perform, toy with the cellophane and get the tape on your middle finger (Fig. 54). There is so much scrap cellophane around these days that no one pays any attention to it. The tape makes it easy to open the center fold with your

left hand. You can then read the name when you replace the scraps in your left hand and reach in your pocket for a match with your right.

profane eyes. Turn your back while the name is being printed. When your victim is finished, tell him to fold the sheet both ways. Pause a moment. Then, face him and hold out your hand for the paper, which you immediately proceed to tear into bits. Place these in an ash tray and light them with a match. While they are burning, chant another spell in a rhythmic monotone. The moment the flame dies, look your victim straight in the eye and suddenly pronounce the name.

This is made possible by an exceptionally clever device known as the *center tear* (Fig. 52). Figs. 53 and 54 show how to obtain possession of the central fold and open it long enough to read the name or question written by The Sitter.

Note the use of two-sided cellophane tape. You can perform many other impossibilities with its aid. For example, you can attach a golf ball to your palm and hold your hand perfectly flat without dropping the ball. You can then free the ball in an instant simply by bending your hand.

THE THEORIES OF MAGIC

Folklorists divide magic into two types: "homeopathic" and "contagious." Homeopathic magic is supposed to work on the principle that like causes produce like effects. Thus, savage witch doctors sprinkle water on the ground to bring rain.

Civilized spectators are not apt to believe in the efficacy of homeopathic magic, and most of them have never even heard of it. In spite of this, they will instantly recognize it as appropriate. In *Fan-tastic*, for example, you do not need to lecture on the homeopathic theory to make your audience appreciate the relationship between a change in the color of the fan and a corresponding change in the color of a handkerchief.

Contagious magic is supposed to operate on the principle that anything done to a part of a person, animal, or object will affect the whole—even though the part has been cut off. This is illustrated by the way the lock of hair is treated in the following illusion. The use of the doll introduces an element of homeopathic magic. Combinations of principles are common in the rites performed by "real" sorcerers.

THE VOODOO DOLL

This illusion requires a full stage. The doll is made of rolled and crumpled wax paper (Figs. 55–58). Its head is covered with tissue paper and painted with melted wax. The dress is pasted together from red and blue tissue paper. These are authentic voodoo colors. Keep the doll in a box which rests on a small table. You will also need a long hat pin, a brazier, and the cabinet in Fig. 59. The flame is provided by a can of Sterno, which is available at any hardware store.

Your girl assistant has been "hypnotized" during a previous routine. A spotlight in the rear of the auditorium focuses on you, and the stage lights go out. As you walk toward the footlights, the traveler curtains close behind you, and a stagehand pushes the brazier on from the wings. Behind the curtains, the cabinet is brought on. Fig. 61 shows the arrangement.

Remark that although you hold your degree in goetics from the University of Salamanca and served your internship as a thaumaturgist in the Carpathians, you have just begun to dabble in voodoo sorcery. For some time, you have wanted to try a full-scale experiment. This seems to be a good opportunity. As you say that, strike a match and light the brazier.

Invite a gentleman from the audience to assist you. While he is coming forward, the curtains part. Walk up to the cabinet and open the front door.

Ask the volunteer to help you move the cabinet to the center of the stage. Turn it around as you do so to let the audience see all sides.

Cross to the table. Open the box and take out the doll. Explain that voodoo sorcery is fascinating and sometimes terrifying. For example, this is one of the dolls used by witch doctors to injure their enemies. If the witch doctor wants to give his enemy a pain in the left leg, he simply runs a long pin through the corresponding leg of the doll. If he intends to kill his enemy, he runs the pin through the doll's heart. Illustrate these methods by running a hatpin through the appropriate parts of the doll.

"However," you continue, "these actions are harmless until the doll has been identified with a particular person." This requires obtaining a lock of that person's hair.

Hand the doll to the volunteer. Command your hypnotized assistant to come to the center of the stage in front of the cabinet. Take a narrow strand of her hair and snip off half an inch.

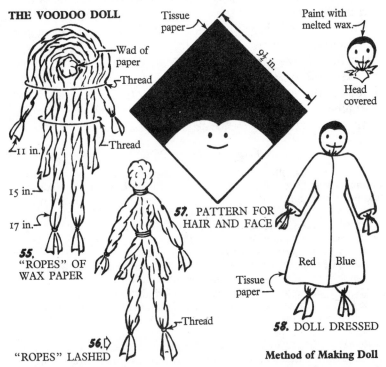

THE VOODOO DOLL

Wad of paper

Thread

Tissue paper

9¼ in.

Paint with melted wax.

Head covered

11 in.

Thread

15 in.

17 in.

55. "ROPES" OF WAX PAPER

57. PATTERN FOR HAIR AND FACE

Red | Blue

Tissue paper

58. DOLL DRESSED

Thread

56. "ROPES" LASHED

Method of Making Doll

"The hair," you explain, "is rubbed into the wax from which the doll is made." Start this operation yourself and then give the doll back to the volunteer with instructions to "Rub it well in."

Wheel the brazier toward the center of the stage but not far enough to obscure the audience's view of the cabinet. Command your assistant to enter the cabinet and face front. Close the door. Direct the volunteer to set fire to the doll and drop it into the brazier. While it burns, face the cabinet and chant,

> Way yah-yah, woe.
> Gro ko-ko mah kahck.
> Jen jah me, yah-way.
> Yah-way toto, feenee bah-ko.

As the flame from the burning doll begins to die, walk to the cabinet and fling the door open. The girl has gone. Nothing remains but a wisp of smoke!

THE VOODOO DOLL (Cont.)

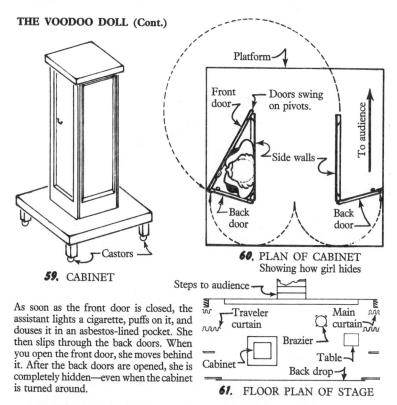

59. CABINET

60. PLAN OF CABINET
Showing how girl hides

As soon as the front door is closed, the assistant lights a cigarette, puffs on it, and douses it in an asbestos-lined pocket. She then slips through the back doors. When you open the front door, she moves behind it. After the back doors are opened, she is completely hidden—even when the cabinet is turned around.

61. FLOOR PLAN OF STAGE

Get into the cabinet, push open the back doors, and walk through. With the aid of the volunteer, turn the cabinet around a second time.

In many routines, it pays to give a volunteer credit for his performance and let him share your applause. That is not practical here. The best procedure is to step toward the footlights so that you are directly between the audience and the cabinet. In this position, you obscure the spectators' view of the volunteer without actually standing in front of him. This lets you take all the attention yourself without seeming rude.

Bow, thank the volunteer and dismiss him. While he is going back to his seat, look at the audience and remark, "You know, a man could lose more assistants that way!"

Fig. 60 reveals the secret. This cabinet has the exceptional advantage of being completely free from fakery. Your volunteer Helper can examine every detail minutely without finding anything to arouse suspicion.

Chapter 7
MYSTERY WITHOUT MAGIC

Our ancestors believed that almost any strange phenomenon was caused by magic. However, we cannot expect modern audiences to agree. Hence, we must treat magical themes as fantasy, and the suspension of disbelief becomes a major problem. Fortunately, other and more plausible types of themes are available. They make conviction easier, and illusions based on them seem much fresher.

These advantages are partly offset by the fact that non-magical themes do not combine well with each other. They are excellent for individual impromptus, but if you want to use them in an act, you should stick to one type of theme throughout. This is not always easy. Some types permit so little variety that they can hardly serve as the basis for a complete act.

Occult Phenomena

Occult themes come close to magic but differ from it in one important respect; for every American who believes in magic, many thousands have blind faith in some form of occultism.

Spiritualistic phenomena are easy to imitate, but they should normally be confined to single routines. If you present a whole act of this type, conviction will either break down or become overwhelming. Sitters at a mock seance often refuse to be undeceived and insist on regarding the manifestations as genuine in spite of anything the conjurer can say. Conan Doyle always contended that Houdini was an unconscious medium and flatly rejected Houdini's protestations that his spiritualistic demonstrations were mere tricks.

A comic treatment avoids this sort of embarrassment. Here is an example which has the added advantage of turning an old trick into an amusing illusion.

ANCESTRAL AID

Confess that you have no magical powers yourself. However, you are a direct descendant of the remarkable French card expert, Charlier (pronounced Shar-lee-ay). Great-great-great-granddaddy started life as a card sharp, but he developed his skill to such a fantastic extent that it passed over the borderline into downright magic. "The old boy loves to show off. Sometimes I can persuade him to come back and do it. I'll try anyway."

Let someone shuffle the deck. Tell another spectator to cut and place the cut-off packet on the table. Have him display the bottom card of the original pack. Point to the cut-off packet and say, "Complete the cut and square the deck."

When this has been done, continue, "No matter how well a crooked gambler stacks a deck, a cut changes the order of the cards. If the gambler or his partner can do the cutting, he can reverse the cut secretly, but once the deck is squared like this one, he cannot tell where to divide the cards. However, that didn't stop Granddad Charlier. I don't expect you to take my word for it, but I can prove it. Watch."

Look upward toward the ceiling and say, "All right, Grandpappy, how about it?" Slap the table and add, "Come on." [*Slap.*] Cut the cards. [*Slap.*] "Do your stuff!" [*Slap.*]

The pack will mysteriously divide. When the top packet is lifted by a spectator, its bottom card will be the one previously shown.

The secret lies in a pinch of common salt, which you carry in your pocket. Get a few grains between your thumb and forefinger. Have the pack shuffled and cut. While the spectator is looking at his card, point to the bottom packet, saying, "Replace the cut on top and square the deck." As you point, drop the salt onto the top of the bottom packet. When the cut packet is returned, the grains of salt act as little ball bearings and permit the top packet to roll on the bottom one. Slapping the table jars the cards and provides the power that makes the packet roll.

Most fortune-telling requires nothing but a glib tongue and a willing dupe. However, it can be used to dress up a routine that would otherwise be too weak to present. The illusion which follows is another example of how an almost trivial trick can be turned into first-rate entertainment by adding meaning.

THE BOOK OF THOTH

Although tarot cards are still employed for fortune-telling and serious attempts at sorcery, conjurers make almost no use of them. The reason is that they are so large, stiff, and thick that sleights become almost impossible. One solution is a *stacked* deck. However, this requires convincing the audience that the cards are innocent. A false shuffle is impossible. Switching will not help because it has no effect unless the fair deck is first used enough to prove that it really is fair. Our routine provides a stratagem which avoids these objections.

Take the tarot cards from their case and spread them face up in a ribbon so that their order is not changed. Say, "Many adepts believe the tarots to be the famous Egyptian *Book of Thoth* which contains all wisdom when properly interpreted. A pack consists of seventy-eight cards. Four suits of fourteen cards each including the Knights, twenty-one trumps, and a Fool. Students of the tarot disagree as to whether the Fool counts as a trump. However, it is certainly an important card."

Display each card as you speak of it. Take out any trumps that you mention and pass them around, but leave the suit cards in place.

Explain that the four suits are "Cups," "Coins," "Crowns," and "Swords." The higher magic of the tarots lies in the trumps, but the whole deck possesses arcane powers. These powers are not inherent in the printed pasteboards but must be conferred on them by an elaborate ritual lasting nine days and nine nights. The old Gypsy woman from whom you bought your pack assured you that it had been prepared by this ritual. You were skeptical, but she proved it. You propose to supply proof in the same way.

Once tarot cards have been treated by the ancient ritual, they become prophetic. Each person's future may be foretold from a "significator." With treated cards, a seer can know in advance what the significator of the next sitter will be—even though he has no idea whom he will meet.

Take a sealed envelope from your pocket. Lay it on the table saying that it contains the significator for the next sitter.

Decide whose fortune you will tell. Draw out half a dozen more trumps from the face-up deck saying that trumps play no part in the next step. Sweep up the remaining cards and turn the deck face down. Tell The Sitter to cut three times and complete the cut. Give him (or, preferably, her) your penknife and tell him to thrust it into the deck. He is then to note the cards above and below the knife. If one happens to be a trump, tell him to ignore it and take the next suit card. Have him add his two cards, counting Jacks as 11, Knights as 12, Queens as 13, and Kings as 14. The sum will indicate his significator.

When he announces that the answer is 15, laugh and say, "That corresponds to the trump known as 'The Devil.' Now let's see if I predicted your significator correctly." Slit open the envelope and remove the card. It is Trump XV, The Devil, just as you claimed it would be. Go on to make up a reading for The Sitter based on this card.

The caption to Fig. 62 explains how the deck can be stacked so that the cards at any cut will always add up to either 15 or 16. The illustration shows an envelope which will enable you to reveal either Trump XV, The Devil, or Trump XVI, the House of God.

The interest aroused by the strange deck, the detailed explanation of individual cards, the fact that some of the trumps are carelessly pulled out and discarded, and the triple cut all tend to kill the idea of a stacked deck and to make your audience overlook your failure to shuffle the cards.

Three traditional methods of telling fortunes with tarots are given in *The Pictorial Key to the Tarot* by Arthur Edward Waite, and there are many others. Unfortunately, they are all too elaborate to suit the needs of the conjurer. I recommend the following simplified procedure.

Keep the significator face down until you place it in front of The Sitter. Arrange for it to fall with the top of the picture toward him. Tell him to turn it over. Point out that it is "reversed," i.e., the picture is upside down. This reverses its meaning. Hence "The Devil" now signifies an angel to protect or bless. "The House of God," which shows two people being thrown from a building that has been struck by lightning, indicates when reversed either construction of some sort or an averted calamity. Reversal is necessary, because these are the only two trumps that fit the device and neither one can have pleasant connotations if interpreted at its face value.

THE BOOK OF THOTH

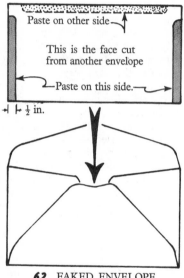

1. Cut the front from one of two identical envelopes. Apply a half-inch wide strip of paste along the sides of its inside face (*A-A*, Fig. 62). Slide this fake into the other envelope. Place a weight on it and let it dry. Put Trump XVI, The House of God, between the fake and the front of the whole envelope. Slide the card well down to the bottom. Lift the top edge of the fake and smear a half-inch of its under side with paste (*B*). Press this against the face of the main envelope. When the paste is dry, put Trump XV, The Devil, into the envelope and seal it.

2. If you now slit the top flap with a knife, Trump XV will drop out. If you tear a narrow strip off one end, you can shake out Trump XVI. In either case, "accidentally" expose the inside of the envelope so that the audience can see that it is empty.

3. To stack the deck, lay two of the Aces aside; they will not be used. Also remove the trumps. Arrange half of the suit cards like this: Ace-King-2-Queen-3-Knight-4-Jack-5-10-6-9-7-8-8-7-9-6-10-5-Jack-4-Knight-3-Queen-2-King. Arrange the other half in the same order and put the halves together. With this setup, any two adjacent cards will total either fifteen or

62. FAKED ENVELOPE

sixteen. Put Trumps XV and XVI in the envelope. Stick the remaining trumps into the stacked deck at random, and you are ready to perform. If The Sitter cuts cards that add up to fifteen, open the top of the envelope. If his cards add up to sixteen, tear off either end.

After the significator is revealed, announce that you will also use the trumps corresponding to the cards above and below the cut. Suppose, for example, that the cut is made between The Knight (12) and a three. That gives The Devil for the significator and adds The Hanged Man and The Empress. Note which ones are reversed from the viewpoint of The Sitter.

Use anything that appears on the three cards as a clue in your reading. This includes minor details which differ from deck to deck. With my cards, the above example might be interpreted as follows:

"The tarots contain hidden wisdom, and we must not read them superficially. Thus, the fact that your significator is reversed means that the cards are to be interpreted in a sense opposite to their obvious meaning. The Devil itself is an extremely lucky card when reversed and means good fortune or protection against some evil. As The Empress is also reversed, we have two negatives which make a positive. In this aspect, The Empress is interpreted as lucky and promises some important blessing such as an empress might bestow. The Hanged Man is a card of contradictions. He is upside down but not hurt or suffering. In association with the other two trumps, this card stands for suspense. It means that the good fortune promised will not come soon. Also, as all three cards indicate reversal, it will probably be a blessing in disguise; something which appears to be disastrous at first will prove highly beneficial in the end."

If you like this routine, practice inventing imaginary fortunes before trying it in public.

PARAPSYCHOLOGICAL PHENOMENA

Anyone who believes in the occult usually takes parapsychology seriously, but this does not work the other way. Plenty of people are convinced that parapsychological phenomena are genuine, although they have no faith in the occult. Themes based on parapsychology can be sufficiently varied to permit a whole act in this field. The conjurer then bills himself as a mentalist.

Telepathy, clairvoyance, "thought control," and "precognition" or the ability to foresee events, are so closely allied that psychic researchers like Professor Rhine of Duke University find great difficulty in distinguishing them. Thus, if *Mental Television* were genuine, the "psychic" could never be sure whether: (*a*) he "saw" the drawing with his "inner eye," (*b*) read the subject's mind, (*c*) knew in advance what design would be drawn, or (*d*) subconsciously influenced the subject to draw a particular design. Most mental effects can be ascribed to any one of these phenomena by specifying it and perhaps making slight adjustments in the routine.

The proper choice will depend on the illusion itself. *Dial Information* goes best as an experiment in telepathy. This leads The Participants to concentrate and hence to identify themselves with the performance. That, in turn, builds atmosphere and tends to suspend disbelief. *Mental Television*, on the other hand, must be offered as clairvoyance in order to stress the need for making the lines of the drawing "good and strong."

The following illusion gives the performer an opportunity to create an impression of frankness by professing uncertainty as to the exact nature of his power.

PREVIEW

This works best for a fairly large audience. As each spectator arrives he is asked to write his name on a slip, fold the slip, and drop it through a slit in the top of a cardboard box which has been sealed with cellophane tape.

Begin the routine by announcing that your next experiment was designed to test your ability to foresee the future. You will record a prediction and then ask a spectator to make certain choices. If your predictions match his choices, you believe that it will demonstrate your powers of what parapsychologists call precognition. However, in the interest of scientific accuracy, you must admit that another explanation is possible. It may be that, after writing your predictions, you unconsciously exert some form of mental control over the person who makes the choices so that he is led to select the items which you have predicted. You have never been able to determine which view is correct. Perhaps you read the spectator's mind in advance; perhaps you control his choices. In either case, the experiment offers an interesting parapsychological phenomenon—if you succeed. Unfortunately, you are not always able to do this.

Invite A Helper to come up onto the stage. While he is doing so, display a large sheet of cardboard and a crayon. Announce that you will write the name of a color, the name of a flower, and a number. Do so without showing the result. When the volunteer arrives, give him the cardboard and tell him that he may look at it but that he must keep it turned away from the audience.

Choose A Second Helper seated near the rear of the auditorium. Ask him to get the box of names and fetch it to you. Go down off the stage to meet him. Supply him with a penknife and tell him to cut the cellophane. Lift off the lid. Give the bottom of the box to this Second Helper. Have him offer it to anyone he chooses. Ask this person to draw a name without looking. As soon as this has been done, retrieve the bottom of the box and return to the stage.

Recapitulate. Members of the audience have written their names on slips and deposited them in a sealed box. Your helper has offered it to another person who drew a name at random. At present, no one knows what this name is.

Call upon the spectator who drew the slip to unfold it and read the name. Ask the owner of the name to stand. Remind him that you listed a color, a flower, and a number on the card held by the volunteer before anyone could possibly know who would be chosen as a subject for the experiment. He is not to guess what you have written. Instead, he is to name the first color that pops into his head. He says, "Purple." You write this on a second piece of cardboard and ask him to name a flower. He chooses "Carnation." Write that and call for a number. He names "Seven thousand, three hundred and eighty."

PREVIEW

Use a candy box with a deep lid (*A*). Cut a slot in the top of this lid. Get a smaller box (*B*). Paint the inside gray. Make an opening in the top. Glue the smaller box under the lid of the large one. Write your confederate's name on a number of slips and place these in the bottom of the large box. Put the lid on the box and keep it in position with strips of cellophane tape. Be sure to have a knife in your pocket so that you can cut the tape.

63

OM BILLET-CHANGING BOX

Remark that although the test was not completely successful you came close enough to demonstrate that the power is genuine. Ask The First Helper to turn his sheet of cardboard around and display yours at the same time. They read:

Your Prediction	Spectator's Choice
Violet	Purple
Carnation	Carnation
738	7380

Do not point out that "purple" is close to "violet" and that you got all of The Subject's number except the final zero. The spectators will recognize this themselves. If you appear slightly disappointed, they will assume that you are usually more accurate. At the same time, your near misses convince them that the experiment was genuine.

This depends on an especially clever procedure for introducing a confederate who acts as The Subject and names predetermined items. I owe the idea to my friend Major Winton A. J. Carroll. Although the selection seems exceptionally fair, only the confederate can be chosen. The simplest way to assure this is to prepare two identical boxes. One receives the slips signed by the spectators. The other already contains a number of slips naming the confederate. As the box remains at the rear of the auditorium during the entire act, there is ample opportunity for a second confederate to switch boxes. If this method is used, you need not leave the stage or touch the box yourself, but can let your innocent Second Helper handle it and allow anyone to draw a slip.

If you prefer to work without a second confederate, you can use the OM billet-changing box invented by Otis Manning and pictured in Fig. 63. In that case, however, you will have to open the box yourself to make sure that the lid is not turned upside down.

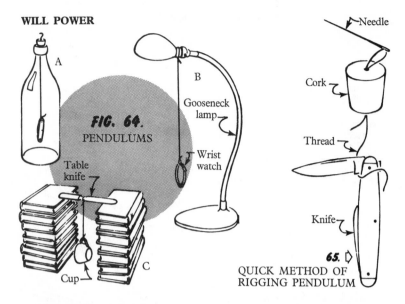

FIG. 64.
PENDULUMS

A

B
Gooseneck lamp
Wrist watch

Table knife
Cup
C

Needle
Cork
Thread
Knife

65.
QUICK METHOD OF
RIGGING PENDULUM

"Psychometry" is another parapsychological phenomenon that can easily be imitated by conjuring. The method given on p. 39 is simply an adaptation of *Horoscope*. Annemann's version (*The Jinx* No. 9, p. 36, and *Practical Mental Effects*, p. 150) is better, but it requires prepared envelopes. This prevents it from being presented "impromptu" except in your own home or office.

"Psychokinetics" is the power to affect physical objects by mental force. The following example is elaborate and calls for both showmanship and acting ability. However, it demands no skill whatever, and its impact is tremendous.

WILL POWER

Arouse interest in psychokinetic force by mentioning Professor Rhine's experiments with dice at Duke University. Rhine has his subjects throw dice and try to control their fall by exerting mental effort. He finds that the desired number comes up more often than the laws of chance predict.

Some spectators will probably accept Rhine's experiments as valid. Others will find fault with them. Align yourself with the latter group by pointing out that John Scarne (pronounced Scarn-e), the great expert on cards and dice, has criticized Rhine's findings severely. If the Rhine effect were genuine, it would show up at crap tables in gambling joints. When a dozen or more bettors are ardently urging the dice to win, the result should decrease the percentage won by the house. Actually, that does not occur. This is an extremely interesting point merely as conversation. It shows that you are well informed on the subject.

Add, "Scarne considers dice too crude for a scientific experiment. Why not try something more delicate, such as a balanced arrow like those used in carnival games ? If mental force is strong enough to control dice, it should certainly be able to deflect the arrow."

Try to have spectators think of even more sensitive instruments. A Geiger counter might do, or a gold-leaf electroscope. Point out that an equally responsive and much simpler device is available—a pendulum. Suggest trying an experiment. "It's no trouble to rig a pendulum. If we can't make it swing, Rhine is definitely wrong."

Rig a pendulum as shown at *B*, Fig. 64 and place it on a bridge table. Seat the spectators around the table. Indicate with your finger the direction in which they should will the pendulum to swing. Tell them to give it rhythmic mental pushes. Soon, a movement is perceptible, and in a minute or two, the swing is large enough to be beyond argument.

However, you remain skeptical. There must be a vibration from trucks passing in the street. Have The Participants try to swing the pendulum in another direction while you rig a second pendulum. They make the attempt and find that they can swing the pendulum as easily in the new direction as they did in the old.

When you place the second pendulum on the table, suggest trying to make this one swing while the first hangs motionless. While they are doing this, successfully, you rig a pendulum in a bottle to avoid any chance that someone is working the pendulum by blowing on it (*A*, Fig. 64 and 65).

The third pendulum proves as easy to influence by will power as the others, but you remain unconvinced. The Participants have been sitting with their hands on the table. This can hardly make one pendulum swing while the others are still. Nevertheless, the experiment will not be conclusive so long as any physical contact exists. Have The Participants move back and fold their hands in their laps.

Choose a pendulum. Tell everyone to direct his mental force against it. It swings.

Admit that matters are getting too uncanny for you. You have had enough. Start dismantling the pendulums. Anyone who wants to experiment further can do it with his own pendulums.

This is most effective in your home where the props can be arranged so that you are able to assemble the pendulums without making the action drag.

The first four experiments work like *The Sympathetic Pendulum* through minute impulses supplied subconsciously by The Participants. As each thread is a different length, each pendulum will swing at a different rate. Hence, impulses that move one will damp out the vibrations of the others.

The fifth experiment is faked by using a *plate lifter* or *palpitator* sold in most novelty shops. This is a rubber tube with a soft bulb on one end and a harder bulb on the other. Arrange this under the carpet. Put one leg of the table over the soft bulb and have the other bulb just behind the front of the chair where you will sit. You can then press this *very* gently with your heel and make the chosen pendulum swing.

SUPERNORMAL FACULTIES

A few people have developed ordinary abilities to a point where they seem almost miraculous. The Lightning Calculator of *Number Please* impersonates a man with extraordinary talent for arithmetic. Other roles that can be faked are The Juggler, The Strong Man, The Pickpocket, and The Man with the Giant Memory.

Faculties like color-touch and the ability to "eat" fire also come under this head. Although they must always be faked, onlookers can be persuaded that they are genuine. The line between the fake supernormal and the parapsychological is narrow, but it has a definite effect on the attitude of an audience. The layman who accepts color-touch regards it as essentially scientific. The layman who accepts *Mental Television* tends to connect it with mysticism and perhaps with religion.

This dividing line appears most clearly in the distinction between circus fire-eating and fire walking as practiced by religious cults in Asia. The average spectator believes that the fire-eater has toughened his skin by some physical means such as rubbing it with chemicals. On the other hand, the ability of religious fanatics to walk on fire is attributed to the power of faith.

This distinction should govern your presentations. Make an effect like *Chromavoyance* as rational and "scientific" as possible. There is a good deal of genuine evidence that the skin really is an undeveloped organ of light. The more of this you can find and use, the more convincing your performance will be. Illusions like *Mental Television* go better with a semi-mystical approach. Believers in parapsychology talk about science, but it never rings quite true. Their real argument is that they have gone beyond science. Your explanations for *Mental Television* and *Preview* should pretend to be scientific, but never fail to remind the audience that you are on the borderland of science and entering the undiscovered country of the mind.

SUPERINVENTION AND SUPERSCIENCE

These phenomena are exhibited by the apparatus rather than by the performer himself. Many stock devices sold by dealers can be adapted to fit such themes. The conjurer may appear as a man who has been captured by the crew of a flying saucer. When the saucer was wrecked, he was lucky enough to escape. He salvaged part of the equipment and proposes to demonstrate its marvels. Other useful roles are, a Mad Scientist, a Crackpot Inventor, and a Demonstrator for the World of Tomorrow who displays the latest marvels. The use of a definite characterization and an over-all theme ties the act together and makes it much more interesting than a series of unconnected illusions would be.

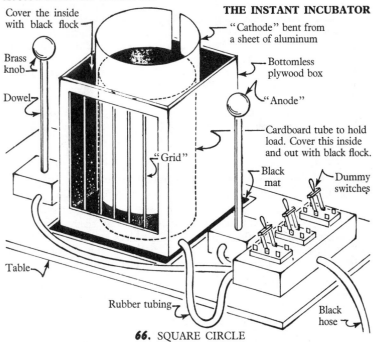

THE INSTANT INCUBATOR

Cover the inside with black flock

"Cathode" bent from a sheet of aluminum

Brass knob

Bottomless plywood box

Dowel

"Anode"

Cardboard tube to hold load. Cover this inside and out with black flock.

"Grid"

Black mat

Dummy switches

Table

Rubber tubing

Black hose

66. SQUARE CIRCLE

The "cables" and "anodes" have no practical function, but they contribute greatly to the atmosphere and they make suspension of disbelief possible. The heart of the device is the central tube. When the box is lifted, the "cathode" hides it. When the box is replaced and the "cathode" is lifted, the tube is invisible. This is partly because it is black against black and partly because the grille helps to conceal it. Experiment with the weight of this grille. The bars should be as slender and as far apart as possible while still being heavy enough to disguise the black cylinder. The grids in most square circles weaken conviction by being unnecessarily thick.

If you use one of these ideas, do not go about it halfway. Remodel your apparatus so that it looks scientific or like an inventor's working models and carries no suggestion that it was originally made by a manufacturer of conjurer's supplies.

Your costume, make-up, and manner—and those of your assistants, if any—must also fit the theme. Crackpot Inventors are not assisted by shapely girls in tights. On the other hand, if you are demonstrating The World of Tomorrow, a lavish production and curvaceous colleagues will be just the thing.

THE INSTANT INCUBATOR

This is arranged for An Inventor, but it could easily be adapted to a superscientific theme.

A heavy electric cable leads from backstage to supply power for your inventions. One of these looks like Fig. 66. Introduce it as your latest electronic device. You have discovered that if you enlarge the components of an ordinary radio tube and apply much more power than anyone ever used before, you do not need a vacuum.

Point to the "grid" and the "anodes." Lift out the cylindrical "plate" or "cathode," and display it in such a way that the audience can see through it. Replace the "cathode."

"One of the more interesting effects," you assert, "is the acceleration of biological processes." Show a small egg. Place it within the "cathode," throw the switch, and take out a dove.

Your "invention" is simply a redecorated version of the well-known *square circle*. As a square circle will hold much more than one dove, you can use it for a whole series of demonstrations including:

Carefree Cleaning. Lower soiled, rumpled handkerchiefs into the "cathode," throw switch, and remove clean, pressed ones. The clean handkerchiefs should be starched. Press them flat without folding, and bend them to fit inside the black cylinder.

Teleportation. You can use two square circles for this. Place an object in one, throw the switch, and take the object from the other.

An act like this offers many chances for comedy. For example, you try to teleport an object but it fails to arrive. Go back to the sending apparatus and remove the object. It has burned to a crisp. Shake your head and say, "Too much power." Then try again and succeed.

Chapter 8
PROVIDING THE PROOF

The function of the effect is to prove the phenomenon. Thus, the phenomenon in *Mental Television* is clairvoyance. The effect consists of duplicating a sketch which you could not possibly have seen. This proves your clairvoyant powers.

As the object of the effect is to convince the spectators, their interpretation of the evidence is the only thing that counts. When the effect consists in taking a cannon ball from an empty hat, the audience must believe that the hat is empty and that the cannon ball is heavy. If the spectators accept this, a one-ounce half-globe of papier-mâché is as good as a twenty-pound iron sphere; if they regard the ball as an imitation, iron is no better than papier-mâché.

It may be easier to convince people that the twenty-pound ball is genuine, but even this is not necessarily true. When a performer knows a thing is real, he is apt to take its reality for granted. Unfortunately, audiences tend to be skeptical. They need to be convinced, and they are likely to assume that even the most genuine element in a performance is spurious. Thus, I have had native British and German actors criticized by spectators for their "phony" accents.

This works the other way as well. If a strong enough atmosphere is created, imitations may be more convincing than the real thing. I once staged a scene in an operating room. Ether was not used or even mentioned. Nevertheless, several spectators left the audience at each performance "because they could not stand the smell of ether."

These spectators were undoubtedly stupid. But their decisions were final. If a playgoer is made ill by the smell of ether, I have no way of assuring him that the ether is imaginary. If he believes that an actress straight off the boat from Hamburg speaks German with a fake accent, she is just as unconvincing (to him) as though her acquaintance with the language were limited to one semester in high school.

We cannot prevent individuals from jumping to foolish conclusions, nor should we worry much when they do. However, the audience as a whole is always right. Once it forms an opinion, the fact that this is completely unfounded is of no consequence whatever.

This is a fundamental principle of showmanship. When we offer to entertain—and convince—an audience and fail to do so, the fault is ours. If the audience does not like our material, we cannot complain of its taste but must take the blame for choosing unwisely. If the audience is stupid, we must find ways to be especially clear. If the audience is inattentive, we must manage to capture and hold attention. An audience may be difficult, but there is no such thing as a bad audience Anyone who performs before an audience has undertaken to please that audience. If he bores it, he has not lived up to his obligation.

On the other hand, it is poor showmanship to trouble about matters which cannot affect the spectators. The performer who does so is thinking less about the impression he will make on his audience than about the impression he will make on himself. Thus, some conjurers disdain to use substitutes for real articles on the ground of professional pride. This is topsy-turvy thinking. The conjurer is in the business of making people believe in things which are not true. The more his effect departs from reality, the greater his justification for pride. Anyone can learn to persuade an audience that a twenty-pound cannon ball is a twenty-pound cannon ball.

IDENTIFYING THE EFFECT

You cannot hope to create a convincing effect unless you first decide what that effect is to be. Nevertheless, conjurers constantly ignore this obvious requirement. Consider *The Antigravity Hat*, for example. Stop now and ask yourself exactly what effect The Magician creates when he turns the hat over and no water runs out ?

A little thought shows that there are at least three. Each of these implies a different phenomenon, and each one requires different behavior on the part of the performers.

1. The water vanishes because the hat is magical and protects The Magician automatically. In this case, The Magician simply puts the hat on and gives no sign of even suspecting what has occurred.

2. The Magician's art informs him of the Boy's prank and magically transfers the water back to the original container. For this, we need a *lota bowl*, which is a device sold by dealers. The Boy inverts the bowl over the hat. This apparently empties the bowl completely. The Magician turns and raises an eyebrow at The Boy to show that he knows what has been done. He taps first the hat and then the bowl with his wand, presumably returning the water to the bowl. To "prove" that this has actually occurred, he turns the hat over to show that it is now empty. Finally, he pours the water from the bowl into some other container. The construction of the bowl makes this possible.

3. The Magician knows what The Boy has done. He makes three circles inside the hat with his wand and remarks, "Antigravity spell." When he turns the hat over, nothing runs out. He holds the hat high enough for the boy to peer up into it and says, "See, it stays in the top." He inverts the hat again, taps it with his wand and adds, "Watch!" With that, he tips the hat to one side and pours the water back into the original container.

In this case, one effect may be as good as another. However, the impression made on the audience will be blurred unless we decide on a specific effect and then make our choice clear by words and/or actions.

The first step in identifying an effect is to determine its basic type. Although many effects are available, they all fit into a comparatively small number of categories. My classification is given below, but it will pay you to make your own. No two people analyze material in exactly the same way. My headings may not match your way of thinking, but those that you choose yourself cannot help doing so.

PRODUCTIONS

When a conjurer makes something appear, he is said to *produce* it. Taking a rabbit from a hat is a typical production.

Two effects which are not strictly productions may, nevertheless, conveniently be considered under this heading. The first is *growth*, in which an object is magically enlarged. *The Expanding Rabbit* is a representative example. Note that if you omitted the baby rabbit and merely took the large one out of the hat, it would cease to be a growth effect and would become a production effect. If you substituted a "rabbit egg" (Easter egg) for a baby rabbit, you would have an incubation-plus-growth effect. Although the mechanics are the same in each case, the attitude of the audience—and hence the real effect—differs significantly.

Also under "production" we may list *multiplication*. Thus, many conjurers start with a single billiard ball and multiply it by producing others from it, one at a time.

VANISHES

Conjurers speak of *vanishing* something when they make it disappear. The device which causes the disappearance may also be called a "vanish." The cabinet in *The Voodoo Doll* is a vanish.

Effects in which objects *diminish* in size may be classified under "vanishes." Although a few excellent routines fit into this category, reduction is essentially an undramatic process. It is not a field that deserves much attention unless you happen to hit on an exceptionally good idea.

TRANSPORTATION

Transportation occurs when an object passes invisibly from one place to another. When a square circle is used to "teleport" an object invisibly, this is a transportation effect (p. 100). Note that although the red handkerchief in *Twentieth-Century Nylon* disappears, the effect is a transportation and not a vanish. *Passe-Passe Dice* illustrates double transportation or *transposition*.

TRANSFORMATION

Turning a white handkerchief into a dove is a typical transformation effect. Another example occurs in *The Haunted Conjurer* where the dice become guinea pigs. This effect combines a transformation with a transposition; the white guinea pig with black spots takes the place of the black die with white spots and vice versa. Although there is no objection to combining categories, there is no advantage in doing so. Whether the combination is good or bad will depend on the particular case.

From the standpoint of the conjurer, transportations, transpositions, and transformations are merely a combination of one or more vanishes and productions. I have even heard experienced performers deny that they were separate effects. This is a serious mistake. When you set out to transform a silk handkerchief into a dove, you must convince the audience that the handkerchief becomes the dove. If the spectators think, "How clever he was to make the handkerchief disappear and produce the dove," you have failed. You set out to achieve one effect but created two quite different effects. If you want a transformation effect, you must think and act as if you were transforming something. If you think and act "Vanish-plus production," you cannot expect your audience to think, "Transformation."

Invulnerability

Pure illusions of *invulnerability*, such as the bullet-catching feat, are rare. However, several more popular types are conveniently classified under this heading.

One of these is *restoration*, which itself has several subheads. Thus, we have cases of *cutting without harm*, such as *Sawing a Woman in Half*. Another variety of restoration is *solid-through-solid*. A typical example of this is *The Linking Rings* in which solid steel rings are apparently linked and unlinked without effort. *Escapes* like those which made Houdini famous can best be regarded as instances of solid-through-solid penetration. *Reversals* belong in the same category as escapes. The escaper frees himself completely. The reversed object is only partially freed, but this is enough for it to turn over. The most common examples are card tricks in which a chosen card seems to have mysteriously turned face up in a face-down deck.

Control of Force

This includes levitations, knots that untie themselves, psychokinetic effects like those in *The Sympathetic Pendulum*, *Ancestral Aid*, and *Will Power*. It also covers tests of strength such as *The Strong Man's Secret*.

IDENTITY

This category comprises more effects than all other types put together. Most mental effects and many card tricks end with the performer identifying a selected card, name, or number. Effects where the performer matches items chosen by chance or a spectator come under the head of *identity*.

When dealing with identity effects, make sure that you know just what you are pretending to identify. In *Horoscope*, for example, you actually fit each notebook sheet to its owner and then fit his characteristics to him. However, if The Sitters see the effect in this light, it will fall flat. From their point of view, you must first determine each one's characteristics from his birthday and then identify The Sitter from his characteristics.

Each of the main headings listed above includes several subheads. It will pay you to work these out for yourself. Your classification will then provide a check list that can prove extremely helpful when you are seeking an effect for a routine. An outline like the one given below is the easiest type of list to prepare and use. I have added examples to explain what I mean by the headings, but you would not need these in an outline that you make for yourself.

Class 7. IDENTITY
- A. Discovery
  - I. Mental
    - a. Telepathy. *Dial Information.*
    - b. Clairvoyance. *Mental Television.*
    - c. Precognition. } *Preview*
    - d. Thought control. }
  - II. Supermental. *Number Please.* (The answers supposedly computed by the performer are identical with the true answers.)
  - III. Spiritualistic. *Ancestral Aid.* (Cutting point identified by spirit.)
  - IV. Pseudoscientific.
    - a. Direct. *Chromavoyance.*
    - b. Indirect. *Horoscope.* (The performer is not primarily concerned with identifying a person who has a given birthday, but with showing that the character of a person born on that day coincides with the character determined by astrology.)

B. Location. *The Singing Glass.* (This heading is largely confined to card effects. The card is located by some physical means, such as being found face up in the deck. Usually, the performer does not know, or pretends not to know, the identity of the card until it is located.)

C. Coincidence. *The Singular Singletons.* (The cards appear to be controlled by pure chance. Nevertheless, by a remarkable coincidence, singletons occur much more often than the audience considers likely.)

This outline does not pretend to be exhaustive. You may find more types, or you may feel that some of mine should be subdivided.

DIVINATION

Nine out of ten effects of identity involve some form of divination. Although the phenomenon may range from realistic science (as in *Arithmagic*) to the occult (as in *The Sigil of Solomon*), the conjurer's technique shows only minor variations. This technique is so useful and so flexible that it can probably be employed in more illusions than all the other conjuring devices put together.

Divination has such a wide range of applications that even the simple effect of revealing a chosen card illustrates its basic principles. Imagine that you are endowed with mental vision, but that you "look" through a whirling mist which makes your sight blurred and fragmentary. Sometimes you "see" a physical object. At other times, you get only an intangible impression. The various aspects are revealed to you in a random, illogical order. Some of your glimpses and feelings are so indefinite that your interpretation of them is guesswork. Others are sharp and clear.

When you divine the card in an illusion like *I Scry*, do not state flatly, "This is the Jack of Hearts." Instead say something like, "I get the impression of a picture. I can't see it; I only know that it is a picture. Now I feel warmth. That often means a red card . . . usually a heart. I'm beginning to see something! It's a symbol . . . a symbol like this." Take a pencil and sketch the symbol ♂. Then ask, "Does anybody know what that means?" If no one answers, exclaim, "Oh, I know now! It's the symbol biologists use for 'male.' Picture, male. . . . It must be a face card and either the King or Jack . . . red King or red Jack. Wait a minute! I see it better now. It is a Jack, and I was right. It's the Jack of Hearts."

Exactly the same principles apply when you divine a name in a routine like *The Sigil of Solomon*. If the name is "Jack Nelson," you might say, "I get an initial . . . M? W? And there's an N somewhere. I see another initial. It looks like a U, a broken U. Does that mean W?" Trace J in air with your forefinger. "No, the front part is missing. It must be a J. Am I right? J–A, J–A, James? No, its Jack. Jack W–N, W–L–N. There's an S, too. That would make it Wilson, Jack Wilson. Is that the name?"

This can be reduced to a set of working rules:

Break the information up into fragments.
Dole these out in an irrational order.
Be doubtful about some points.
Ask questions to check your "vision" when The Sitter knows the answers.
Make an occasional mistake or near miss ("Wilson" for "Nelson").

This procedure must be modified in pseudo-scientific illusions like *Arithmagic*. Visions and impressions are out of key with such phenomena. Nevertheless, it normally pays to show at least a little uncertainty and to make a near miss now and then. Thus, if the card in *Arithmagic* is a seven, you might "compute" it as an eight—especially if you plan to repeat the effect and get it right the second time. The near miss will convince skeptics that you did not know the card.

Most conjurers experiment with divination technique, but many of them soon abandon it. There are several reasons for this:

It does not work with tricks. Divination comes as a climax. You cannot create atmosphere at a climax, you can only strengthen it. As a trick has no atmosphere, there is nothing to strengthen.

The technique bores conjurers, who know it is fake. Hence, the man who tries it on his conjurer friends finds that it misses fire. He, therefore, abandons it before testing it on a lay audience, which might be deeply impressed.

Both acting ability and showmanship are essential. As few beginning conjurers have acquired either one, their early attempts at divination are ineffectual and they drop the technique without giving it a fair chance.

Finally, when a divination fails, it falls completely flat.

The proper approach is to use divination only when working with laymen and only after you have established a definite atmosphere. Make your first trials brief. "I see a card ... a spot card.... There are four ... no, five spots ... red spots ... Hearts. It's the five of Hearts."

Mastery of divination technique will come neither quickly nor easily, but it richly repays the trouble of acquiring it. An impressive divination not only intensifies the atmosphere but creates a certain amount of suspense. It appears to contradict any idea that you knew the facts in advance or learned them by reading what The Subject has written in a routine like *The Sigil of Solomon.*

There is also another advantage, and one which is of vital importance when you offer character readings in an illusion like *Horoscope.* Divination techniques permit you to give impressive performances when you must analyze a stranger about whom you know almost nothing.

CHARACTER READINGS

Illusions which provide character readings are popular with lay spectators, especially women. Prepare each reading in advance while you have plenty of time to think. You are already accustomed to size up people subconsciously. Train yourself to put your impressions into words. A stranger's apparent age tells you something about his interests and problems. His clothing provides hints as to his wealth, his social position, and his desire to impress others. You normally have a chance to hear a person talk for some time before you need to give him a reading. His speech will tell you much about his education and may reveal the section of the country in which he was raised. Almost every remark he makes will provide some clue as to his character and opinions.

Even when you learn almost nothing about a stranger, you can eke out your skimpy information with remarks that fit virtually everyone. This may seem impossible, but highly intelligent people have testified that such stock readings showed deep psychological appreciation of their characters. The following items are worth memorizing:

"You are more easily led than driven."

"You are often critical of yourself."

"You like to think independently and do not accept the statement of others without adequate proof."

"You dislike being hindered by restraints."

"Although you recognize weaknesses in yourself, you more than compensate for these in other ways."

"You feel a strong need to be liked and admired by others."

"You normally appear to be self-controlled, but you are often worried and unsure of yourself."

"You have many abilities which you have never fully developed."

"You are occasionally suspicious and withdrawn, but at other times you are open and sociable."

"Although you are a good judge of character, you are sometimes wrong about people because you follow your heart rather than your head."

"You appreciate the finer things of life, but you are not always able to gratify your tastes because you put the needs of other people above your own." (This is especially good for women.)

FISHING

Experts lead sitters to answer their own questions without realizing that they have done so. This technique is called *fishing*. The Medium makes some vague statement, but uses a rising inflection so that the remark can be interpreted as a question. Thus, if A Sitter is asking about a person, The Medium may say, "You are thinking of a woman . . ." The normal Sitter will take this to mean, "Are you thinking of a woman?" He will either start to answer or will give some indication of whether the guess is right or wrong. If his expression tells The Medium that she is correct, she quickly adds, ". . . a dark woman." If she has been wrong, she says, ". . . but this woman is not the chief figure in your thoughts. Your real question centers about a man." In either case, The Sitter assumes that The Medium's words form a single statement, and he fails to suspect that she changed her tactics in the middle of a sentence.

In many cases, The Medium uses the fishing technique like a child playing "hot and cold." In our example, she might begin by saying, "You are thinking of a woman . . . a dark woman." If The Sitter does not respond, The Medium adds, "No, she is in shadow. I see her more clearly now. Her hair is lighter. . . ." Should this still fail to register, The Medium goes on to say, ". . . perhaps with a touch of red." If The Sitter now shows interest, The Medium is on firm ground and states flatly, "It is red. I see her in full light now, and her hair is a rich auburn."

The following card routine will provide you with opportunities to practice both character reading and fishing.

SIGNIFICANT SELECTION

Explain that a person's character governs everything he does. If you know his character and the situation, you can even guess what card he is most likely to choose. Tell him to look through the deck and select the card which has the strongest appeal for him. It must be a deliberate choice. Have him show the card to the other spectators and then return it.

You need to learn the name of this card. There are many ways to accomplish this. The simplest is to shuffle the pack yourself and note the top and bottom cards while doing so. Have The Sitter pick a card, replace it on top of the deck, cut once, give the pack one riffle shuffle, and cut again. The chosen card will be between the two you noted. Usually, it will be the only one in this position, but if your luck is very bad, there may be half a dozen others as well. This need not worry you, if you know how to fish.

Turn the deck over and spread it out. Let us suppose that the following cards have fallen between the two you used as *keys*:

4H, KD, 2C, 4D, 10S, 3S, KH

Ask The Sitter a few questions such as his favorite color, the number of his brothers and sisters, and his place in the family. Say, "People like you generally tend to avoid the obvious. I'd say that you picked a spot card. Am I right?"

Nine times out of ten, his expression will reveal whether he is going to say "Yes" or "No." If you see that he disagrees with your statement, cut off his reply by adding quickly, "However, I think you're a bit different. You'd choose a face card." If he is about to agree, state flatly, "Yes, I feel sure you'd prefer a spot card."

This eliminates the Kings and leaves:

4H, 2C, 4D, 10S, 3S.

Give a brief character reading here. Then say, "Your type of person is apt to prefer color to black-and-white. You probably chose a red card." Watch The Sitter's face, and try to anticipate his answer. In any case, either his expression or his reply will tell you whether your guess is right or wrong.

Let us suppose the card is red. You now know that it is one of the fours. Make a few more statements about The Sitter's character. Remark that as he has shown a warm temperament, his card is probably a Heart. If his expression fails to reveal whether you are right, ask flatly, "Is that correct?"

If it is a Heart, you know that it must be the four. However, from the standpoint of the audience, it may be any spot Heart. You can, therefore, proceed with your reading without asking any more questions. For example, "You like things to be balanced. This indicates that you probably picked an even-numbered card. You tend to avoid the obvious. That means you would prefer a card that was low but not too low. I'd guess that you're the sort of person who'd pick the four of Hearts."

Answering Questions

Routines like *The Sigil of Solomon* are most impressive when sitters ask questions which The Seer answers. As you rarely know the answer, it may seem impossible to give one. However, there are several ways in which you can provide an apparent answer, and this is all you need.

The principal technique consists in restating the question so that it sounds like an answer to everyone except the person who asked it. This may not satisfy the questioner, but he will be amazed by the fact that you seem to have read his mind.

Thus, if The Sitter in *The Sigil of Solomon* writes, "Will I go to Europe this summer?" you can reply, "I see a journey. A long journey . . . to an eastern country. . . . At least the traveler moves in an easterly direction. Perhaps it is only to England or France. This trip seems to be in the future. I would say that it is some three or four months away."

A question about the future can usually be "answered" by giving advice. Thus, "Will my child get well?" may be taken to mean, "What should I do to give my child the best chance of recovery?" The answer is, "Follow your doctor's instructions implicitly. Any carelessness on your part may prolong your child's illness."

In most cases, it is easy to give advice that will be recognized as sound. There is an old receipt that guarantees success in life. "Never do anything that you know is foolish, and do everything that you know is wise." Most people ask the advice of others because they are not prepared to act on their own. Either they want their opinion confirmed, or they hope the advisor will find some excuse for them to avoid doing what they know they should do.

When someone asks a question that can be interpreted as a request for advice, inquire what he considers the right answer. This will at least give you an important clue as to the proper response. If you need to keep your reply short, say, "You don't really need to ask me that question. You already know the answer in your heart. You just aren't willing to face it."

Here are a few more stock replies to common questions:

"Worry comes from thinking about your troubles without trying to correct them. Either analyze the problem and seek a practical solution or turn your attention to something else."

"Your desire for sympathy leads you to confide private matters to people who will gossip about you. Learn to keep your own counsel."

"You are letting your friends impose on you. Real friends never ask favors that they do not expect to repay."

"I feel that you are not asking the right question. Analyze your situation more deeply and try to learn more facts. Once you arrive at the true question, you will be able to answer it yourself."

"You are crying over spilled milk. Learn to face the facts and stop torturing yourself by thinking about what might have been."

"Never criticize anyone unless you feel sure you can help him. If the fault cannot be cured, or if the other person is unlikely to act on your advice, any criticism that you give will do more harm than good."

"You are letting yourself be guided by your feelings rather than by your good sense. Also, you are seeing only your side of the case. Try looking at the other fellow's side before you make up your mind."

When some sitter insists on an answer instead of accepting advice, there are several ways to avoid giving a definite reply. For example:

"I cannot see that far into the future. Everything is misty . . . blurred."

"The influences are favorable, but they are not strong enough for me to feel justified in making a definite prediction."

"The future is not preordained but depends on your actions. If I predict an event, and you expect it to occur without any effort on your part, your failure to promote it will actually keep it from taking place. Then, instead of realizing that you are at fault, you will denounce me for a false prophet."

"The event does not depend on you alone. Someone else has a powerful influence. Do you know a person whose name begins with J?" Most sitters will think of someone at once. If yours does not, you can say, "J need not be a friend. He, or she, may be some stranger. Perhaps a clerk at a travel agency or an official connected with passports."

If a sitter persists, say, "I prefer not to answer that question in public. There is at least one phase of it—one of which you are not fully aware—that I am sure you would rather have me take up with you privately." As you should end every session of realistic conjuring with an illusion-breaker, you are safe. You have achieved conviction during the routine, and that is all you set out to do. If some overcredulous sitter does approach you afterward, you can assure him that it was merely a trick without spoiling the entertainment.

Honest conjurers give readings only for entertainment. Never let yourself be tempted to provide a definite prophecy. Professional spirit mediums and fortune-tellers often make predictions; they know that their accidental hits will be remembered and that most of their misses will be forgotten.

This sort of thing can do a greal deal of harm. I have a spiritualistic pamphlet before me which recommends saying to anyone who seems in good physical condition but who asks about his health, "Change your diet and follow the correct laws of nature. Yes, you will reach the ripe old age of 80 or 81. A stomach disorder will occur about the age of 49. With your resistance, you will recuperate from this in a short time." That is good advice for the person who interprets every tummy-ache as cancer. But it is downright murder if the victim really has cancer of the stomach during his late 40's.

Even on minor matters, never give a flat answer. Some people insist on taking predictions seriously, no matter how hard you try to disillusion them at the end of the session. I know one woman who has watched a number of conjurers, but who still asks at regular intervals, "Are you *sure* that's *only* a trick?" Tell one of these credulous souls that he is, or is not, going to Europe, and you may cause him a great deal of inconvenience and worry for nothing.

ELIMINATING OTHER POSSIBLE EXPLANATIONS

An effect is not proof of the phenomenon unless all other explanations are eliminated. One of the most embarrassing moments in my early attempts at conjuring occurred when I went through a trick perfectly only to have a twelve-year-old boy point out a much simpler way in which it could have been done. Nothing but Houdini's magnificent showmanship kept his needle trick from suffering the same fate; the dentist who examined his mouth could have been a confederate who switched the loose needles for the threaded ones. Houdini established such a strong atmosphere that most people completely overlooked this possibility; it did not occur to me until I was writing this book some forty years later. Nevertheless, in the hands of anyone but a master, the dentist would have been a weakness rather than a source of convincing proof.

Unfortunately, spectators are prone to accept the wildest explanations rather than admit that they have been fooled. "It's all done with mirrors," or "It went up his sleeve," satisfies many people, even when it should be obvious that neither device could possibly achieve the effect.

There is no way to avoid such absurd "explanations" entirely, but try to decide what suggestions will be offered and then arrange your routine to prove that they are impossible.

Chapter 9
DEVICES FOR DECEPTION

A device is the means of achieving an effect. Conjurers and laymen alike tend to overemphasize the importance of devices. The idea seems to be that because the device is the secret of an illusion, it is the only thing that matters. This is like saying that rosin is all there is to playing the violin. No one can coax a tune from a violin without this vital substance, and no one can understand how a violin works unless he knows the secret of rosin. Nevertheless, although rosin is essential, the art of the violinist begins where the rosin leaves off. Conjuring requires devices, but the art of illusion starts where the devices leave off.

SELECTING A DEVICE

We have already seen that a basic routine like *Horoscope* can be dramatized to fit a wide range of different themes. Similarly, most effects can be produced by a variety of devices. Here are a few examples that enable you to perform routines of the *Horoscope* class:

1. Use any kind of paper and distinguish the sheets by tiny pencil dots.

2. Use index cards and mark their edges with pencil. Such marks are almost invisible when the cards are separated (as they are in the hands of the spectators) but stand out clearly when the cards are stacked (as they are when you hold them yourself).

3. Many of the inks used to rule paper or index cards are soluble in water and blur when moistened. Make your code by wetting a quarter-inch of a different line on every sheet. If the ink on your paper will not dissolve, you can erase a little of one line on each sheet.

These are only a small sample. Any device which identifies each Sitter with either a birthday or a piece of paper will make the effect possible.

If a device is successful, the audience is not even aware of its existence. No spectator can tell whether it is ingenious or conventional, whether it takes years of practice or can be mastered in a minute, whether it costs several hundred dollars (like some electronic equipment used by mind readers) or only a few cents (like the notebook sheets for *Horoscope*). As the audience does not know these things, it cannot be influenced by them. Hence, they are of no importance to anyone but the performer himself. This is the one phase of conjuring for which we do not need to consider the viewpoint of the audience. If an audience has any viewpoint about a device, the device is worthless.

A device is only a means to an end. Its sole function is to provide the effect, and it has no value in its own right. An ideal device is effective, indetectable, foolproof, easy, and inexpensive. Qualities such as simplicity, ingenuity, and fine workmanship are worth noting because they usually make the device more effective, more indetectable, more reliable, or easier. However, they occasionally interfere with the really important qualities; when they do, they are liabilities, not assets.

Effectiveness is, of course, the first consideration. A device that fails to create the desired effect convincingly serves no purpose at all.

No device is completely indetectable and foolproof. Even the coded notebook sheets in *Horoscope* may be suspected. Or some Sitter may inadvertently enlarge a tear and thus destroy part of the code. Although such possibilities are always present, we should not allow too much leeway. Unless a device comes reasonably close to being both indetectable and foolproof, it is not worth considering.

The difficulty involved in using a device is not always obvious. The device in *Horoscope* requires no skill at all, but the ability to give entertaining readings is not acquired overnight. You may find it easier to perform illusions that rely more on skill and less on showmanship.

When judging the difficulty of a device, consider also its usefulness. For example, the ability to hide a card or other small object in your hand by *palming* can be applied in so many illusions that it may repay hours of practice. On the other hand, a device that serves for only one routine will not justify much effort unless you are in a position to perform that routine for many audiences.

Before investing time or money in equipment, do not ask yourself, "Is the apparatus worth it?" but "Will the illusion that it enables me to create be worth the cost?" Then go on to ask, "Can I get the same or a better effect at a lower price?"

Stage and club performers must also consider appearance. Crude props will prejudice an audience against an act. On the other hand, attractive, well-finished apparatus often makes an audience consider the performance better than it really is. Innocent equipment, such as scarves and tables, usually affects the cost more than the devices do, but there is no clear division between the innocent and the secret. Thus, the device for *The Voodoo Doll* does not depend on the cabinet itself but on the way it is used.

All devices for deception belong to four basic types: *sleights*, *prearrangement*, *secret apparatus*, and *arcana*.

SLEIGHTS

Sleights are secret moves made by the conjurer. A catalog of sleights would be endless, and new ones are devised every day. Nevertheless, if you acquire skill in using a dozen easy sleights, you will be able to present nine card effects out of ten. With these, you can achieve enough excellent illusions to last your lifetime.

There are strong reasons for limiting yourself in this way. Real mastery of a few sleights is worth more than the ability to perform a hundred adequately. Acquiring a large repertoire of sleights takes many hours, and keeping in practice is a never-ending chore. The same amount of time and effort spent on perfecting your presentations will undoubtedly pay bigger dividends.

On the other hand, there is something to be said for acquiring a number of different sleights. If you can produce the same effect by several methods, you can sometimes throw skeptical spectators off guard. Again, with a wide range of sleights at your disposal, you can meet challenges and slip out of difficulties in ways that the master of a few sleights could never hope to equal. In spite of these advantages, I doubt if it will pay you to acquire many sleights unless you are a professional and specialize in card tricks.

Sleights have been devised for coins, thimbles, cigarettes, and almost every other small object that a conjurer can conceivably use. However, for our purpose, it will be enough to describe a few of the workhorses needed for card conjuring.

When learning these sleights, follow the directions and illustrations with a deck of cards in your hands. The sleights are so easy that you can probably do them the first time you try. In spite of this, even the simplest sleight requires careful practice.

This brings us to a basic principle which governs many aspects of all the performing arts. It is so vital that it deserves to be printed in capitals: NEVER PRACTICE IN PUBLIC.

A performer has much to think about during his act. He cannot concentrate on these things if his mind is distracted by technical details, which he should have mastered so thoroughly that they require no more attention than he gives to tying his shoe laces. If he needs to spare them a moment's thought, he has not practiced enough. A pianist who thinks about his fingering never gives a good performance. Neither does the conjurer who thinks about his sleights.

The *break* permits you to identify a card in the middle of the deck without letting the audience suspect that you have done anything. Allow someone to choose a card freely and memorize it. Have the card returned. When it is about two-thirds of the way in, squeeze the deck. This keeps the card from being shoved home. At the same moment, withdraw the deck slightly and push the card in with the first three fingers of your right hand. As you do so, press one finger into the crack between the projecting card and the upper packet (Fig. 67). This makes a break in the deck above the chosen card. Slide the little finger of your left hand into the break. If you hold the deck as illustrated in Fig. 68, neither the break nor the finger can be detected by the audience.

The *pass* was formerly regarded as the most useful card sleight. A pass may be defined as a secret cut; the part of the deck below the break is brought to the top without the knowledge of the audience. Unfortunately, even the easiest methods

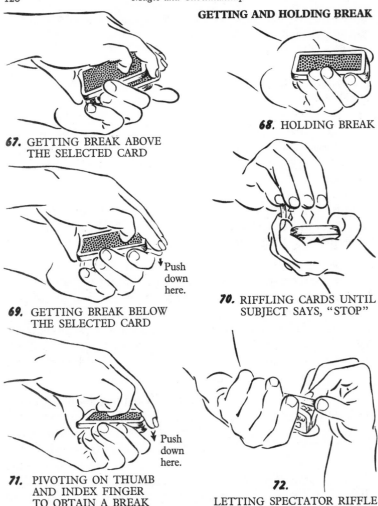

GETTING AND HOLDING BREAK

67. GETTING BREAK ABOVE
THE SELECTED CARD

68. HOLDING BREAK

69. GETTING BREAK BELOW
THE SELECTED CARD

Push down here.

70. RIFFLING CARDS UNTIL
SUBJECT SAYS, "STOP"

71. PIVOTING ON THUMB
AND INDEX FINGER
TO OBTAIN A BREAK

Push down here.

72.
LETTING SPECTATOR RIFFLE

of making a pass are extremely difficult. Few performers can carry out this move indetectably unless the attention of the audience is diverted at the crucial moment. To meet this objection, modern card men have developed substitutes for the pass. These are easier and, for most purposes, better than the original.

Let us suppose that you are holding a break above the chosen card and want to bring this to the top of the deck. Cut the deck casually at the break and shuffle it, being careful to leave the chosen card on top after the shuffle. The most thumb-fingered manipulator can accomplish that with an overhand shuffle like the one in Fig. 10. Omit the toad stone, take a batch of cards from the middle of the pack and shuffle them back into the middle leaving the top and/or bottom cards untouched. A *riffle shuffle* is slightly more convincing but no more difficult (Fig. 73). A shuffle is not only much easier than a secret pass, but the shuffle itself reinforces the idea that the chosen card is literally "lost in the shuffle."

While shuffling, you can easily retain a packet of four or five cards on the top or bottom of the deck. If you want to keep more cards, or even the whole deck, in order, you can do it by substituting an open cut for the shuffle. Cutting brings a different card to the face of the deck, but it does not change the sequence of the cards in relation to each other. Many card effects depend upon this important fact.

Although a cut is less impressive than a shuffle, it is usually above suspicion. To be on the safe side, make a double cut (Fig. 75). This is a small thing, but it will fool people who know that a conjurer's cut is not always so innocent as it seems.

Some illusions require bringing the chosen card to the bottom of the deck. This is done by getting your break below the card as in Fig. 69.

RIFFLE SHUFFLE

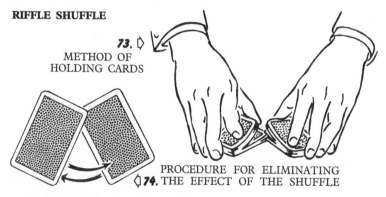

73. ◊
METHOD OF
HOLDING CARDS

PROCEDURE FOR ELIMINATING
◊**74.** THE EFFECT OF THE SHUFFLE

The technique in Fig. 73 can be used for a fair shuffle. You can also control one or more cards on the face of the deck by dropping them first, and/or one or more cards on the back by dropping them last. If you swing one packet on top (Fig. 74) instead of shoving them into each other, the result is a false shuffle that leaves the whole deck in its original order. The natural action of the hands hides the sleight. Also, you can divert attention from it by staring at the cards as you riffle and then suddenly looking up and asking a question at the moment when you swing one packet over the other as shown by the arrows in Fig. 74.

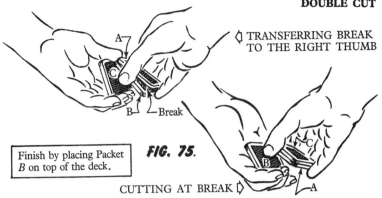

◊ TRANSFERRING BREAK
TO THE RIGHT THUMB

A

C

B — Break

Finish by placing Packet
B on top of the deck.

FIG. 75.

B

C

A

CUTTING AT BREAK ◊

If you habitually use the same technique for card control, it will soon become obvious. Here is another method of securing a break beneath the chosen card. Hold the deck as shown in Fig. 70 and riffle the ends of the cards, saying, "Tell me when to stop." At the command, "Stop!" display the next card and say, "That's your card. Remember it."

Press your left thumb and forefinger into the break between the front ends of the two packets. Let the upper packet go, and then push down on its far end (Fig. 71). This makes it pivot on your thumb and forefinger in such a way that the rear end kicks up and leaves a break. Thrust the end of your little finger into this break and immediately square the deck.

The method in Fig. 72 applies the same principle but is

Push up top card with left thumb.

76.

GLIMPSING TOP AND BOTTOM
CARDS DURING THE SHUFFLE

more subtle. Show a spectator how to riffle one corner of the deck. When he does this, tell him to stop wherever he likes and to peep at the index of the exposed card. After he has found his card and lets the upper packet fall, your first finger acts as a pivot. Press down on the front of the deck. The rear of the upper packet will tip up far enough for you to get the end of your little finger under it.

Both of these sleights make a break below the chosen card. Shuffling or cutting will bring this card to the face of the deck.

A card controlled to the bottom can easily be *glimpsed* by tipping the deck slightly. Fig. 76 shows an easy way of glimpsing the top card while shuffling the rest of the pack.

Here is a completely realistic illusion that is made possible by card control:

LIE DETECTOR

After a game of cards, bring up the topic of lie detectors. Explain, if necessary, that these are machines which record changes in the subject's pulse, blood pressure, breathing rate, and sometimes other reactions as well. State that for many purposes, no apparatus is really needed; fairly accurate results can be secured by merely feeling the subject's pulse.

Offer to demonstrate. An expert usually begins by convincing his subject that the procedure really works. He is told to draw a card and then to answer "No" to every question the operator asks. While you are explaining this, pick up the deck and fan it to let your Subject choose a card. Tell him to show it to the other spectators and remember it himself. Hold out the deck for him to replace his card. Shuffle the deck "absent-mindedly." Glimpse the card as you do so and drop the pack on the table.

Put your fingers on The Subject's pulse. Concentrate on this during the rest of the routine. Ask, "Was your card red?" Even if it happens to be the Queen of Hearts, he will obey your instructions and answer "No." Ask, "Was it a Diamond? A high card? A face card? A King? A Queen?" In each case, he replies, "No." Drop his hand, smile, and say, "Unless I've missed out somewhere, you drew the Queen of Hearts."

The *force* is a method of requiring a spectator to select a particular playing card, number, or whatnot while convincing him that he has a free choice. In *Preview*, for example, the

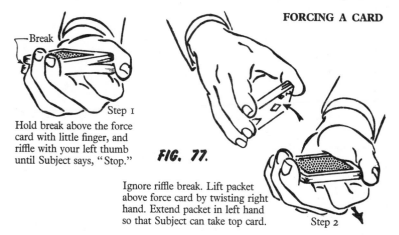

FORCING A CARD

Break

Step 1

Hold break above the force card with little finger, and riffle with your left thumb until Subject says, "Stop."

FIG. 77.

Ignore riffle break. Lift packet above force card by twisting right hand. Extend packet in left hand so that Subject can take top card.

Step 2

person who draws a slip from the box believes that he picks one at random although he must actually choose one bearing the name of the confederate.

There are dozens of good card forces. If you expect to do much work with cards, you should master at least three so that you can vary your technique. Thus, you can repeat *Lie Detector* with several Subjects if you use different methods to force cards on each one. Or you can force cards on some Subjects and use control-and-glimpse techniques on the rest. This reinforces the suggestion that the method of handling the cards has no significance. The force in Fig. 77 is probably the easiest.

Even with the few sleights given here, you can present five location- or discovery-effects without using the same sleight twice.

PREARRANGEMENT

Prearrangement consists in placing apparatus (usually cards) in some order which the conjurer knows but keeps secret. The term covers everything from simply noting one or two key cards, as we did in *The Singing Glass*, to stacking the whole deck as we did for *The Book of Thoth*.

A stacked deck becomes much more deceptive when you execute a false shuffle. The one in Fig. 74 is quite easy and is as effective as any.

Normally, you will not only shuffle but will also let a spectator cut the deck. This does no harm in some routines. But if you need a *stock* of several prearranged cards on the face or back of the deck, a cut is fatal unless you can cancel its effect. Do this by *crimping* the bottom card diagonally as shown in Fig. 78. Cut the deck yourself and ask a spectator to cut again. He is almost certain to cut at the crimped card. However, if

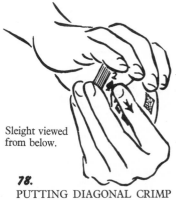

Sleight viewed from below.

78.
PUTTING DIAGONAL CRIMP IN THE BOTTOM CARD

he fails to do so, cut a third time yourself making sure to cut at the crimp.

A completely stacked deck is the key to many of the most mysterious illusions that it is possible to perform. Some *setups* are designed only for particular tricks. However, there are also general-utility setups which can be used in many ways. The one named after Si Stebbins is especially good. I recommend it strongly. Some other setups have more advantages, but they require memorizing the whole deck so thoroughly that you know the relative position of each card without thinking. This may be justified for the professional who keeps in constant practice, but it is hopeless for anyone else.

To prepare the Si Stebbins setup, divide the cards into suits. Count Jack as 11, Queen as 12, and King as 13. Arrange the cards so that each one is 3 higher than the one before it, and the suits rotate in the order Clubs, Hearts, Spades, Diamonds. This is the sequence of their initials in the word CHaSeD (see Fig. 79, and the accompanying description of the setup and how to use it).

With such an arrangement, you can fan the deck face down and let a Subject draw any card. When he does so, cut the deck at that point and glimpse the card above the cut (now the bottom card) as you square the deck. Adding three and naming the next suit will give you the name of the chosen card. Thus, if the glimpsed card is the four of Diamonds, the seven of Clubs was drawn; if the glimpsed card is the Queen of Hearts, the spectator selected the two of Spades.

Unfortunately, the Si Stebbins setup has one serious weakness. The faces of the cards cannot be shown; the fact that the colors alternate makes prearrangement obvious. I devised the following subtlety to overcome this. As it requires an extra mental step, I do not recommend it to those who employ the setup only occasionally. But for anyone who has much use for a stacked deck, the advantage more than repays the slight extra effort.

When you lay out the cards, interchange suits for the Aces, Kings, Queens, and Jacks. Switch minor suits (Clubs and Diamonds) so that the high Clubs occupy the places of the high Diamonds and vice versa. Do the same with the major suits (Hearts and Spades). With this setup, the colors come in unequal batches.

You can now fan the deck facing The Subject and let him draw a card. Glimpse the next card by bending its index corner

SI STEBBINS SETUP

AC,	4H,	7S,	10D,	KC,	3H,	6S,	9D,	QC,	2H,	5S,	8D,	JC,
AH,	4S,	7D,	10C,	KH,	3S,	6D,	9C,	QH,	2S,	5D,	8C,	JH,
AS,	4D,	7C,	10H,	KS,	3D,	6C,	9H,	QS,	2D,	5C,	8H,	JS,
AD,	4C,	7H,	10S,	KD,	3C,	6H,	9S,	QD,	2C,	5H,	8S,	JD.

LOCATING ANY CARD IN A SI STEBBINS DECK

To find the position (P) of the wanted card (W) when you know the card (F) on the front of the deck. First find the suit number (S) by counting clockwise around the circle in Fig. 79 from the suit of the known card to the suit of the wanted card. Thus, if the card on the front

79. SUIT ORDER

of the deck is a Heart and the wanted card is a Club, the suit number is 3. If both cards are the same suit, the suit number is 0. Multiply this by 13 ($3 \times 13 = 39$; $0 \times 13 = 0$). Subtract the wanted card from the front card and multiply the result by 4. If, for example, the card on the front of the deck is a Queen (12) and the wanted card is a nine, $12 - 9 = 3$, and $3 \times 4 = 12$. Add this to the product of the suit number times 13. The result is the position of the wanted card counting from the top. This is much simpler than it looks in print. The formula is:

$$P = (13 \times S) + 4(F - W).$$

Example: The front card is the King of Spades and the wanted card is the eight of Clubs. The suit number (count "Diamonds, Clubs") is 2, and 13 times 2 is 26. Subtracting 8 from King (13) gives 5, and 4 times 5 is 20. Then, 26 plus 20 is 46, which is the position of the Club eight.

When the wanted card is higher than the known card, add 13 before subtracting. Thus if F is the four of Diamonds and W the Jack of Clubs, we get:

$$S = 1; 13S = 13.$$

$4 + 13 = 17$; $17 - 11$ (Jack) $= 6$.
$4 \times 6 = 24$.
$13 + 24 = 37$.

When the total is more than 52, subtract 52. Suppose, for example, that the Spade ten is on the front and the wanted card is the Heart Ace. Then:

$$S = 3; 13S = 13 \times 3 = 39.$$
$10 - 1 = 9$; $4 \times 9 = 36$.
$39 + 36 = 75$; $75 - 52 = 23$.

Naming the card at a particular position is a little more complex, but very little. Dividing the position number (P) by 4 gives the quotient (q) and a remainder. The remainder is the suit number (S). Thus, if the card on the front is a Spade, the 14th card from the back must be a Club (14 divided by 4 gives a quotient of 3 and a remainder of 2). Subtract the quotient from the card on the face and add three times the remainder (suit number). For example, when the card on the front is the Spade 10, the card 14 from the back must be the Club King. The computation goes like this:

$14 \div 4 = 3\frac{2}{4}$; the quotient is 3 and the suit number is 2.
$(F - q) + 3S = W$, $10 - 3 = 7$;
$7 + (3 \times 2) = 13$ (King).

When the quotient is larger than the card on the front, subtract the latter from the former and then subtract the result from 3 times the suit number (remainder). Thus, if the card on the front is the Club 2, what is the 43rd card from the back?

$43 \div 4 = 10\frac{3}{4}$; the quotient is 10, and the suit number is 3.
$3S - (q - F) = W$; $3 \times 3 = 9$;
$10 - 2 = 8$; $9 - 8 = 1$.

The wanted card is the Diamond Ace.

up with your thumb (Fig. 80). The rule for the suits is simple. Whenever you glimpse a high card, change its suit before making your computation. Whenever the result of the computation is a high card, change the suit before naming the chosen card. The examples that follow should make this clear.

Card glimpsed	4H	AS	9C	JS
Think of it as	4H	AH	9C	JH
Apply formula	7S	4S	QH	AS
You name	7S	4S	QS	AH

The Si Stebbins setup permits you to name the card at any position in the deck or to give the position of any card named. The following routine lets you work out the necessary arithmetic on paper. Once you get the knack, you can make the computations in your head and produce some of the most baffling illusions in the whole field of conjuring.

THE MONTE CARLO METHOD

State that the law of averages can produce information from random data by statistical techniques. No one knows when you will die, but insurance actuaries can tell almost exactly how many men your age will die next year. Workers in operations research can advise the captain of a destroyer how to hunt for a submarine although he must guess at such apparently vital facts as her size, her speed, and the mentality of her commander. The process is called *The Monte Carlo Method*. All of this is true.

Offer to demonstrate. Place a Si Stebbins deck before someone after glimpsing the bottom card. Ask him to name a card. Then, have each spectator guess where that card lies in the pack. Remark that the more guesses you have, the more accurate the Monte Carlo Method is likely to be. Record the guesses but otherwise ignore them and use the formulas given on p. 126. Make a near miss;

80. GLIMPSING CARD IN DECK

if you learn that the card is the twenty-first from the top, announce that it is the twentieth. When you find it, explain that the method does not pretend to be exact. If you interchange suits, the rule given above also applies here. The procedure may seem involved. But after working out a few examples, you will find it quite easy.

The stage conjurer has no trouble in introducing a stacked deck. The man who works close up can carry the prearranged deck vertically in a side pocket of his coat. After a duplicate deck has been proved fair by repeated shuffling and use in several routines, the conjurer casually drops it into his pocket as though the performance were over. This deck goes in horizontally so that the stacked deck sticks up above it and is easy to grasp. If the performer is asked to continue, he simply takes out his stacked deck and is set for a miracle.

SECRET APPARATUS

Young performers usually start with tricks which depend on secret apparatus because dealers' advertisements lead them to believe that these devices are self-working. This is never wholly true. In many cases, handling the apparatus calls for more skill than you need for simple sleights. Furthermore, although some devices achieve their effects without help from the performer, no device has built-in showmanship.

Duplicates are perhaps the most widely used type of secret apparatus. The handkerchief on The Assistant's leg in *Twentieth Century Nylon* is a typical example.

A *gimmick* is a piece of apparatus which the audience never notices, and which is so secret that its existence is never suspected. The salt used in *Ancentral Aid* is a gimmick. So is the harness in *The Expanding Rabbit.*

Fakes are pieces of equipment which seem fair but which are actually doctored to permit results that would be impossible if they were innocent. The looped string in *The Strong Man's Secret* and the dice in *The Haunted Conjurer* are representative examples.

ARCANA

The fourth main category of devices covers all those that work by secret knowledge alone, without the aid of sleights, prearrangement, or apparatus. Although many of the most indetectable devices fall into this category, conjurers have never developed a technical name for it. However, as ancient sorcerers and alchemists called secret knowledge arcana (singular *arcanum*), we shall use this term. A number of examples have appeared in previous pages: singletons are not rare but occur in five deals out of six; cutting a deck does not disturb the order of the cards; tearing a folded scrap of paper both ways leaves the center intact.

Anyone who takes conjuring seriously will do well to keep notes of all the promising devices he finds. List only devices, not whole routines. Describe each one on a separate 3 by 5 index card or a sheet of a small loose-leaf notebook. This will enable you to arrange them by types, and to rearrange them from time to time as your collection grows and your ideas of classification change. Thus, you may start by keeping all card sleights together, but when you have twenty or more, you will need to reclassify them under subheads such as, "Forces," "Methods of Control," and so on. Still later, you may want to subdivide "Methods of Control" into "Card to Top," "Card to Bottom," and "Card to a Predetermined Number."

Notes of this type are invaluable when you work out a new routine or revise an old one. All the relevant material is collected in one place, and you do not need to wade through notes on other matters to find it.

Chapter 10

THE GREAT SECRET

An illusion is, by definition, untrue. In every field, we detect untruth by inconsistency. We recognize statements as false when they contradict themselves. An actor who does something which is not in keeping with his role falls out of character, and the spell of the play is broken. If a conjurer's words and actions fail to match the powers he claims, he pricks the bubble of illusion; he may still entertain his audience with a trick, but he loses the magic of drama. *Consistency is the key to conviction.*

Consistency is also the key to entertainment. In entertainment as in physics, we achieve the greatest effect when all the available forces are directed toward the same goal. You would take no pleasure in a football game if the teams stopped after every play and performed a comedy skit. The game might be dull and the skits might be good, but you would still be irritated by the interruptions. You enjoy a parade between halves, but that is because it fills time while the players are resting. The same principle governs a play or a conjuring performance. You make the best impression when you present a unified routine built around a definite theme and give it a consistent treatment throughout.

THE "AS IF" PRINCIPLE

Consistency implies a standard. We cannot merely be consistent; we must be consistent with something. In creating an illusion, our standard is the theme. Once you realize this, you will find that the theme provides a guide to every detail of your presentation. This is a tremendous asset. It answers many questions almost before you can ask them.

The treatment provides a second standard, but even this is largely governed by the theme. Although *Horoscope* allows several kinds of treatment, *Dial Information* must be handled seriously and *The Haunted Conjurer* is worthless if it is not funny.

These facts give us a working rule: *Plan a routine as if every element of the theme—personalities, phenomena, purpose, and proof—were literally true. Select a treatment appropriate to this theme. Make every detail of the presentation, however trivial, consistent with your theme and treatment.*

In most situations, this rule is a welcome aid. It not only helps us to make decisions, but suggests ideas. Thus, the effect of *The Haunted Conjurer* came directly from the theme. How would An Obeah Man with a sense of humor jinx *Passe-Passe Dice*? By providing a different but appropriate climax. What should it be? Have him transform the dice into something else. What? Black-and-white animals. Rabbits? Too large. Hamsters? Too small. Guinea pigs? O.K.

Consistency of purpose is an especially helpful guide. When you give a demonstration, treat it exactly as you would if you were a salesman demonstrating a new appliance, or a teacher demonstrating a scientific principle to his class. This allows plenty of room for showmanship.

When I stage a play, I try to make each point so clear that the dullest spectator cannot help understanding it. I like to think of this dullest spectator as "The Deaf Old Lady in the Back Row." If she can follow the action without effort, no one else will have any difficulty.

Demonstration is as much an art as drama. The demonstrator's "Deaf Old Lady" may be a harried housewife or an inattentive school boy. His "back row" may be no further away than his elbow. Nevertheless, there is always one spectator who is especially hard to reach. The demonstrator's job is to make each point clear to that spectator without boring the others.

A good demonstrator wants his presentation to be interesting, impressive, and memorable. All of these qualities require showmanship. In short, the only difference between the demonstrations given by salesmen and teachers on the one hand and conjurers on the other is that the former demonstrate genuine phenomena, and the latter demonstrate false ones.

The following illusion is based on an old parlor trick. However, it is extremely deceptive and supplies a fine example of a straightforward demonstration.

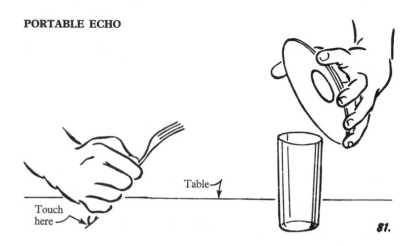

Table

Touch here

81.

PORTABLE ECHO

Introduce the subject of acoustics. Pick up a table fork. State that all forks are really tuning forks. Ordinary forks, however, give so little sound that we can barely hear them. Prove this by striking the tines of your fork on the edge of the table and holding it to your neighbor's ear.

Remind your audience that resonance can amplify sound. For example, if a violin lacked a sound box, it would not be audible ten feet away. But with the sound box, a violinist can make his music carry to every corner of an enormous concert hall.

Point out that although most people know about tuning forks and resonators, comparatively few are aware that sound can be reflected in the same way as light. Actually, whispering galleries, such as those in the United States Capitol and St. Paul's Cathedral in London, reflect the sound like concave mirrors and focus it on one spot.

You propose to demonstrate reflection by the use of a saucer and resonance with the aid of a tumbler. Place the tumbler on the table and hold the saucer over it (Fig. 81). Strike the fork against the table. While it is still vibrating, tip the saucer back and forth until the sound is reflected into the glass, which then becomes a resonator and hums loudly. However, when you move the saucer a fraction of an inch from the correct position, the sound is cut off.

This is a convincing demonstration. Glasses can act as resonators, and curved surfaces do reflect sound. The whole procedure might be followed for a class in physics except for one thing—the phenomenon is false. Strike the tines of the fork and then touch the butt against the table. The table top amplifies the sound. Lift the butt a sixteenth of an inch, and the sound stops. The glass and saucer are merely window dressing.

EVERY LITTLE BIT HURTS

Although the "as if" rule is an inspiring guide, it is also a strict taskmaster. Consistency is essential to any suspension of disbelief. No conviction is so deep that it cannot be destroyed by a discrepancy in presentation. On the contrary, the more profoundly the spectators are enthralled by a performance, the more likely they are to be jerked back to reality by anything which is not in harmony with the illusion.

Furthermore, even the most trivial discrepancy may provide a clue that reveals a device and destroys the illusion. As the creation of an illusion is the whole aim of dramatic conjuring, overlooking a discrepancy is like failing to oil one bearing in a motor. If that one bearing burns out, the whole motor stops; if one discrepancy reveals your device, your illusion fails.

Conjuring illusions are more delicate than drama. A play is long; if the spell is broken, it can usually be rewoven. Also, the spectators do everything in their power to suspend their own disbelief. Once a conjuring illusion is destroyed, it has gone forever. There is no time to rebuild it, and the spectators offer no help. They want to be fooled, but they want to be fooled in spite of themselves. The audience at a play supplies willing credulity. The conjurer's audience is deliberately skeptical.

In many cases, complete consistency is attainable. In *Horoscope*, for example, The Astrologer's procedure is exactly what it would be if he could actually analyze people's characters from their birthdays. Of course, those who take astrology seriously insist that it is necessary to know the precise minute of birth and to go through the elaborate business of casting a horoscope. However, there is nothing to prevent a conjurer-astrologer from posing as A Superastrologer, provided that his proof substantiates his claim. *Dial Information, Chromavoyance,* and *Mental Television* are other examples of completely consistent illusions.

Perfect consistency is possible only when the performer controls the conditions. In *Horoscope*, he must provide the paper on which the birthdays are written. In *Dial Information*, he must arrange to have one of his coins used for the test and must dial The Telepath's number himself.

Unfortunately, complete consistency is rare. Some discrepancies are normally unavoidable. In such cases, our course is clear. We must either find a way to conceal the flaw, or we must abandon the routine. Avoidable discrepancies are more insidious. For example, the performer may invent a witty remark or a striking bit of business. It does not fit his theme, but he is so enamoured of it that he uses it anyway. If his audience responds favorably, he persuades himself that his judgment was sound. Actually it was false.

In mathematics, the whole is always equal to the sum of its parts; two and two invariably add up to exactly four. In the arts, however, the whole is either much more than the sum of the parts or much less. The face on the Mona Lisa is not especially beautiful. But if some fool painted in lovelier features, Leonardo's masterpiece would cease to be a great picture. This is true of every art. Many dramas have been ruined by actors who tried to enliven serious scenes by being funny. The spectators laughed at the comedy, but they were bored by the play. The same law holds for conjuring: *No matter how effective an inconsistent part may be, the damage that it does to the routine as a whole more than offsets whatever advantages it may have in itself.*

This principle is easy enough to grasp in theory. Unfortunately, as in all other cases where conservation is needed, practical applications are apt to be overlooked. Directors and performers alike are so flattered by hearing an audience laugh or exclaim over some line or action that they blind themselves to the harm it does to the play or the illusion.

Laziness also leads us to minimize the havoc created by discrepancies. It is so much easier to ignore them than to eliminate them. Even when a friend points out a flaw, we tend to reply confidently, "The audience never notices that." This ostrich-like attitude is fatal. A discrepancy may escape conscious notice and still weaken conviction. The suspension of disbelief is a subconscious process. No one says to himself, "If I am to enjoy this performance to the full, I must accept it as true and close my mind to the fact that I know it to be false." Spectators can be led to adopt this attitude, but they must do so without thinking—and without realizing that they have done anything of the kind.

I cannot stress the harm done by discrepancies too strongly. My whole procedure as a showman is based on a technique of hunting for faults and ruthlessly eliminating them. This may seem like a strange way to go about a creative art, but I can assure you that it works beautifully in practice. The good parts of a play or routine take care of themselves. If I see a way to improve them, I do so. But I never worry about them. Instead,

I concentrate on spotting and correcting the flaws. *These are the places that offer the greatest opportunities for improvement. Hence, they are also the places where time and effort devoted to improvement will produce the greatest results.*

In a surprising percentage of cases, correcting a discrepancy pays a double dividend. We not only eliminate the flaw, but the solution provides some positive improvement as a free bonus. In *Chromavoyance*, for example, it is plausible to insist on shiny objects, but not to limit them to pencils. Complete conviction requires determining the hue of at least one other object. The simplest procedure is to use a confederate, and the best confederate is a close friend. But choosing a friend as A Subject would be a serious discrepancy. *Booby Trap* gets around this by: (*A*) having the friend volunteer, and (*B*) having him seem to play a trick on the performer. This not only eliminates the weak spot in *Chromavoyance* but adds a strong proof of the performer's powers. Furthermore, it provides a procedure which can be used to climax a wide variety of routines that have no connection with color touch.

DETECTING DISCREPANCIES

The tendency to ignore discrepancies is extremely strong. Although hunting for them has become almost a way of life with me, I am occasionally chagrined to discover that I have overlooked one in material on which I have been working for weeks. Fortunately, there is a simple technique which will enable you to spot most flaws almost automatically.

Jot down an outline of your routine as if the theme were genuine. You can then see what departures from perfection will be forced upon you by your devices. A theoretically ideal sequence for *The Strong Man's Secret* might run like this:

OUTLINE A

1. Borrow a piece of string.
2. Have a spectator cut it into two pieces.
3. Demonstrate that they are undeniably separate.
4. Take one end of each part between your thumb and two fingers.
5. Have spectators pull vainly on the other ends.
6. Prove that the string has not been switched by releasing the joined ends to let them be pulled apart.

Obviously, you cannot live up to this ideal. Nevertheless, every departure from it is a discrepancy. The illusion is possible only because these discrepancies can be disguised. Some of them are made to seem natural. Others are hidden by actions which divert the attention of the audience at the crucial moment.

Let us examine the departures in detail:

1. You supply the string instead of borrowing it. This is made plausible in two ways: (*A*) No one else is likely to have any. (*B*) You begin by taking out the string and toying with it. That familiarizes the spectators with the string and leads them to take its innocence for granted. This impression is reinforced by the fact that the string reminds you of the strong-man's stunt rather than the other way around.

2–3. The string looks like a knotted loop. The audience automatically assumes that cutting the loop and untying the knot *must* divide the string into two parts. This appears to be confirmed when you "carelessly" toss the string onto the table leaving four "ends" plainly visible. Note, however, that the method of cutting the loop is definitely inconsistent with a genuine demonstration. Ideally, you should let a spectator do the cutting. Furthermore, if you divide the string yourself, you should cut it at a single point. Snipping off a small piece is unnatural and irrational. This flaw is made inconspicuous by the technique in Fig. 8.

4–5. You must begin with a demonstration in which you hold the string in your fist. This would be unnecessary in a genuine demonstration; you could use the two-finger grip at once. However, two factors make the fist grip appear reasonable: (*A*) No one knows what you intend to do; the fist test looks like the real demonstration, and holding the "ends" with a thumb and two fingers seems to be an afterthought. (*B*) The fist test is interpreted as legitimate showmanship leading up to the more spectacular demonstration of holding the string between your thumb and fingers.

6. You cannot release the "pieces" to show that they are separate but must put them into your pocket immediately and change the subject. This may be a serious discrepancy. What can you do if someone says, "Show me that again," or "Let me try it."? Situations like this are the test of a real showman.

The hack merely shoves the string into his pocket and hopes for the best. The fair performer plans some way to change the subject quickly and divert attention from the string. The real expert also does this, but he goes further and provides himself with an *out*. While performing the stunt, he plants the idea that he has not done it for some time and is uncertain of success. When he does succeed, he puts the string in his pocket, saying, "Whew! They almost pulled loose that time. I didn't think I was going to make it." He then introduces some new topic, but he does not rely on this to take attention from the string. If someone says, "Do it again," he replies, "Not a chance. I might not get away with it next time." He then takes a duplicate, cut string from his his pocket and adds, "But you can try it yourself if you like." By suggesting the possibility of failure, he provides himself with an out—which he may not need. At the same time, he strengthens the conviction that the string is in two parts. Furthermore, he adds interest by making the audience uncertain whether he will succeed or fail.

Note that many of the suggestions given above concern subtle and apparently trivial details. *Attention to details is the essence of expert showmanship.* Slydini lets a spectator tie two handkerchiefs together with several knots. He then takes the handkerchiefs and gently pulls them apart. He not only makes no false moves but also appears to do nothing whatever except to separate the handkerchiefs. He has taught this trick point by point to many competent conjurers. In their hands, it is a good trick, but it is just a trick. Slydini makes it a miracle. The difference lies in details so subtle that, with the best will in the world, Slydini cannot teach them.

Details which seem too minute to affect the audience, even subconsciously, nevertheless deserve the attention of the performer. For one thing, he may underrate the astuteness of his audience. For another, a discrepancy which is too small for the spectators to notice may be large enough to throw the performer out of character. An audience never misses that.

In *Lie Detector*, for example, you should not be content to hold the spectator's wrist but should actually feel his pulse. When you do this, no spectator with medical knowledge can accuse you of having your fingers in the wrong place. Also, when you fail to feel the pulse, you must act as though you feel it, and you may not succeed. But when you really do feel it, acting is unnecessary; there is no way to go wrong.

You cannot call yourself a real showman until you form, and maintain, the habit of treating every discrepancy as important. The temptation to let details slide is so strong in all of us that we must never let ourselves yield to it. The performer who says, "Spectators never notice that," is training himself to overlook inconsistencies which will be obvious to most of his audience. That is a frame of mind which no one who aspires to showmanship can afford.

DIGRESSIONS

A word or action which is not inconsistent with the theme but which does not either clarify or enrich it is a *digression*. Digressions are not so bad as discrepancies, but they are poor showmanship. Aristotle pointed out that anything which does not add will detract. In over two thousand years, no one has found an exception to this rule.

I know one man who stops in the middle of every trick to tell a joke. His jokes are good and he tells them well, but they are out of place. People lose the thread of the trick while he is telling the joke, and they rarely laugh at the joke because they are thinking about the trick.

Few conjurers are so careless as this, but many of them throw in extraneous comic remarks. Thus, when a performer wants the deck cut, he may turn to someone and ask, "Have you got a jackknife?" When the spectator says, "No," the performer continues, "Then, I guess it's safe to let you cut the deck."

This sort of thing may be desirable in a series of mild tricks where the conjurer's flow of light banter is as important as the tricks themselves. However, it will not do for even the thinnest illusion because it destroys the atmosphere and breaks the spectators' train of thought. In fact, the funnier a digression is, the more harm it does. After laughing at something outside the routine, the spectators have to go back and pick up the thread of the action. They rarely succeed completely.

There is, of course, nothing wrong with comedy, but keep your comedy within the framework of the routine. The best plan is to stick to ideas that you need anyway but phrase them in some comic fashion. In *The Expanding Rabbit*, for example, you must have The Boy look into the hat. However, instead of merely saying, "Look inside the hat," you could say, "Make sure it is really empty. If there happened to be a fox inside the hat, it might eat the rabbit. Then you couldn't pull the rabbit out of the hat. Besides, the fox might bite you." This is amusing, but it is not a digression. On the contrary, it not only makes the point that the hat is indeed empty but makes it more forcibly than a straightforward statement could do.

Incidental effects are excellent at the beginning of a routine. They make it longer without letting it grow dull, and they strengthen the atmosphere. For example, you might prepare for *Twentieth-Century Nylon* by presenting a routine in which you use three green scarves. You could then ask your assistant for a red scarf. When she replies, "Oh! I forgot to bring one," you can shrug and turn a green scarf red.

However, if you did the same thing in the middle of the routine, it would be a serious source of distraction—especially if it came just before the climax. Thus, in *Twentieth-Century Nylon*, you might start with three green scarves, tie two of them together and have the girl stuff them into her bodice. You could then hold up the third scarf and say, "I shall now toss this toward my assistant. When it reaches her, it will knot itself firmly between the two scarves which she now has. But perhaps you can follow it better if it is a different color." Whereupon, you proceed to turn it red.

Although this is the same stunt, it now interrupts the smooth flow of the action. Many spectators will forget what you did with the first two scarves. Some may even imagine that you tied a red scarf between the two green ones in the first place! This may seem unlikely, but I assure you that spectators are capable of even wilder absurdities. If you want to keep them on the right track, you must eliminate every source of distraction.

Flourishes are especially distracting. I have seen men stop in the middle of a trick to pull a fan of cards from behind A Helper's ear. If this falls flat, it bores the audience. If it amazes anyone, it takes his attention from the routine and makes him forget what has gone before. Even minor flourishes are distracting. After having a card chosen and returned to the top of the deck, conjurers often bury it by giving the pack a fancy cut with one hand. This destroys the atmosphere. It throws The Subject out of character. He is no longer A Subject for a Demonstration but becomes An Onlooker at a Juggling Feat. Furthermore, the mental gymnastics involved in shifting roles often causes him to forget his card.

Chapter *11*

ELIMINATING DEPARTURES

When you have outlined what you would do in an ideal presentation if the theme were genuine, and have listed your departures from this ideal, your next job is to discard digressions and either get rid of discrepancies or at least find ways to conceal them. No detail is too small to deserve attention. Anything that the audience suspects will be held guilty without a trial.

Take each inconsistency in turn and ask yourself, "Is this really necessary?" You will often find that it adds nothing at all. In *The Inseparable String*, for example, the conjurer usually gives a spectator his choice of ends. At first sight, this makes the puzzle more baffling. In reality, however, it provides a clue to the solution. If the string were fairly cut, the idea that there was any difference between the pairs of ends would not occur to anyone. Hence, the performer would never think of offering a choice. By doing so, he raises the point. This may be all a shrewd spectator needs to realize that the string has been faked. The same reasoning applies with even more force to *The Strong Man's Secret*. Admittedly, the risk of discovery is not great. But why take a chance by introducing a discrepancy which adds nothing from the standpoint of the audience?

Departures from the ideal are justified only when they are forced on us by the devices. When you have weeded out all the rest, take up the devices one by one and try to find substitutes which will not involve discrepancies. For example, earlier versions of *Mental Television* were worked either with carbon paper or with waxed paper, which leaves visible traces when it is placed on a shiny surface and a drawing is made over it. Handling the special paper always introduces discrepancies. These may be concealed in clever ways, but it is obviously better to get rid of them entirely. The use of a paperback book does this perfectly—if the performer makes sure that no more suitable surface is available to support the paper on which the drawing is made.

When a discrepancy cannot be eliminated, it may often be placed beyond suspicion. *The Sigil of Solomon* provides an example. Requiring the subject to confine his writing to the center of the slip is a discrepancy. Most methods of handling this do more to arouse suspicion than to allay it. The sigil, however, makes the requirement seem inevitable.

Unfortunately, few conjurers adopt any systematic procedure for detecting and eliminating discrepancies. The rest not only tend to overlook inconsistent words and actions, but some of them go out of their way to introduce inconsistencies. This sort of thing would be impossible for anyone who first formed a clear idea of his theme and then wrote out the points of his routine as it would be if the theme were genuine.

Although every illusion presents its own problems, certain discrepancies are so common that you should learn to watch for them and discard them automatically.

WORDS BETRAY

Careless playwrights sometimes provide such lines as "You rant like a ham actor in a bad play." A speech of this type destroys the illusion by reminding the audience that it actually is watching actors in a bad play. The same thing happens whenever a conjurer uses any word which remotely suggests trickery.

If your theme were genuine, words like "trick," "illusion," "routine," and "act" would not enter your mind. Indeed, you would rarely have any occasion to mention the nature of your performance. Should such an occasion arise, you can always refer to "this demonstration," "this experiment," or whatever your purpose may be.

Cases like *The Strong Man's Secret* and *The Haunted Conjurer* are exceptions. Here you create the illusion of performing one trick while actually performing another. Note, however, that if these themes were genuine, you would naturally use words like "trick" and "stunt." Hence, in these special cases, the use of such terms is consistent with the themes.

Words like "gimmick," "force," and "setup" are probably out of place in any type of illusion. Even if extraordinary circumstances make their use plausible, they cannot strengthen conviction and may weaken it. The same thing is true of technical terms like "silk" for "handkerchief" or "scarf," or "vanish" for "make disappear." In fact, if you speak of "vanishing" something when talking to laymen, they will simply assume that your grammar is at fault.

Try to avoid figures of speech which may lead spectators' minds in undesirable directions. If you use the words "I see" while wearing a blindfold, some skeptic may be reminded that the remark could be literally true. If you say, "I am beginning to get an impression," while presenting *Mental Television*, a quick-witted spectator may realize that a ball-point pen will make an impression on a paperback book.

Titles for illusions are equally taboo. I have found names for the illusions in this book so that I could refer to them conveniently, but do not use them while addressing an audience. If the phenomenon you are simulating were genuine, you would have no reason to select a special title for any particular exhibition of it. In fact, it is usually best to pretend that you have invented the demonstration or experiment on the spur of the moment. *Will Power* illustrates this technique.

There is a special reason for not mentioning the titles of routines which require preparation. If a friend requests *Chromavoyance* by name when your faked pencils are not available, you are in an embarrassing position. But if he merely asks you to demonstrate your sense of color touch, you have a fair chance of fobbing him off with either an excuse or a substitute.

CONCEALING SKILL

Some performers specialize in creating illusions of skill. For example, they may give demonstrations of crooked gambling which appear to require great or even impossible dexterity, but which are actually done with a stacked deck.

In all other types of illusions, *your skill should be your most cherished secret.* As long as you conceal it, you can appear to work miracles. Once you expose it, skill drains all the magic out of conjuring, and you reveal yourself as nothing more than an entertainer with nimble fingers. Even a suspicion of skill may be fatal; when a spectator guesses that his card was forced, his curiosity is allayed, and he loses interest.

Resist the temptation to parade your deftness by making *card fans*, *ribbon spreads*, and other fancy flourishes even when you are merely warming up. While shuffling, cutting, or dealing, try to seem slightly awkward. Nothing is gained by appearing actually clumsy, but give the impression that you are not accustomed to handling cards. Careful performers also speak of "mixing the cards" instead of saying "shuffle them," and direct a helper to "lift off a few cards" rather than telling him to "cut the deck." These points may seem trivial, but remember that the smallest clue can arouse suspicion—and that any suspicion automatically weakens conviction.

Suspicious Apparatus

Apparatus is another common source of spectator suspicion, and therefore another potential illusion-breaker. Anyone who has ever looked into the window of a novelty shop believes that by paying ten cents, or ten dollars, he can acquire push-button magic that would place him in a class with the pros.

Furthermore, as Darrel Fitzkee has pointed out, spectators today live in a world of magic gadgets that are infinitely more amazing than anything a conjurer can offer. The woman with a pocket radio knows that it works by batteries. Her curiosity stops there. Why should she marvel when you show her another magic box? From her standpoint it is just one more ingenious gadget. As she does not own the thing and would have no use for it if she did, she is not even interested.

Borrowed apparatus is free from suspicion. But borrowing is not always practical. In close-up work, no spectator may have what you need. Stage performers find that borrowing wastes time and makes an act drag. The next best solution is to use commonplace props. Of course, they need not be commonplace, but the audience must regard them as such. When you have serious doubts that an article will be taken on faith as genuine, you can usually persuade the audience to accept it if you let some volunteer handle it.

Apparatus which is really commonplace may seem suspicious merely because of the conditions under which it is introduced. There is nothing extraordinary about clothesline. But if I attend a party and "just happen" to have three feet of clothesline in my pocket, only the most gullible guest will believe that the clothesline is innocent.

Another method of allaying suspicion is to construct your apparatus during the routine, or have your assistant do it for you. The production number which follows can start with an almost bare stage and end with most of the apparatus that you will use in the rest of your act.

MINIATURIZATION

The stage is empty except for two tables draped with silk scarves. One holds nothing but an empty tray. The other supports an 18 by 36 inch sheet of magenta construction paper and a 17 by 36 inch sheet of pea-green paper.

Announce that this is the age of miniaturization. We have microphones which can be concealed in a folder of matches and computers which will fit into a thimble. However, magicians have been doing this sort of thing for four thousand years. King Solomon had a tent that could be folded into a packet no larger than a handkerchief or opened out to shelter his whole court, complete with servants and dancing girls. This has become almost a lost art but you are trying to recover it and have made some progress.

While you talk, roll the magenta sheet into a cylinder 18 inches high and 9½ inches in diameter. Hold it in shape by attaching a paper clip at each end. Give this to your assistant, who handles it so that the audience can see through it. Roll the green paper into a slightly larger cylinder and fasten it with paper clips. Take the magenta cylinder from the assistant and drop the green one over it. Give the green one to your assistant who now holds this so that the audience can be sure it is empty. Stand the magenta cylinder on the table.

Bring a small box from your pocket, and announce that it is full of miniaturized objects. Pick up a tiny object (actually a small bead) and identify it as a miniaturized apple. Drop it into the green cylinder. Make a pass with your wand, murmur a spell, and take out an apple. Give this to your assistant. Continue to enlarge miniaturized objects in this way until the tray is full, and your assistant has to take the magenta cylinder in her hand to make room. She then crosses to the other table, puts down the full tray, and picks up an empty one. After this, she returns to you. Exchange cylinders with her and proceed to "enlarge" more objects.

The secret is revealed in Figs. 82–84. Notice the use of the wire *servantes* from which the loads are procured. The usual servante is a shelf or bag placed behind a chair or draped table. These are general-purpose gimmicks which can be used for vanishes, productions, and transformations.

If you use *Miniaturization*, try to arrange your act so that all the later routines will be performed with objects which can be compressed into one of the two loads. This requires careful planning, and it may force you to eliminate one or two pet

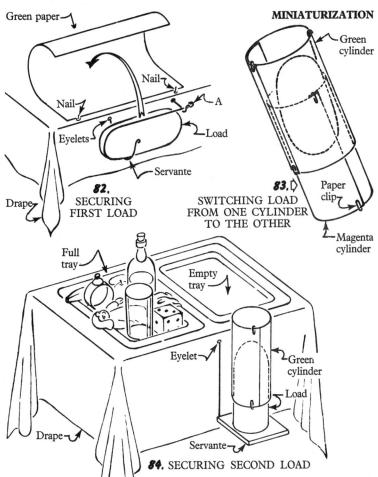

82. SECURING FIRST LOAD

83. SWITCHING LOAD FROM ONE CYLINDER TO THE OTHER

84. SECURING SECOND LOAD

1. Fig. 82 shows the first table. The load is assembled along a 14-in. length of coathanger wire. This is bent at the left to keep the load in place and has a hook (*A*) at the other end. Two pieces of the same wire provide a servante to support it. Shorten two 6-penny nails to ¾ in. and drive them into the table top just ahead of the rear edge. Let the heads project about $\frac{3}{16}$ in. Eyelets in the drape permit it to fit over the servante and the nails.

2. After rolling the magenta cylinder, place the green sheet so that the nail heads keep it from slipping off the table. Raise the front edge with your right hand. As soon as it is high enough to hide the load, lift this with your left hand and place

it on the paper. Roll the paper into a cylinder with the hook caught on one edge (Fig. 83). Drop the green cylinder over the magenta one in such a way that the load goes inside. The hook catches on the rim of the magenta cylinder, and the load remains inside this cylinder when you pull it out.

3. When your assistant takes the full tray to the other table, she holds the green cylinder in her left hand. As she puts the tray down, she "accidentally" lowers the cylinder behind the table and picks up the load by pinching the sides of the cylinder. The cylinder is never out of sight, the action is natural, and the attention of the audience is on you at the time.

146

routines. Nevertheless, it repays both the effects and the sacrifice because it is a great help in maintaining the magical atmosphere throughout.

DELIBERATELY AROUSING SUSPICION

A scientist performing a genuine demonstration or experiment normally takes the belief of his audience for granted. If the phenomenon seems incredible, he may be prepared to have some observers question the validity of his claim. However, he almost never expects anyone to doubt his good faith. The honest salesman demonstrating an appliance is in much the same position. The dishonest salesman is accustomed to suspicion, but he does everything in his power to avoid it. Similar considerations apply to virtually every role the conjurer can play.

Any actor will tell you that his own sincerity affects the belief of the spectators. They accept him at face value as long as he stays completely in character. They lose interest the moment he thinks of himself as playing a part.

Far from applying this principle, many conjurers deliberately introduce material to arouse suspicion. Statements like "Watch me closely" and "Which hand is it in?" amount to saying, "I'll fool you if I can." The conjurer who indulges in them knocks himself out of character. Instead of leading the spectators to share his own (apparent) sincerity, he infects them with his actual knowledge that it is faked. This is sure to weaken or destroy any suspension of disbelief.

One all-too-common method of calling attention to devices is the *sucker trick*. In this, the conjurer performs a feat by some apparently crude method, but when a spectator points out the obvious device, the conjurer triumphantly proves him wrong.

Children enjoy this sort of thing. They like to match wits with the performer, and repeated defeats fail to dampen their ardor. As most conjurers start by entertaining children, they find that sucker tricks go well with small fry. If they later turn to performing for adults, they never discover that grown-ups do not react like children.

Even if mature audiences were enthusiastic about sucker tricks, routines of this type would be poor policy because they destroy any hope of an illusion. Would you believe anyone who went out of his way to make you suspect him, even though he later demonstrated that the maneuver was only a joke?

The weakness of sucker tricks depends on the fact that the performer obviously baits his trap deliberately. If we can eliminate this fault, we will have the advantages of a sucker trick without its weakness. One of these advantages is the fact that such routines can be used to squelch the man who believes he knows how everything is done, and who insists on sharing his theories with the rest of the audience. The performer gives a sincere and straightforward demonstration, but he opens a path down which the heckler's unworthy suspicions lead him into a booby trap of his own making. There is all the difference in the world between this type of subtle snare and the sucker trick for children in which the performer has obviously gone out of his way to dangle the bait in front of his audience. Here is one routine for discouraging the heckler at an "impromptu" performance.

THE INDESTRUCTIBLE MATCH

Hold up a match and say, "To the profane eye, this appears to be an ordinary kitchen match. Nevertheless, it is a magic match, because it has been purified seven times—by the mystic rites of earth, air, water, fire, sulphur, mercury, and blood. These rituals have imbued it with unique properties as I shall now demonstrate."

Cover the match with a handkerchief as you continue, "This arcane rite must not be witnessed by the eyes of the vulgar. However, if the match is concealed, I can separate its atoms by breaking it into two halves." At this point, you appear to snap the match, saying, "But these atoms immediately recombine, and, as you see," snatch off handkerchief, "the match is as whole and perfect as ever in spite of its ordeal."

The heckler is almost sure to swallow the bait and to say, "I learned that in the first grade. You have another match hidden in the hem of your handkerchief."

Turn to the others and say, "Aha! We have a skeptic in our midst." Drop the match into your pocket. Swing back to the heckler and remark, "I could, of course, prove that you're wrong. However, for the sake of argument, let's assume that you're right. Will you admit that I'm a real magician if I make the match disappear from the hem of the handkerchief?" He will probably smell a rat, but he can hardly refuse to agree that if you can get rid of the match in the handkerchief you are pretty good.

Tell him to make a ring with his index finger and thumb. Pass a corner of the handkerchief through this ring and draw the whole handkerchief through slowly while you mumble, "Sator, Arepo, Tenet, Opera, Rotas." Drop the handkerchief on the table. The heckler will probably snatch it up and examine it incredulously—because there is no match in the hem.

This is the strongest version. Use it on a loud-mouthed heckler who deserves a sharp setback. For a milder type, which needs only a warning, either borrow a handkerchief or use one with a hem too small to hold a match. You can then omit the step with the spell. Merely drop the handkerchief on the table where he can reach it and let him discover for himself that his solution is absurd.

To work this, you must wear a four-in-hand necktie of some thin material. Insert a duplicate match into the hem of your necktie. Hold the handkerchief near the front of your coat and get the tip of the tie under it. Break the match in the tie and let the tie drop. Nothing is left for the audience to discover.

EXPOSURE

Conjurers who protest against exposure usually do so on the ground that once a trick has been exposed, it can no longer be presented successfully. This is questionable. Most laymen either do not learn of exposures or promptly forget them. No trick has been more thoroughly exposed than the one where a girl crouches in a box while the performer thrusts swords through it from all angles. Nevertheless, as experienced conjurers keep the item in their programs, it must amaze the average audience.

Furthermore, by making some small change in his method, a conjurer can fool those who know the original. A familiar trick has a built-in interest. The informed spectator watches for the device he knows so that he can feel superior. Then, when it becomes obvious that the usual procedure is ruled out, he is more deeply puzzled than if he had no idea of the secret in the first place. *Sawing a Woman in Half* is a good example. The early methods required putting the girl in a box and sawing through the box. When someone discovered a way to eliminate the box, people familiar with the old devices were more astonished than those who had never seen the trick before. Cases like this have led some to assert that exposure is good for conjuring because it forces performers to invent new ways of achieving their effects.

These arguments, both pro and con, miss the main point. If we wish to create an illusion, *it is not enough to conceal the particular device used; we must conceal the fact that any device exists.*

Realistic routines like *Dial Information* and *Horoscope* may succeed completely. In *Ancestral Aid*, *The Haunted Conjurer*, and other fantastic illusions, concealment will never be more than temporary. In spite of that, we can keep our audiences from speculating about the devices while the routine is being performed.

From this standpoint, exposure is undoubtedly harmful. Every time a person sees a trick exposed, he becomes less apt to suspend disbelief and more apt to concentrate on trying to detect the devices. This prevents him from fully appreciating the entertainment. It also increases the chance that he will see through the next routine.

Worse still, most exposures give the layman a poor opinion of conjuring. He does not know that the simplest devices are also the most ingenious, and he cannot realize that the device plays only a minor role in the illusion. If you describe Robert-Houdin's bullet-catching feat as the Arabs saw it, a layman may regard it as too marvelous to believe. But if you try to convince him by revealing the device, he ceases to admire it and concludes that "it was all done with fake bullets."

Once he forms that opinion, you will never be able to persuade him that the wax bullets were a minor factor and that the real secret lay in the Frenchman's almost superhuman combination of patriotism, poise, courage, ability to make quick decisions, ingenuity, knowledge of human nature, and skill in dramatizing a situation. Each time you expose a device, you decrease the capacity for awe in your audience.

Those who condemn exposure usually confine themselves to that which is done deliberately. But this is only one type. For each secret exposed on purpose, a hundred are revealed inadvertently through the carelessness, ignorance, or incompetence of performers.

The man who uses a device before mastering it so thoroughly that he can handle it without thinking, risks exposure every time he performs. The dealer who advertises, "You can present this five minutes after you get it," is urging his customers to disclose his secret. A purchaser may be able to work the apparatus at sight, but presenting an illusion is a different matter. Commercial apparatus is rarely accompanied by directions sufficiently complete to provide every detail of a routine. The best directions must be adapted to the performer's characterization and style of presentation. In any case, the routine should be rehearsed until it becomes completely familiar. No one can do all that in five minutes.

The conjurer who uses one or two weak tricks in an act which is otherwise composed of strong illusions risks exposing the illusions. The weak tricks prevent any suspension of disbelief. They create an atmosphere in which many spectators become more interested in solving puzzles than in being entertained. Under such conditions, the performer rarely gets through his act without having some spectator see through at least one of his illusions—and the perceptive spectator is almost sure to boast by explaining the secret to his friends.

Finally, a number of performers vary their acts by inserting a parlor trick that fools only one spectator and gives the rest a good laugh. This can be highly entertaining, but it destroys the suspension of disbelief and therefore weakens the impact of every illusion that follows.

Chapter 12

CONSISTENCY IN CHARACTERIZATION

All of the most successful showman-conjurers agree that you must believe in your own magic; you cannot hope to convince an audience unless you first convince yourself. Unfortunately, they do not supply directions for achieving this miracle. As you know that the phenomenon is false, how can you possibly persuade yourself that it is true? Well, actors—even second-rate amateurs—do this sort of thing as a matter of course. If they can do it, so can you.

The secret of convincing yourself is the same as the secret of convincing an audience—consistency. When everything you do is consistent with your assumed character and with the phenomena which you exhibit, you will find it easy to suspend disbelief in your own marvels.

The first step is to plan your characterization in detail. This is essential even when you play Yourself. If you played your real self in *Horoscope*, for example, you would think of yourself as a conjurer. Actually, you must regard Yourself as An Astrologer. The differences are genuine, and your audience will be quick to sense them. The slightest suspicion of trickery will keep spectators from believing that you are reading their characters from their birthdays.

Once you have decided on the characteristics which you plan to display, check them to be sure they are consistent with each other. This is particularly important when you present several routines at a sitting. The matter-of-fact Amateur Psychologist who demonstrates his skill in *Lie Detector* ceases to be plausible when he claims occult knowledge and represents himself as An Astrologer in *Horoscope*.

Although a fantastic effect makes a good illusion-breaker

after a serious routine, the two types should not be combined in your main act. A man who has amused his friends with *Ancestral Aid* may go on to demonstrate his sense of color touch, but he will have a hard time persuading anyone that he is sincere. Even if the characteristics required by such divergent roles can be reconciled, the routines call for entirely different atmospheres. He may possibly establish both, but one will certainly weaken the other. These facts give us another working rule: *Portray only one character in any given series of routines.*

PUTTING THE CHARACTER INTO THE ROUTINE

When you are satisfied that your character is consistent, go through your routine and ask yourself what you would think and feel at each step if you were really the person you pretend to be. You need not worry much about what to do; when you understand your character's thoughts and feelings, his actions normally take care of themselves.

If you once realize this important fact, most of your acting problems will vanish. When an actor asks, "What do I do with my hands at this point?" I invariably reply, "I don't care. All that matters is what you think and feel at that point." If he asks himself the right question, the answer is usually obvious. His hands respond in character, and his uncertainty about what to do with them no longer exists.

You must decide on your thoughts and feelings at *every* step in every routine, but a few key steps from *Dial Information* will suffice as examples:

Q. How do I feel when I suggest making the test with coins?

A. I suspect that The Telepath can work only with cards. I name coins because they are the first things that pop into my head which are similar to cards and easily available.

Q. How do I feel when The Telepath identifies the object as a coin?

A. I am surprised, but I still believe he is working some trick.

Q. How do I feel when he first describes A Participant?

A. I am astonished and try desperately, but futilely, to imagine any trick by which he could have acquired this knowledge.

The planning required is straightforward and logical. It does not need to be clever, and it takes no great amount of imagination. I never met an actor who could not do it, although I have met many who did not do it until I insisted.

Furthermore, unlike the actor, who plays a wide variety of roles, your range will probably be small. Close-up work requires changes of attitude rather than different characterizations. The Skeptic whom you impersonate on Tuesday in *Dial Information* may be essentially the same person as The Believer you portrayed in *Horoscope* on Monday. If you give stage performances, you can adopt radically different personalities; you may appear as A Haunted Conjurer one season and as A Master Mentalist the next. Nevertheless, you will not make such changes often, nor will you need to create many roles in a lifetime.

To some extent, you should remain in character during the whole of any given session, even though you present only one brief routine. However, when not performing, you need merely avoid remarks or actions which contradict your characterization; when you have any thought of ending an evening with *Horoscope*, do not begin it by ridiculing everything connected with the occult.

Active plans for your characterization should start with the moment when you, in your assumed role, introduce your theme. They must then continue until conversation about the illusion ceases, and the spectators turn to some other topic. In *Horoscope*, for example, you play An Astrologer. You believe in astrology and like to demonstrate its wonders. Experience has taught you that you cannot afford to introduce the topic bluntly, or people may laugh at you. Hence, you begin obliquely by mentioning palmistry and numerology as stalking-horses to test the attitude of the spectators toward the occult. If their attitude proves favorable, you speak of astrology and indicate that you possess some skill in the field. Give your readings. When your are through, answer questions politely but say that doing astrology in your head is tiring, and you prefer to pursue some other subject. Such prologues and epilogues are vital because you are on stage from the moment you start leading up to a routine until the audience abandons the whole idea and turns to something else.

On top of this, you may need a little time to get into character before you even begin to introduce your theme. Many actors can fall into character instantly, but others take a few seconds or even a few minutes. If you find that you require an appreciable interval to get into character, allow for it in planning your presentations.

When you use an assistant, work out her characterization with the same care that you devote to your own. Do not look on this as a chore. Planning an assistant's characterization can be fascinating. While doing it, you are almost certain to improve the one you have chosen for yourself.

HANDLING TECHNICAL PROBLEMS

Once you learn to ask yourself about your character's thoughts and feelings, most of the answers will be easy. These answers will then determine your actions. However, there are always a few points where your actions are controlled by technical considerations and do not, at first sight, fit your character. Such situations are the weakest spots in your routine. In *The Sigil of Solomon*, for example, you must unfold and read the center of the paper although this is necessarily inconsistent with what you would do and think if the effect were genuine.

Sometimes you can eliminate a discrepancy by changing your characterization. It is out of character for A Diviner to confine himself to one type of apparatus, even something as ordinary as a handful of lead pencils. But a person with color touch might reasonably be expected to use the only shiny objects available. Hence for *Chromavoyance*, you drop the role of A Diviner and assume that of A Person with Especially Sensitive Fingers.

MOTIVATION

When you cannot eliminate an action which is technically necessary but out of character, you must *motivate* it. A motivation is a plausible reason why that character would perform that act. Thus, in *The Inseparable String*, the conjurer must ask The Helpers to pull the ends. But this is illogical. He proposed to restore the string; for this purpose, a pull can be expected to do more harm than good. In *The Strong Man's Secret*, on the other hand, the pulling is perfectly motivated; it is the whole point of the stunt.

A motivation is a reason, not an excuse. When a trickster disposes of something by going to his pocket for imaginary "magic woofle dust," it is obviously an excuse. But when the performer in *The Strong Man's Secret* returns his penknife to his pocket and carries the bit of glued string along with it, the action is so thoroughly motivated that it is almost sure to pass unnoticed. A motivation must be made clear before you perform the action which it explains. Discrepancies inspire curiosity. When you do something odd in daily life, people notice it and wonder why. Once their curiosity is aroused, they will make every effort to satisfy it—and they cannot be fobbed off with a half-baked explanation. On the other hand, when the explanation is offered beforehand, no one is sufficiently interested to examine it closely. Unless it is palpably absurd, most people accept it without thinking. After they have accepted it, the action which it "explains" does not seem peculiar and fails to stimulate their curiosity.

Chromavoyance illustrates this. If you demonstrate your ability without first explaining why you use pencils, someone may guess that the pencils are faked. Hence you must say, "I can't feel color unless the surface is shiny. We need things which are all alike so that I can't get any clue from their shapes. Let's see, what can we use? Oh, I know. I have some pencils that will do." This motivates the pencils so thoroughly that their use seems accidental. Only the most skeptical spectator can suspect them of being the key to the mystery.

NEGATIVE MOTIVATIONS

Finding a reason for doing something is usually easy. Finding one for not doing something is more difficult. Such problems abound in conjuring and solving them may require real ingenuity. For example:

Q. Why not let The Subject in *Lie Detector* simply think of a card?

A. You want him to draw a card and show it to the other spectators so that they can follow the demonstration.

Never stress a motivation. All you need is to convince the audience that an adequate motivation exists. Thus, in *Lie Detector*, you should say, "The quickest test is the one used by experts. Here, take a card and show it to the others so they can understand what's going on." This keeps The Subject from inquiring why you do not merely let him think of a card—and it does this without letting him suspect that you have answered his question before he could ask it.

FINDING MOTIVATIONS

Most conjuring motivations arise out of the theme. When you build a presentation around a theme, you normally find the motivations built in. Thus, in *The Instant Incubator*, you want to demonstrate that your apparatus is "empty" without arousing suspicion by calling attention to that fact. The theme supplies an obvious motivation. In order to explain your invention, you take it apart and assemble it again. This is completely natural and completely convincing.

When a theme fails to supply motivations automatically, a careful study of it will often reveal one. In *Ancestral Aid*, for example, the theme does not require you to slap the table. Nevertheless, this is a natural action in anyone who calls on the spirit of a forebear to demonstrate his power.

Props supply excellent motivations, as the penknife in *The Strong Man's Secret* proves. Sometimes you will need to add a *motivating prop* merely to provide a motivation. A motivating prop should be commonplace, and the need for it should be obvious before you use it. In *Miniaturization,* for example, your assistant must go to the spare table and lean over it to pick up the second load. You motivate this by having her use two small trays as motivating props. When the first one is full, she puts it on the spare table and gets the second tray. The audience recognizes the need for this action as soon as the first tray becomes overcrowded. Hence, the business of changing trays (and picking up the second load) seems perfectly natural.

The best way to learn motivation is to study an illusion which makes great use of it. That given below is one of the most convincing in the book when properly performed, but almost every detail must be motivated. Some of these motivations may seem needlessly elaborate to anyone who has not learned from experience how convincing such careful attention to detail can be. As the process of devising this routine was largely an exercise in motivation, I have described the course of my thoughts so that you can recognize each discrepancy as it appears and appreciate how it is covered by its motivation.

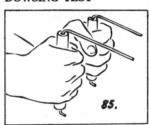

85.

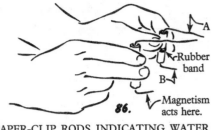

86.

A

Rubber band

B

Magnetism acts here.

PAPER-CLIP RODS INDICATING WATER

FULL-SCALE DIVINING RODS IN "READY" POSITION

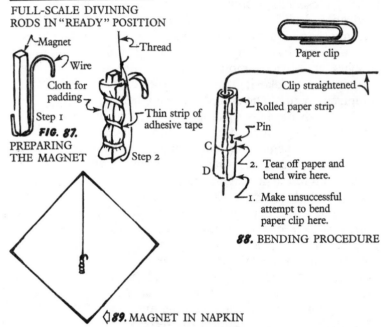

Magnet

Wire

Thread

Paper clip

Cloth for padding

Clip straightened

Rolled paper strip

Step 1

Pin

FIG. 87.

PREPARING THE MAGNET

Thin strip of adhesive tape

Step 2

C

D

2. Tear off paper and bend wire here.

1. Make unsuccessful attempt to bend paper clip here.

88. BENDING PROCEDURE

89. MAGNET IN NAPKIN

DOWSING TEST

Divining rods are used primarily to locate water underground. They have received much attention in recent years because Kenneth Roberts, the novelist, wrote several books about his friend, Henry Gross, who gave evidence of remarkable powers in using a rod. The practice is called "dowsing." Is there any way to imitate actual dowsing and still have an effect that can be presented in a private home or on a stage? Yes. I can use several empty glasses and one which is half full of water. If I cover the glasses with a napkin and pick out the one with the water, I shall simulate actual dowsing.

Old-fashioned dowsers, like Henry Gross, used a forked stick as a divining rod. However, the type made from bent wires is better for our purpose (Fig. 85). Miniature versions of these can be improvised from paper clips (Fig. 86). As paper clips are magnetic, they will respond to a magnet hooked over the rim of the glass which contains water (Fig. 87).

The magnet can be concealed by the napkin without difficulty (Fig. 89).

When I experimented with this arrangement, it refused to work; the horizontal parts of the clips are too far from the magnet (*A*, Fig. 86). I can correct this by bending the lower ends of the clips (*B*). This works perfectly. The movement of the rods is decidedly eerie, even though I know that a magnet is responsible. Unfortunately, a genuine dowser would not need to bend up the lower ends of the rods in this way. He might make short bends to keep the wires in the handles, but I need lower legs that are half as long as the upper parts of the wires. As over-long lower legs serve no apparent purpose, they are apt to arouse suspicion. They cannot be hidden or disguised. The only other solution is to find some motivation which will make the audience accept them as natural.

The problem is difficult, and the answer turns out to be complicated. However, complex motivations are not objectionable unless they need to be explained. This one does not.

I open out the first clip and slip a tube on the short end (Fig. 88). When I start to hand the rod out for examination, I hold it by the long end and the tube falls off. I put the tube back and try to keep it in place by bending the wire at Point *D*. I do this by pressing the wire against the fleshy part of my index finger, *not* against my thumbnail. Under this treatment, the wire refuses to bend at *D* but gives at the original bend (*C*). This also bends the tube. I remove the tube and tear off the bottom part. I replace it and bend the wire at the easiest point (*C*). I then prepare the other rod to match. This is precisely the way I might fumble around if I were really improvising miniature rods from paper clips. The turned-up ends are motivated by my desire to hold the tube on the rods, and their length is explained by the fact that I tried to make them shorter and failed.

This may seem like an elaborate maneuver to cover a small point. However, it is the key point; the unnecessarily long lower legs of the rods are the only clue to the device. Anything that makes these legs seem reasonable is well worth the trouble.

Every bit of apparatus (except completely concealed gimmicks like the magnet) must be motivated. *Dowsing Test* is not apt to be convincing unless glasses, a napkin, and water (or some other fluid) are available without any suggestion of preparation on the part of the performer. This normally limits the presentation to the dining- or living-room of a private home. Clips, paper, and rubber bands cannot always be found in living-rooms, and they are even rarer in dining-rooms. Hence, the performer must provide them himself. To avoid suspicion, he needs to make his possession of these props seem completely accidental.

My solution is to carry a packet of old letters in my pocket. These are held together by a rubber band. Two of the letters consist of two sheets each and are held together by clips. One of the clips is nickled and the other is copper-colored (my copper-colored clips are magnetic). I also carry a pin in my lapel.

I introduce the apparatus like this: "I can't explain dowsing clearly without some wire. Anything at all will do, even a couple of paper clips in a pinch. Does anybody happen to have some?" If I can borrow the clips, so much the better. If not, I add, "Wait a second, I have a few letters in my pocket. Maybe one of them . . . yes, here's one. That will be enough to show how a divining rod is made. I can't . . . Aha, here's another clip. We're in business."

I then tear two strips of paper off an envelope and roll these into tubes for the handles. One handle is held in shape with a rubber band from the envelopes. The other is fastened with the pin. Props produced in this way look like makeshifts; few spectators will suspect that each item and each move has been carefully planned to produce just this effect.

Is the routine now complete? No. Someone else must cover the glasses so that I can find which one holds the water. But then how am I to get the magnet onto the glass? The answer is that I must change my role. I must be the one to arrange and cover the glasses (and incidentally insert the magnet). The spectators will then act as Subjects and try their luck with the divining rods.

This requires changing the theme. Instead of demonstrating my dowsing ability, I shall conduct a series of experiments to see whether any of the spectators has this power. The new theme provides audience participation and is both more interesting and more convincing than the old one.

However, I am not yet through with the problems of *Dowsing Test*. The fact that I am always the person who arranges the glasses and covers them with the napkin is suspicious. How can avoid I this suspicion? By saying that only 15 per cent of the population has dowsing ability, and that I am one of the ungifted 85 per cent. This puts me out of the running as A Subject and automatically casts me in the role of Laboratory Assistant. That requires me to arrange the apparatus, but gives me no real part in the experiments.

The illusion will be more impressive if only two or three spectators succeed. I can cause a failure by not putting the magnet in any glass. However, in order to permit a subsequent success, I must rearrange the glasses. As the glasses are hidden, there is no real need to rearrange them. What motivation can I find for doing so? Answer: After each test, I can lift up the napkin to show which glass holds the water. The next Subject must then turn his back while I rearrange the glasses. This lets me remove and replace the magnet for each "test."

Getting rid of the magnet at the end presents no real problem, but even here a little attention to motivation can be helpful. I plan to have the last Subject fail. After the last successful "experiment," I drop the napkin (with the magnet) to my lap. This seems completely natural; people put napkins on their laps from force of habit. As I pick up the napkin for the final "test," I leave the magnet in my lap. Later, when every eye is fixed on The Subject's futile attempt to dowse, I slip the magnet into my pocket while I reach for a match or a handkerchief.

A routine that offers little chance of exposure is said to be "clean." You will never find a cleaner one than this. The only false moves are those with the magnet, and they are completely covered. Apart from these, there is no clue except the excess length of the lower legs on the divining rods. This seems so unimportant and is so thoroughly motivated, that only the shrewdest and most knowing spectator will notice it at all.

If *Dowsing Test* had been written up in the usual manner, it would have been confined to the basic procedure and a description of the gimmick. The motivations would not have been mentioned. Nevertheless, they are the things that make it impressive. In short, the conventional explanation stops at the exact point where the art of illusion begins.

MOTIVATING ASSISTANTS

If you use an assistant, her motivations are as important as your own and may be harder to find. Your role keeps you busy and gives you plenty of chances to suggest motivations, but the girl has many idle moments. Also, she may need to move for reasons which would not exist if the phenomena you are exhibiting were genuine.

The first step is to work out her character. Without a character, she can have no motives. Pay especial attention to her attitude toward you. The attitude of A Typical Magician's Assistant towards her boss is entirely different from that of A Sorcerer's Apprentice towards her master.

Next decide what she would naturally do if the phenomena were genuine. Note the departures required by your devices and those demanded by stage technique. This will give you a list of the points where she needs motivation.

Most of these motivations will have to be supplied by something you say or do. Suppose, for example, that your assistant in *Twentieth-Century Nylon* has been characterized as beautiful but dumb. It would take a girl of this type several seconds to recognize the object between the handkerchiefs as a stocking and several more to decide that it must be hers. She might never think to check by lifting her skirt. But effective timing requires her to gasp when the audience identifies the object as a stocking and to raise her skirt the instant after that. You must motivate her by saying, "It's your stocking!" and then look down at her legs.

MOTIVATING VOLUNTEERS

Volunteers must be kept in character. The Helper who suddenly decides to cast himself as An Inspector can be a major nuisance. The first rule is: *keep him busy.* Try to arrange the routine so that he has no time to get into mischief. If he must remain idle, give him something to hold. The second rule is: *keep him near you.* He will be more apt to embark on some out-of-character action if he gets off by himself.

Make your directions clear. Most of the mistakes made by volunteers are caused by failure to understand their roles. When his actions are at all complex, explain one step at a time and have him execute it before you explain the next. Thus: "Lift off part of the deck." [*He cuts.*] "Take the next card." [*He does so.*] "Look at it and remember it." [*He at least looks.*] "Show it to the others without letting me see it." [*He holds it up.*] "Now, replace it." [*He puts it back.*] "Cover it with the top half." [*He obeys.*] "Now square the deck." [*He pats the sides.*]

When you can conveniently do so, go through the action yourself while giving directions. In the above example, you could make the motions without using the cards. Reverse your actions right to left so that he can follow them as though he were watching himself in a mirror.

Occasionally, a volunteer must be motivated more subtly. In routines like *The Sigil of Solomon*, for example, The Sitter writes something that The Mentalist must read at a glance. Unfortunately, it is often a mere scrawl which no one could read. *The Sigil* handles this by stressing the necessity for observing every detail of the rite precisely and by making the letters E H Y H, and the word ADONAY part of the design. This enables The Magician to explain that all writing must be done in roman block capitals because the ceremony was devised before small roman letters were invented. The term "roman" should be repeated in the hope of luring someone to object that Solomon presumably wrote in Hebrew. The Magician then retorts that the diagram is used in many arcane rites and that this one was perfected by the great fourth-century adept Optimus Montanus. The Sitter will misinterpret this as byplay, but it leads him to use block capitals without being specifically required to do so by the performer.

KEEPING THE AUDIENCE IN CHARACTER

As the audience has its own role to play, you should do everything in your power to keep it in character. This applies to the audience as a whole as well as to individual volunteers.

Treat everyone precisely as you would if the theme were genuine. For example, in *Lie Detector*, you tell the exact truth when you say that experts begin by detecting a chosen card. If a spectator doubted this, you would try to convince him even though you did not intend to give a demonstration yourself. You should adopt the same attitude toward your claim in *Chromavoyance* in spite of the fact that it is completely false. You have always taken it for granted that everyone could recognize hues by touch. You never happened to mention it to anyone before because the sense is too weak to be much use. You believe Your friends have the same ability, and You are quite sincere in your assertion that You can prove it by letting them make the test. You do not offer to demonstrate Your own power until You are challenged. You *know* that you can feel color; You do not need to convince Yourself. If you handle this properly at least half of your victims will expect to feel color and will be disappointed when they fail.

Apply the same treatment even to fantasy. Decide how the audience would act if the theme were real, then seem hurt or indignant when they refuse to respond properly. Thus, if The Obeah Man in *The Haunted Conjurer* really did turn the dice into guinea pigs, The Conjurer would be annoyed when the spectators laugh at his discomfiture. He might protest openly, or he might try (unsuccessfully) to hide his attitude. He might even pretend to take credit for the magic. Nevertheless, it would be only a pretense, and you should contrive to let the audience know that. In an act of this sort, the audience laughs at your role, not with it. The best way to get laughs is to stay completely in character. The act may be fantasy, but you should always treat your own part with complete realism.

THE SILENT SCRIPT

Control of your conscious actions is a straightforward matter. Anyone can do it who takes the trouble. However, you cannot hope to be convincing unless you can control your subconscious actions as well. This is why Slydini is so much more impressive than his imitators. When he separates knotted handkerchiefs, it looks like a miracle; when they do the "same" thing, they are obviously performing a clever trick.

How can anyone control subconscious actions? A false inflection, the wrong tension in a muscle, or a mistimed pause can give the game away—and there are dozens of such chances for failure in the shortest routine. Even if he could list them all, no actor or conjurer could remember every one during a performance. Fortunately, there is an extremely easy technique which makes control of subconscious actions almost automatic.

After an actor has worked out his characterization, he has no trouble staying in character as long as he has lines to speak. The lines force him to think the character's thoughts. While he does this, he is not apt to fall out of his role. But the moment he stops talking, he begins thinking his own thoughts. This throws him out of character; he cannot be two people at the same time.

Once we recognize the difficulty, the solution becomes obvious: every performer needs lines to think whenever he is silent. Providing such a *silent script* is a simple matter. Virtually all my actors—including some who were far from bright—mastered the knack after one easy lesson. I see no reason why conjurers should not find the same solution equally effective and equally easy.

The technique consists of writing out on paper enough lines to fill all the gaps in your speech. Then recite these lines mentally while you perform. Do not attempt to memorize them exactly, just get the basic ideas in mind. A silent script to fit the situation on p. 159 might run like the example below. Probable interruptions by spectators are included because you must be prepared for these. The silent part is in capitals and small capitals. Italics represent stage directions and comments. Tom and Sue are typical Spectators.

You. I can't explain dowsing clearly without some wire.

TOM. Wire? I thought dowsers used forked sticks.   [*As you must think about Tom's words here, you do not need any of your own.*]

You. That's old-fashioned. The modern boys use two rods of wire bent out of coat hangers. I could show you what they are like if I had some soft wire. [*Looking around the room.*] HAIR PINS, STIFF ELECTRIC WIRE, ANYTHING. Even a couple of paper clips in a pinch. Does anybody happen to have any?

SUE. I have bobby pins, will they help?   You. [*Not listening.*] WAIT A SECOND. I HAVE A FEW LETTERS IN

TOM. There's some radio wire in   MY POCKET. MAYBE ONE OF
the basement.   THEM. . . . [*Find first clip.*]
YOU. Don't bother. I have a clip. That'll be enough to show how a
divining rod is made. I can't . . . [*Find second clip.*] AHA, HERE'S ANOTHER
CLIP. That's all I need. It's all right, folks. I have two clips. We're in
business.

Note that although both the spoken and silent scripts fit
your assumed character, the silent lines do not fit your real
situation at all. You would not, in your own person, think that
hair pins or stiff electric wire will do. You know they will
not. Nor would you think that one of the letters in your
pocket *may* have a paper clip. You know you have two clips. It
is precisely on points like these that you must forget the facts
as they are and think as you would if the facts were what you
pretend them to be.

The silent script also provides an easy way to believe in your
own miracles. While you watch Sue test her dowsing ability,
you know that the magnet is in place. You know that she will
succeed, and your only worry is that she may somehow discover the magnet. Nevertheless, you cannot afford to think
those things. Instead, your thoughts must run something like
this: "I WONDER IF SHE'LL MAKE IT? IT'S FUNNY HOW PEOPLE
DIFFER AS WATER FINDERS. IT DOESN'T SEEM TO HAVE ANYTHING
TO DO WITH INTELLIGENCE OR EMOTIONAL SENSITIVITY. [*The
rods jump.*] AHA! GOOD GIRL. SHE DID IT!

Silent scripts are by no means confined to realistic "impromptus." Here is an example from the point in *Twentieth-
Century Nylon* where you "toss" the red scarf.

YOU. And now, ladies and gentlemen, I will cause this red scarf to travel
invisibly to the young lady's bodice where it will tie itself firmly between
the two green ones already there. Watch! Or rather, don't watch because
you won't see it go. One . . . two . . . three! [*Make tossing motion. Release
pull subconsciously while you think.*] RIGHT THROUGH THE AIR AND DOWN.
WAIT A MINUTE. SOMETHING'S WRONG. OH, WELL, CAN'T STOP NOW.
[*Cross to assistant and draw out first green scarf.*] I GUESS IT'S O.K. THERE'S
SOMETHING TIED ONTO THIS, AND IT COULDN'T BE ANYTHING ELSE BUT . . .
[*Stocking appears.*] WHAT THE DING DING? [*Gasp. To Assistant.*] It's
your stocking! [*Looks down at her legs.*] How did that . . . ? WHAT'LL I SAY
TO THE AUDIENCE? [*Assistant lifts skirt and reveals scarf tied as garter.*]
WELL WHAT D'YOU KNOW. SO THAT'S WHAT HAPPENED. BETTER GRAB
CREDIT FOR IT QUICK. I'm sorry, ladies and gentlemen. That never hap-
pened before, but—you see—I've been using a silk scarf for this demon-
stration. The one I used tonight is actually made of nylon. Nylon is more

slippery than silk. It must have missed its grip of the green scarves and barely managed to knot itself around my assistant's leg. But magic never lets me down, so the stocking came up to complete the demonstration. Tomorrow, I'll go back to using silk.

If you try writing silent scripts, you will find that the work goes quickly. The words do not need to be polished or amusing. Just write what you would say if the phenomena were real.

You will also find that your performance shows an immediate and marked improvement. When I teach this technique to an actor, I watch him at the next rehearsal. If he is not noticeably better I know that he has either failed to work on his silent script or has missed the idea.

There are only two ways to go wrong. First, you can mix your own thoughts with those of your character. Thus, in *Twentieth-Century Nylon*, you should *not* say and think, "One . . . two . . . three. RELEASE PULL. RIGHT THROUGH THE AIR. . . . DID THE PULL JERK THE SILK OUT OF SIGHT? . . . AND DOWN. YES, IT'S HIDDEN." This is a sure way to throw yourself out of character.

The second type of error is more insidious. A silent script must not be written in the third person. You must think, "RIGHT THROUGH THE AIR AND DOWN," not "HERE HE THINKS, 'RIGHT THROUGH THE AIR AND DOWN.'" When you use phrases like "HERE HE THINKS" and then put your thoughts in mental quotation marks, you are looking at your character from the outside. This is fatal. No one normally thinks of himself as "HE."

Saying to yourself, "HERE I THINK," is equally bad. In real life, you merely think; you do not annotate your thoughts with stage directions. A silent script will not enable you to feel your character from the inside unless it duplicates real thoughts in every particular.

A silent script is no help unless you actually run through it in your mind during every performance. If something goes wrong, you will have to abandon your silent script long enough to correct the trouble.

When something occurs that is unexpected but not actually wrong, you should be able to improvise a new silent script to cover it. Suppose, for example, that your confederate in *Preview* forgets his number and calls "Eight-three-seven" instead of "Seven-three-eight." Do not say to yourself, "OH LORD, THE FOOL BALLED IT UP!" but "THAT'S STRANGE. I GOT THE DIGITS

BACKWARD. I NEVER DID THAT BEFORE." Even if he forgets completely and says, "Five-six-nine," you can think, "I'M BELOW PAR TONIGHT, ONLY ONE HIT AND A NEAR MISS OUT OF THREE TRIES." These are the thoughts that you would think if the test were genuine.

You cannot stay within your silent script if you let a secret move interrupt your train of thought. This is another reason why you must master sleights so thoroughly that you can perform them without thinking. The mental arithmetic for routines like *Arithmagic* and *The Monte Carlo Method* will break your silent script. For this reason, you should try to handle it while the attention of the audience is on the cards or some other prop and not on your face.

The whole idea of a silent script will seem strange to many conjurers. I can only assure them that it worked wonders for every actor to whom I have taught it, and that none of them ever had any trouble with it once they understood the process.

Chapter 13
CONCEALING DEVICES

Themes and characterizations concern the dramatic aspects of illusion. We are now ready to consider the conjuring aspect, which is the art of concealing devices. The degree of art required depends on the device. The devices behind *Horoscope* and *The Singular Singletons* are virtually indetectable and will be revealed only by gross mishandling. However, this happy condition is not common. Most devices require some concealment, and a few are so crude that the method of concealing them almost becomes the device.

The technique may be physical, psychological, or a mixture of both.

HIDING

The simplest method of concealing a device consists in hiding it in or behind something else. A palmed duplicate card or coin is one example. The loads on the servantes in *Miniaturization* are another.

The routine which follows illustrates three subtle principles of concealment: *shifting screens*, *secret access*, and *concentric transparencies*. It deserves study on that account even if it does not fit your type of act.

THE POLARITY PUMP

You have an undraped table on each side of the stage near the footlights. One is empty. The other holds a tall box with a hinged lid, a small tray, two large tumblers, and the polarity pump (Fig. 90).

State that you are about to demonstrate a working model of the latest scientific marvel. It permits the electronic transportation of fluids and requires no pipes, tubes, or conduits of any kind. The device has two parts. Carry the box to the footlights. Lift the lid and show the box empty. Make sure that several first-row spectators get a really good look. Announce that the box is a model of the "receptor." Walk back to the first table, pick up the tray, place the receptor and the tumblers upon it, and

THE POLARITY PUMP

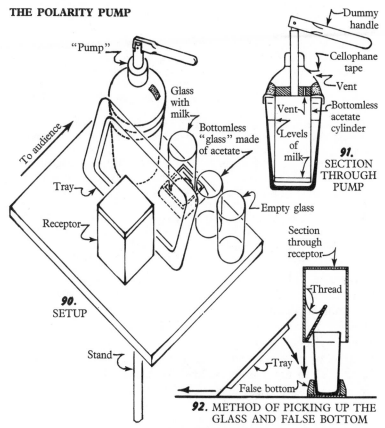

"Pump"

Glass with milk

Bottomless "glass" made of acetate

To audience

Tray

Receptor

Empty glass

90. SETUP

Stand

Dummy handle

Cellophane tape

Vent

Bottomless acetate cylinder

Vent

Levels of milk

91. SECTION THROUGH PUMP

Section through receptor

Thread

Tray

False bottom

92. METHOD OF PICKING UP THE GLASS AND FALSE BOTTOM

When you return the "receptor" to the table, place it over Glass *A* and lower the tray at the same time (Fig. 92). When the bottomless "glass" *B* is put into the "receptor," it fits into Glass *A* and becomes invisible. As you start to "pump," peel off the cellophane tape (Fig. 91). This lets air escape from the acetate cylinder and permits the milk to flow in, so that the level of the visible milk sinks. Open the "receptor" and show Glass *A* filled with milk.

carry them to the other table. Set the tray on the table and put one tumbler into the box.

Return to the first table and show the pump. "This," you announce, "is the transmitter. It is called a 'polarity pump' because it polarizes the ions in the molecules of the fluid and transmits them by teleplasmic magnetism into any container placed in the receptor. At present, the model pump is filled with milk to make the process clearly visible. However, the first practical application of the device will probably be refueling airplanes in flight. In fact, contracts for full-scale pumps are already being let. Here's how it operates. Watch!"

As you work the handle of the pump, the level of the milk falls until you appear to have pumped out enough to fill the tumbler. Cross to the box and lift out the tumbler, which is now full of milk. Prove that the milk is genuine by pouring it into the empty tumbler.

Both the "receptor" with its secret, hinged bottom (Fig. 92) and the bottomless "glass" made of acetate illustrate the principle of secret access. The hole in the lid of the "pump" is a more subtle example of the same principle although it lets air out rather than letting something in (Fig. 91).

The acetate insert in the pump and the fact that the bottomless "glass" is invisible after it has been placed in the real glass of milk illustrate the principle of concentric transparencies.

You employ the principle of shifting screens when you lower the tray at the same time that you place the "receptor" over the glass of milk (Fig. 92). As only the bottom two inches of the "receptor" is ever hidden by the tray, no one can suspect that this is a key move. In my opinion, this is the most deceptive method of stealing a load ever devised. *Miniaturization* also illustrates the principle of shifting screens, once when you pick up the first load, again when you transfer it from one cylinder to the other, and a third time when your assistant picks up the second load.

When a gimmick is used, we cannot be content to hide the gimmick itself, but must conceal any clue that may lead a spectator to deduce the existence of the gimmick. Thus, in *Dowsing Test* it is not enough to hide the magnet; we need to avoid any suggestion of magnetism. The attempt to borrow the paper clips eliminates any suspicion of preparation. When we are forced to use our own clips, the fact that one of them is copper-colored keeps the idea of magnetism from arising in the mind of the average spectator.

DISGUISE

Fakes are devices disguised to resemble something else. The string in *The Strong Man's Secret* is faked to look like a knotted loop, and the collapsible dice in *The Haunted Conjurer* are faked to appear solid.

An object is disguised when it contains any special property which is unknown to the audience, even though this is actually normal. Dealers sell quarters which are specially faked to render them magnetic, but every Canadian nickel is equally magnetic, and so is a copper-colored paper clip. From a practical standpoint, the magnetic quality is disguised in all three cases. Prepared props fall into the same class. Thus, in *Dial Information*, you disguise the fact that you can recognize the date of the coin by noting its denomination.

Duplicates also come under the head of "disguise." The slips in the bottom of the candy box in *Preview* are disguised to look like those signed by the audience.

CAMOUFLAGE

Gimmicks are often camouflaged to blend with their backgrounds. Whole acts are sometimes based on a principle known as *black art* in which white or colorful props are displayed against a black background and supported by black objects or by performers entirely covered in black. Although these make interesting novelty acts, they are not often completely convincing because the secret is fairly obvious. A square circle is really a miniature black-art stage. However, its small size and the presence of a grille make it much more deceptive than its large-scale counterparts.

On a still smaller scale, we can use paint to camouflage gimmicks applied to a prop. Many magic boxes have secret catches which must be pressed at crucial moments. If these are colored to match the box, they may be quite large and still escape notice when the audience can be kept ten feet away.

Small gimmicks intended to be held in the hand should be painted brownish pink. This keeps the audience from *getting a flash* if part of the gimmick is momentarily exposed. Dealers sell the proper paint in spray cans under the name of "flesh color." Make no attempt to match the actual color of your flesh, and do not indicate any details. No matter how artistically the painting is done, it will make the gimmick conspicuous.

Thumb tips are hollow devices which fit over the thumb but leave enough room to hold some small article such as a bit of paper or a cigarette butt. Get a brownish pink tip of spun metal. The "realistic" plastic variety is much less deceptive.

A thumb tip can be used for productions, vanishes, or switches. It is almost invisible when properly handled. Cover the tip in some way whenever this can be done without seeming unnatural. Letting the thumb curl slightly within the fingers is one technique. When the tip must be exposed, keep the hand in motion and point the thumb toward the audience.

MISINTERPRETATION

All the arts depend on misinterpretation by the observer. The painter smears blobs of colored pigment on canvas, and the observer misinterprets these as a bowl of fruit, a beautiful woman, or a landscape. Actors posture before flimsy scenery, and the audience misinterprets them as people moving in a real setting.

Conjuring not only uses misinterpretation in all the ways that drama does but employs it for many purposes of its own. Thus, an effect would not be regarded as proof of a phenomenon unless the audience misinterpreted it. When you perform *Number Please*, your ability to provide instantaneous answers to complex problems is misinterpreted as proof of your ability in mental arithmetic. Actually, all it proves is that you have an accomplice, a desk calculator, and a table of roots.

Misinterpretation is also a powerful device for deception and a method of concealing other devices. If you convince a spectator that you can juggle large numbers in your head, you automatically prevent him from trying to discover your methods.

All of these uses are so closely connected that it is impossible to separate them. Fortunately, this is unnecessary; they all employ the same principles and all work together.

The most powerful, and most generally valuable, method of causing an audience to misinterpret something is to provide a *mock explanation*. This procedure has been largely neglected by conjurers. It often depends on the theme, and conjurers commonly ignore themes.

If you begin by stating your theme, you provide the audience with an explanation of the effect. It may be as plausible as the lightning-calculator "explanation" of *Number Please* (after all, real lightning calculators do exist). Or it may be as absurd as The Obeah Man's whammy of *The Haunted Conjurer*. In either case, it should be sufficiently clear so that if it were true, the audience would accept it as an adequate explanation of the effect.

Thus, a real expert in lie detection might be able to recognize falsehoods by feeling a subject's pulse. A person with a sense of color touch could distinguish hues with his fingers; in fact, a recent news release states that one woman has just furnished persuasive evidence of being able to do it.

Inadequate mock explanations are all too common. Hypnosis accounts for *Sniff-Sniff* and the *Singing Glass*, but it fails to explain levitation or *Sawing a Woman in Half*. Always ask yourself, "If I believed the explanation, would I regard the effect as a natural consequence of it ?"

You do not need to go behind the mock explanation. If psychokinesis exists, will power can swing a pendulum. How the mind operates at a distance is a question for scientists, not for parlor experimenters. Usually, you need not even pretend to know how or why the phenomenon works. It is an adequate explanation if it accounts for the effect.

The completeness needed for a mock explanation varies with the audience. Most groups which are willing to accept *Horoscope* are prepared to believe that character can be read from birthdays. However, if your audience contains a spectator with some technical knowledge of astrology, he will not be satisfied; experienced astrologers do not cast horoscopes without knowing both the year and the hour of birth. In fact, an error of even five minutes is supposed to affect the result. Hence, with such a spectator, you should confess that readings from birthdays are inaccurate and then make enough "mistakes" for these inaccurate readings to seem plausible.

Another advantage of a mock explanation is that it focuses the interest of the audience on some innocent element and thus diverts attention from any weak spot.

THE CLAIRVOYANT DIE

Introduce an odd-looking die. It can be an old-fashioned bone die rubbed with sand to make it seem ancient, or it can be a rough cube like Fig. 93. This was molded from plastic wood and dotted with India ink. State that you found the die one day and carried it as a pocket piece until you accidentally discovered that it has clairvoyant powers. When this is greeted with disbelief, offer to let the spectators judge for themselves.

Have a card chosen and returned. Shuffle the deck and give it to The Subject with instructions to deal six rows of six cards each "because the die has only six faces." Roll the die once and announce, "As the die shows an odd (or an even) number, your card must be in the layout." Hand the die to the spectator and tell him to roll twice. Explain that the first roll will fix the row, counting one for the row furthest from the spectator and six for that nearest him. The second roll will determine the place of the card in the row, counting from the spectator's left to his right. As soon as the die stops for the second time, turn over the indicated card. Figs. 94 and 95 explain the procedure.

In this example, you actually present a card location, but you misinterpret it as a demonstration of the clairvoyant power possessed by a magic die. The same basic effect could be

THE CLAIRVOYANT DIE

Control the chosen card to the top of the deck. When the spectator deals from his left to his right he will put this card in the spot marked *A* in Fig. 94. This makes it the most natural card for you to pick up and use as a trowel. The die may indicate any card (*B*, Fig. 94). Hold Card *A* by a corner with your thumb and middle finger (Step 1). Pretend to flick Card *B* over but really release Card *A* and grip Card *B* with your thumb and index finger. When this is done smoothly, it looks exactly as if you had turned Card *B* face up.

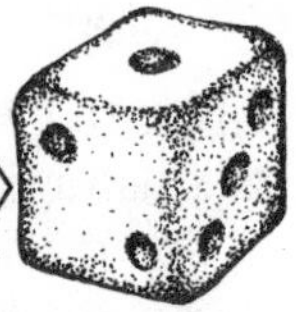

93. DIE

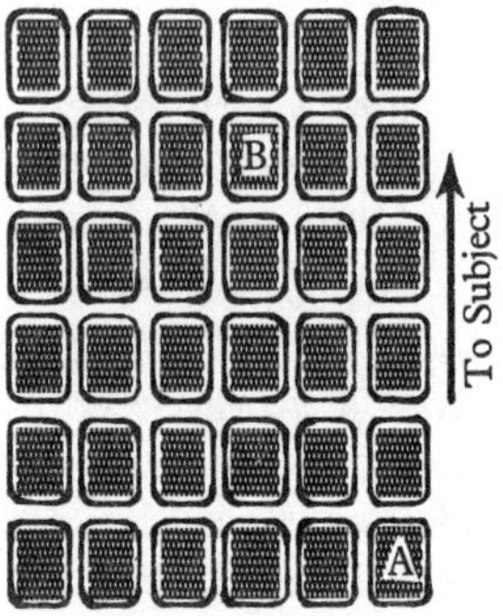

94. LAYOUT

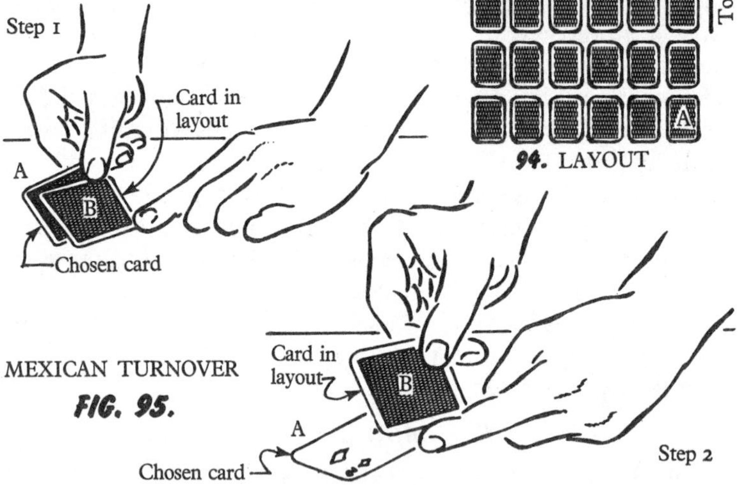

To Subject

Step 1

Card in layout

A

B

Chosen card

MEXICAN TURNOVER

Card in layout

B

A

Chosen card

Step 2

FIG. 95.

presented as a card trick. One Subject might draw a card, a second might name a vertical row, and a third might name a horizontal row. In that case, however, any reasonably astute spectator could guess that the cards must be switched. But when the die is used, it attracts attention and thus keeps the audience from concentrating on the cards.

Mock explanations are not limited to themes. They can occur at any point and can explain props as well as phenomena. Thus, the pencils in *Chromavoyance* are "explained" as being the only shiny, colored objects available for the test. Motivations are essentially mock explanations and lead the audience to misinterpret some statement, action, or piece of apparatus.

All forms of misinterpretation must occur before the spectators notice anything odd and begin to wonder about it. Once curiosity is aroused, it is hard to satisfy—even when the explanation is genuine.

Mock explanations for phenomena are easy to handle in "impromptu" work. You have plenty of time, and the process is misinterpreted as ordinary conversation. Stage performances, however, present difficulties. Mock explanations are highly desirable, but they must be brief and to the point. Try to work them in while you are introducing apparatus or waiting for a volunteer to come up onto the stage. Comedy helps when the treatment permits. A really funny explanation can last a minute or more without seeming excessive.

The best solution is to plan an act around a character like The Haunted Conjurer or The Crackpot Inventor so that all the effects concern the same phenomenon or a series of related phenomena. This reduces the required explanation to a minimum. Furthermore, you can merely sketch it in at first and enlarge on it bit by bit as you proceed.

When a completely unified act is impractical, you may be able to group items so that two or three in succession employ the same theme. This reduces the number of mock explanations that you require.

WHAT ABOUT THE RULE?

The oldest rule in conjuring is: *Never explain beforehand.* Spectators are more likely to see through a trick when they know what is going to happen. As a mock explanation clearly violates this rule, you may feel that mock explanations must be not merely unwise but downright heresy as well. Actually, the trouble is in the rule, itself, which is open to several serious objections.

In the first place, many tricks necessarily reveal their effects in advance. When you have someone draw a card, you cannot conceal the fact that you intend to identify it later. When you perform a repetitive effect like *Dowsing Test*, the dullest spectator has a good idea of what will come next.

Even when the rule can be applied, its primary purpose is to conceal the device. Spectators who do not know what to expect cannot guess what device to look for. Their interest has not been completely aroused, and hence they are not fully alert. This is poor showmanship. Diverting interest from a device by focusing it on something else is sound enough, but any policy that calls for deliberately weakening the over-all interest is hard to justify.

Furthermore, there are other techniques for concealing devices. A mock explanation is one of these, and it usually does a better job. If you present *The Strong Man's Secret* without the strong-man explanation, some spectator is likely to recognize it as a cut-and-restored effect. As he will be thinking along the right line, he has a much better chance of piercing the secret than he would have if you supply the strong-man explanation to lead him down a false trail. Even if you could keep the whole audience from forming an idea of what to expect, any gain in deception would be more than offset by the loss in interest. Think how dull *The Strong Man's Secret* would be if the spectators could make no sense of your actions until after two of them pulled on the string(s), and you then remarked, "See? I can hold two strings so firmly that they can't be drawn out of my fist."

There are, however, cases in which the rule does have important advantages. Thus, in *Arithmagic*, you give The Subject a choice of packets but do not tell him how you intend to use them until he has made his choice. Again, if something goes wrong, you may change your routine as long as you have not declared your intentions. Thus, in most take-a-card illusions, you should first try to force the card. If this works, you proceed as planned; if you miss, you identify the card by controlling and glimpsing it. Obviously, if you begin by saying that The Subject is to take a card and put it in his pocket, a missed force puts you in an embarrassing position.

Fortunately, any conflict between the rule and the use of mock explanation is more apparent than real. The rule forbids giving details of procedure before a device has been used. In most cases, you can frame a mock explanation in such a way that it conveys no clues. Thus, in *Ancestral Aid* you could safely begin by saying that Charlier will repeat The Subject's cut without giving anything away. However, it is better to play doubly safe and avoid being explicit until the upper packet has been replaced and the deck squared. After that, begging your ancestor to duplicate The Subject's cut does not increase the risk of detection, but it does serve to make the climax more impressive.

To sum up: Always provide a mock explanation, but avoid disclosing key details of procedure until after you have worked any device(s) which concern them.

SURPRISE

You may agree that advance explanations have all the advantages I have mentioned and still reject them on the ground that they kill surprise. Many conjurers place a high value on surprise. They believe that audiences enjoy it, and that it increases the air of mystery. Actually, audiences do not like to be surprised. They hate it. They take delight in a "stage surprise," but this differs as much from real surprise as a stage whisper does from a real whisper.

In a real surprise, both the thing that happens and the time when it occurs are unexpected. A stage surprise takes place only after the audience has been duly warned. The performer says, in effect, "I'm going to surprise you. Are you ready? Here it is!"

A stage surprise derives its punch from the fact that two types of material are developed simultaneously. One is introduced but appears to lead nowhere. The other approaches a foreseen climax. However, just as this climax is about to occur, it is sidetracked or abandoned and the climax of the other material is substituted. This involves four elements: (1) The audience is told to prepare for a big surprise. (2) A strong hint is given as to its general nature. (3) Some other event is expected at a specific moment. (4) When the moment arrives, the surprise is substituted for the expected event.

The Haunted Conjurer is typical. (1) The conjurer confesses that he has been jinxed. (2) He adds that almost anything is more than likely to happen. (3) He starts to perform *Passe-Passe Dice*, which leads up to a foreseeable climax at a foreseeable moment. (4) When he displays the transposed dice, they have suddenly turned into guinea pigs.

When you cannot give warning of a surprise, show surprise yourself before the spectators can realize what has happened. Thus, in *Twentieth-Century Nylon*, your face, and the tone of your voice, should indicate that something has gone wrong long before the audience sees that a stocking has been substituted for the red handkerchief.

Stage surprises are excellent for both comedy and drama. But be sure the spectators are prepared for them. The completely unexpected is almost always unwelcome.

Chapter 14

CONTROLLING ATTENTION

Every performer needs to control the attention of his audience. But whereas actors and most entertainers are largely concerned with directing attention toward the point which happens to be important at the moment, conjurers are equally concerned with diverting attention away from some device. This is termed *misdirection*. It is an important part of the conjurer's art, but is largely misunderstood because performers try to study it separately. Actually, direction and misdirection employ identical techniques. The only difference lies in the purpose for which they are used. As we need both, and as we use direction constantly whereas misdirection is required only to cover weak spots, we shall begin with direction.

THE SOURCE OF INFORMATION

A routine is essentially a sequence of *steps*, each of which must be made clear to the audience. The steps of *Lie Detector*, for example, are shown in Outline B as follows:

OUTLINE B

1. You believe that lies can be detected by feeling The Subject's pulse.
2. You are willing to demonstrate.
3. Experts convince subjects by naming a card.
4. Your Subject chooses his card.
5. You feel his pulse and determine the name of his card by a process of elimination.

Most steps contain several *points*. Thus, when your Subject draws his card, you must convince him that his selection is free, that you are indifferent to his choice, that the cards are unprepared, and so on. Each point is conveyed by a *source of information*. You make the point that the cards are fair by shuffling the deck. In that case, the source of information consists of your-hands-and-the-deck. If you then have The Sub-

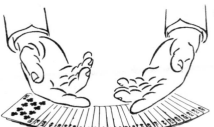

96. ONE SOURCE
This combines three
elements, but the eye
can take them all in
at one glance.

97. THREE SEPARATE SOURCES

ject cut, the source shifts to his-hands-and-the-deck. While you
are telling him to answer every question by "No," your remarks are the source of information. An expert performer controls attention so perfectly that it shifts from one source to
the next throughout the routine.

You can often present several points at once. Thus, if you
display the deck as in Fig. 96, you prove (?) that: (1) the cards
are not fakes, (2) they are not stacked, and (3) your hands are
empty. Nevertheless, even when you convey many points
simultaneously, there can never be more than one source of
information at a time. This may be as small as a pin or as large
as the whole stage, but the audience must be able to grasp it as
a unit. This is easy in Fig. 96, but if you spread your hands as in
Fig. 97, there are three sources and the audience will probably
miss at least one of them. On the other hand, in a bullet-catching
routine one point will be, "The performer is on one side of the
stage, and the man with the gun is on the other side." That will
be completely obvious even though the source of information
is some thirty feet wide, and people in the front rows must turn
their heads to see it all.

In one sense, we create a double source of information whenever we explain a prop or an action; the prop itself is one source and the words are another. From a practical standpoint, however, only the visual source counts.

When someone has drawn a card and you tell him what to do with it, the card is the primary source of information because it is the point on which you want to focus attention. Of course, the words are equally important, but the spectators should take them in subconsciously while their eyes are on the card.

On the other hand, when you explain something without action, your words are the primary source. Spectators pay most attention to your words when they watch your lips, which then count as the visual source of information. This is one reason why you should avoid either covering your mouth or turning your head away from the audience while you speak.

As sources of information are basic for effective presentation, let us examine an example in detail. In the following routine, the visual sources are noted in square brackets.

PSYCHOSOMATICS

Begin a discussion by saying, "The body influences the mind more than most of us realize. Napoleon was right when he claimed that tragedy can be turned into comedy merely by sitting down. If you don't believe it, try making love over the phone while you stand in an aggressive attitude with your fists clenched and a scowl on your face. Or try to bawl someone out while you're leaning back in an easy chair with your muscles relaxed. You just can't do it." [*Your lips.*]

This should start a discussion. [*As it proceeds, each speaker's lips become the visual source of information in turn.*]

When a strong atmosphere has been established, say, "The influence works the other way, too. You can't think a thought without giving some clue through your behavior. No matter how hard you try to fake a thought or emotion, you won't fool anyone who knows what to watch for." [*Your lips.*]

Someone is almost sure to challenge this. [*His lips.*]

Offer to demonstrate. Take a deck of cards from its case. [*The cards.*] Run through it face up to remove the jokers and the advertising card. [*The cards and your hands.*] Turn the deck face down and deal off about ten cards. [*The growing packet now becomes the source of information because the audience wonders what you intend to do with it.*]

Spread the cards in the packet slightly, [*The packet.*] and invite The Challenger to select one. [*First his face, then his hand and the packet, then the drawn card.*]

Tell The Challenger to look at his card and remember it but not to let anyone else see it. [*His face.*] Square the packet while he is memorizing his card. [*This action does not provide a source of information. Although it is not a secret, it can be a source of distraction. Hence, the less attention it receives, the better.*] Have The Challenger replace his card on the packet, [*The card.*] and then cut the packet and complete the cut [*The packet.*]

Drop the rest of the deck on the packet. [*The deck.*] Have The Challenger cut the deck and give it a riffle shuffle, cut and shuffle again, and make one final cut. [*His hands and the deck.*]

Announce that you are now ready for the test. The Challenger is to deal the cards face up as rapidly as possible. As he does so, he is to think of his card and repeat its name over and over to himself. Thus, if he drew the Ace of Spades, he is to think "Ace of Spades, Ace of Spades" while he deals. If he does this, he cannot avoid giving some indication when he recognizes his card. The other spectators are to watch for this sign and see if they can identify the card by The Challenger's actions. [*The source of information here will probably shift back and forth between your lips and The Challenger's face.*]

The Challenger deals. [*For some spectators, the source of information may be his hands. Others will watch his face. In this case, it does not matter which source they watch. However, they should watch one of them. If somebody looks at you or at another spectator, his attention has not been properly controlled.*]

When The Challenger has dealt one card past the chosen one, stop him by saying, "See, he gave his card away that time," and name his card. [*The Challenger's face, because the audience looks to see if he will confirm your statement.*]

This is based on two devices which were first brought together by Jack McMillen for a trick called *The Mind Mirror*. The original appeared in *Expert Card Technique* by Jean Hugard. I have buried the secret one stage deeper and added a theme.

Take the even-numbered Spades and Diamonds from the deck. Arrange them in random order but put the Queen of Spades on top. Also remove the two Jokers and the advertising card. Place four or five indifferent cards face down. Put the even Spades and Diamonds on these. Add a Joker, then about a dozen indifferent cards, then the advertising card, then some twenty indifferent cards. Then the other Joker. Put the remaining indifferent cards on top of the deck.

If you run through this deck face up, no one will suspect that it is stacked. Draw off the cards until you come to the Queen of Spades and let this whole packet drop into your right hand. Discard the next card which is the first Joker. Thumb off the remaining cards in batches. This is actually a crude shuffle, but the order of the stacked cards is not disturbed. Discard the advertising card and the other Joker as you come to them. The whole maneuver brings the stacked cards to the back of the deck.

When you deal off about ten cards, the Queen of Spades goes on the bottom and the rest of the packet is made up entirely of even-numbered Spades and Diamonds. The remaining cards of the stock are on top of the deck.

By placing his card on top of the packet and cutting it, The Challenger brings the Queen of Spades immediately above the card he drew. The later cuts have no effect. Two riffle shuffles mix the deck as a whole, but they do not change the order of the stacked cards. Hence, if you watch for the Queen of Spades while the cards are being dealt, the next even-numbered Spade or Diamond will be The Challenger's card.

THE CENTER OF INTEREST

The source of information is what we want the audience to watch. The *center of interest* is what the audience itself wants to watch. In an ideal presentation, they coincide, but this does not happen automatically. Thus, in *Fan-tastic*, the men in the audience may be more interested in your assistant's legs than in the fan you wave. Except in the most convincing routines, some spectators will try to devote their attention to detecting your device but you must fix it on one source of information after another. The first step in this process is to do everything possible toward making the source of information the most interesting object present.

Certain things are inherently interesting. People are more interesting than things; a helper from the audience is likely to take attention from a piece of apparatus. Sex always attracts notice; a pretty assistant tends to draw every eye, especially if her skirts are short and her legs are shapely. Animals have tremendous appeal. Current topics attract almost everyone. Your apparatus will gain more attention if it recalls the latest fad or the latest scientific discovery, and your words can benefit by the same treatment.

Unfortunately, inherent interest cannot be turned on and off like a light. Your assistant's lovely legs are an asset when you want to throw attention to her, but they are a liability when you want to take attention away from her. Hence, we must learn to subordinate inherently interesting objects when they are not the source of information. Animals, for example, should be kept hidden except for the brief periods when we want to fix all eyes on them.

Subordination is an essential element of showmanship. This is another application of conservation and another hard lesson to learn, especially when the conjurer himself is the thing to be subordinated. Nevertheless, failure to learn it will cost you dear. No audience can watch more than one thing at a time. If you display two centers of interest simultaneously, neither one can make its point properly, and both together will receive less attention than either one would by itself.

Nothing remains a center of interest for long. We must shift attention constantly in order to control it. When A Subject cuts the cards, he is the source of information and should be the sole center of interest as well. A showman-conjurer subordinates himself *entirely* at this point by remaining motionless and saying nothing. He does not even let his hands remain near the deck lest they distract part of the attention from the hands of The Subject who is making the cut. By yielding all the attention in this way, the performer prepares his right hand to be the next center of interest when he stretches it out to take the deck after it has been cut.

The performer who works alone on a stage has more trouble controlling attention because his available centers are limited by the parts of his own body and his props. As the parts of his body—especially his hands and face—are constantly in the eyes of the audience, their capacity to arouse interest decreases rapidly. They cannot regain it, because the performer has no way to turn all attention away from himself—even for a moment. This explains why speakers, who have no props, find it so hard to maintain interest. It also explains why conjurers are wise to call up volunteers or ask some seated spectator to name a card or choose a number.

Although inherent interest is useful, we have little control over it. Fortunately, there is a much more flexible type known as *induced interest*. This arises whenever we give the audience reason to think that something may repay attention. In *The Strong Man's Secret*, for example, you begin by toying with a piece of string. The spectators may notice this casually when you first take it from your pocket. However, as it seems to have no connection with your talk about freak-show performers, they soon ignore it. When you are ready to demonstrate, hold the string up and say, "This piece of string reminds me of one stunt I can do myself." That arouses curiosity. The string becomes the center of interest and every eye turns toward it.

You can make something the center of interest without showing it. Thus, in *Dowsing Test*, you no sooner suggest bending a divining rod from wire than the audience becomes wire-conscious. Mention astrology in *Horoscope*, and most people form the idea of having their fortunes told.

A well-planned routine induces interest in each point in turn because each point leads to the next. As the routine proceeds, interest induced by the action increases and requires less and less control from the performer.

This explains why digressions are so harmful. Even when they are amusing in themselves, they break the sequence of points. If you stop in the middle of *The Strong Man's Secret* to tell what The Sword Swallower said to The Fat Lady, your audience may chuckle—but it loses the thread of the routine. Your power to induce interest in the next step is lost. You may be able to recover it by reminding the spectators of what has happened. However, it will never be so strong as it was before you permitted yourself to get a laugh at the expense of your own illusion.

When you stick to your theme, you will have little difficulty in making the center of interest coincide with the source of information at every point. However, you can never afford to take this for granted. You must have a clear idea of the sequence of points and make each source of information interesting in turn.

The Focus of Attention

An audience gives voluntary attention to the center of interest, but the performer must also control its involuntary attention. If you drop a card, every eye will follow it. No one really cares about the trivial accident, but audiences automatically watch any moving object, especially when the movement is unexpected.

The great conjurers of the past maintained almost complete control of the spectator's involuntary attention. Their successors seem to have forgotten that such control is possible. Fortunately, it is not a lost art. It is part of the stock-in-trade that any competent stage director brings to the theater. I cannot control attention if a bat flies into the auditorium or two drunken playgoers start an altercation. But, barring such interruptions, I can make an audience watch the precise point that I select during every instant of a two-hour play. As the conjurer's problem is both simpler and briefer, he should be able to do at least as well.

The principal techniques for controlling involuntary attention are given in the sections below. However, before considering them, we must recall their purpose. At each moment in a routine, we should offer one—and only one—source of information. We should try to make this also the center of interest at that moment. We must succeed in making it the *focus of attention* as well. If we fail to do this for even one point, our routine will be weakened; if the point is crucial, the routine may fail entirely.

THE PERFORMER'S INTEREST

The performer's own interest is his chief device for controlling attention. Unless there is some strong competing attraction, an audience will watch anything which he treats as important. For this reason he must concentrate—or at least appear to concentrate—on the object or situation that is the source of information at the moment. Exceptions occur, but they are rare; you should give only casual attention to the choice of coins in *Dial Information*, and you obviously must not notice The Mischievous Boy while he pours water into your foo-can hat.

If the conjurer is completely in character, his attention will go to the right point almost automatically. Unfortunately, his thoughts are often claimed by technical matters. He must perform a sleight, obtain a gimmick, or load a prop. If his mind strays to such things, the attention of the spectators will follow it like rabbit hounds on a hot trail. They may not identify the device, but they do know that he has fallen out of character and they also know that he is up to some skulduggery. No illusion can survive these discoveries. The only way to avoid this is to practice all sleights and false moves until they can be done without thinking.

Conjurers who perform a routine many times find that they can do the whole thing, words and actions, while their minds are elsewhere. This is fatal. Audiences are quick to detect the performer's indifference, and they reflect it in their attitude. If a conjurer does not take an interest in his act, he cannot expect an audience to do so.

Furthermore, when a performer's mind wanders, his eyes will continually drift away from the source of information. If the spectators are paying any attention, they will follow his glance. This will make them miss important points.

You may not be able to take an interest in a routine itself, but each presentation of that routine presents fresh problems because the audience is new. Also, no presentation is ever perfect. There is always room for some improvement. If you invariably try to improve your presentation at each performance and also try to adapt it to the peculiarities of each particular audience, you will find that the job demands all your attention. Under those circumstances, boredom becomes impossible.

Your assistant's interest is as essential as your own. It may even be more so because she is normally further from the source of information. If she becomes bored and lets her eyes wander, a spectator who happens to notice her will have his attention carried completely away from the routine. On the other hand, when she concentrates on the source of information, the spectator who looks at her will have his attention directed back where it belongs.

The same principle applies to volunteers insofar as you can control them. When they watch the source of information, the audience is almost certain to follow their lead; when they glance at something else, the audience will do the same thing (Figs. 98 and 99).

POINTING

98. DISTRACTING POINTERS

The scarf is the center of interest, but so many pointers carry attention to the right that most spectators will look at the girl.

Some eyes may even drift past her toward the empty space on her left (the right of the observer).

Pointing

One obvious method of focusing attention on an object is to point at it. Pointing is not restricted to your wand or your

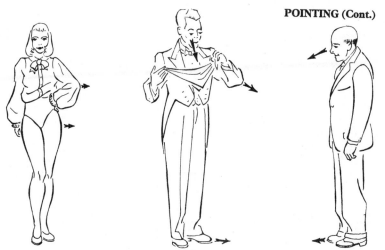

99. A BETTER GROUPING

The girl's elbow now points toward the conjurer, and the volunteer is also led to face him. Note that even if the volunteer actually looks at the girl's legs, he seems to focus on the scarf. However, by facing front, the girl takes too much attention herself and fails to direct enough at the scarf.

finger; almost any part of your body can be used. Figs. 98–103 show examples.

Even a blunt shape can point. Notice how the girl's elbow and hip divert attention from the performer in Fig. 98, but

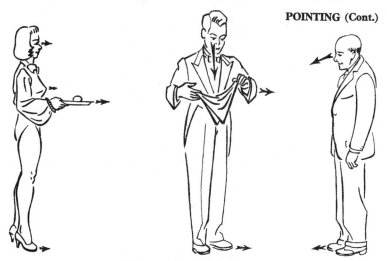

100. AN IDEAL GROUPING

All the pointers are now directed toward the scarf. Note that the performer has lowered the scarf so that the assistant's tray points directly at it.

MORE EXAMPLES OF POINTING

101. ◊
POINTING WITH THUMB

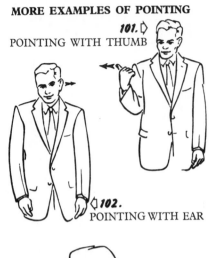

◊ **102.**
POINTING WITH EAR

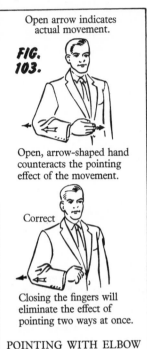

Open arrow indicates actual movement.

FIG. 103.

Open, arrow-shaped hand counteracts the pointing effect of the movement.

Correct

Closing the fingers will eliminate the effect of pointing two ways at once.

POINTING WITH ELBOW

The performer looks at the glass as he sets it down, but his other hand "accidentally" directs attention to the pack which he is about to pick up.

◊ **104.** SMOOTHING A TRANSITION

direct it toward him in Fig. 99. Nevertheless, sharp pointers are more effective. Feet, for example, direct attention better than hips because they are more arrow-like. If you look in one direction and turn your feet in another, you will be pointing in two ways at once (volunteer in Fig. 98). That explains why a young actor is told to make his toes follow his nose. This is not an invariable rule; there are times when you should point in two directions at once. Thus, when you speak to a volunteer about a prop, you point to the prop by looking at it and include the volunteer in the source of information by turning your body slightly toward him and letting one toe point directly at him. Fig. 100 illustrates this. Note also that the conjurer's left elbow points at the volunteer and away from the assistant, who is not part of the source of information.

Any part of the body becomes a pointer when used consciously. For example, an actor who ostentatiously turns his back on another directs attention to the one whom he is attempting to ignore. The conjurer can make good use of this principle when performing a card routine in which he turns away while a spectator does something to the cards. The performer points at the cards most strongly when he stands with his back directly to them. Merely turning slightly away, as many conjurers do, is less effective.

Do not confuse the action of pointing with the points of a routine. Each point of a routine is made by a source of information. The action of pointing is one technique for focusing attention on this source.

Pointers are particularly useful when you shift attention subtly from one source of information to the next. For example, you can make the transition from *Sniff-Sniff* to *The Singing Glass* by simply putting down the glass and picking up the cards. However, the change is less abrupt if you "accidentally" point to the deck as in Fig. 104 just before you are ready to pick it up.

CONTRAST

The intelligent use of contrast provides another technique for controlling attention. Anything that contrasts with its surroundings will draw the eyes of the audience. Attention goes to a moving object when everything else is still. It goes to a vivid color which is contrasted with a dull background. It is attracted by a bright object on a darkened stage. One of the most eye-catching things a performer can do is to strike a match. Even on a well-lit stage, a match seems much brighter than it does in daily life.

Sound also draws involuntary attention. Spectators tend to watch any person who is speaking if only because his voice contrasts with the silence of the other people present. They also look toward the source of any noise that differs from a background of silence or sound. When a full orchestra is playing, a barely audible whisper will draw every eye within earshot.

Anything unexpected or sudden is sure to attract involuntary attention. Nevertheless, the strength of the unexpected and sudden is also their weakness. As we saw on p. 177, we should always warn the audience to expect the unexpected, and the surprise should occur at the precise moment when the audience is ready for it.

The examples I have given are cases where something vivid contrasts with a dull background. This produces the strongest results, but the principle of contrast also holds where the important object is drab and the background is brilliant. Thus, the actor who plays Hamlet is conventionally dressed in black. He finds it easy to command attention in the scenes where his costume is set off by the brightly colored robes of the courtiers. He seems less prominent in the scenes with the guards, where their somber uniforms offer little contrast.

A conjurer in the black-and-white of evening dress will stand out against a stage set with bright-hued draperies, props, and gaily costumed assistants. On the other hand, if he uses such a setting and wears a colorful Oriental costume himself, a volunteer from the audience will receive attention through reverse contrast and may steal the scene.

MOVEMENT

As the eyes of the audience tend to follow any moving object, movement can be used as a technique for controlling attention. But this is only part of the story. Motion is most effective when it contrasts with stillness.

This gives us an important rule: *Make no movement without a purpose.* Every action must be clearly motivated, and the motivation must fit the performer's assumed character. Fidgeting and useless movements, such as putting down your wand and picking it up a moment later, are taboo. They do not fit any character that an intelligent performer would assume.

Competent actors follow the rule religiously. Conjurers must break it to perform sleights and handle gimmicks. However, such out-of-character movements should be disguised as motivated actions if that is at all possible. For example, when you control a chosen card to the top of the deck, you should act as though you are burying the card beyond recovery.

When you rehearse by yourself, you may find trouble in eliminating meaningless movements. Your best plan is to have a friend watch you and point out your errors. If you are a chronic fidgeter, curing the habit will appear hopeless at first. Some people make several pointless actions every minute, and it seems impossible to get rid of them all. Fortunately, correction is much easier than it seems. My experience with actors has taught me that even the worst fidgeters master the habit after five or six rehearsals in which they are frequently reminded of the fault. In any case, fidgeting is one of the worst sins a performer can commit. If you are guilty of it, you must break yourself before you can hope to be more than second rate.

Another excellent rule is: *Make only one movement at a time.* This does not mean that you should keep your whole body still when you move, say, your right hand. Actually, most graceful actions of any size involve every muscle to some extent. The point is that your motions should be coordinated to emphasize a single idea. If you produce a handkerchief with your right hand, do not wave your wand aimlessly with your left.

The rule against simultaneous motions applies even more strictly when two people are on stage. You and your assistant must often collaborate on a single action such as the handkerchief dyeing in *Fan-tastic*, but you should avoid doing two separate things at once. Walking in different directions simultaneously is especially bad. For some reason, audiences consider this funny and will laugh at it even in serious moments.

This does not require you and you assistant to take turns in moving as though you were mechanical toys. The fault lies in starting and stopping at the same time. One should either start to move an instant before the other stops or should wait for a moment or two after the other finishes.

Problems of simultaneous movement are difficult to handle when you must work without a director. Try to get some friend to watch a rehearsal and pay particular attention to this matter. Even an inexperienced observer can tell whether the action is clear and smooth or confused and jerky.

VARIETY

Another important type of contrast is that between the new and the old. This is one reason why variety is so important in any type of performance. Variety need not be great or even definitely noticeable, but try to make each action different from all the others.

An exceptionally clear example of this occurs in routines where the conjurer produces a dozen silk scarves in succession.

Good showmanship requires varying the colors and sizes of the scarves and the movements with which they are displayed. Available colors include: lilac, white, dark blue, orange, dark purple, yellow, light blue, pink, emerald green, red, light green, and magenta. This list arranges the colors so that each contrasts with the one before it, and yet there is enough over-all increase in vividness to give a climatic effect. Nothing is gained by having every scarf a different size, but a few surprising variations do much to add interest. Thus, if most of the scarves are 16-inch squares, use a 24-inch square for the dark purple, a tiny 8-inch handkerchief for the red, and wind up with a magenta streamer a foot wide and eight or ten feet long.

Your own actions can be varied in an infinite number of ways. Hold the production box in your left hand and take the scarves out with your right. Produce two or three in quick succession, pause an instant, peer into the production box, and draw the next scarf out slowly. Pile several on your table. Then start making wider movements which wave a scarf to the right and bring it back to drape over your left arm. Return to piling scarves on your table but finally let one slip off as though the table were overcrowded. When you reach the red handkerchief, stare at it in surprise and tuck it into your breast pocket. Pull out the light-green scarf with a flick. Then put the production box down and draw out the magenta streamer with a hand-over-hand motion.

I doubt if you will ever have a reason for using exactly the same procedure twice. You must sometimes repeat an effect to prove that the first result was not pure luck. But, even in such cases, try to vary the presentation as much as possible. Thus, in *I Scry*, you first divine the card on top of the center pile and then divine the one on the face of a chosen pile.

Triple repetitions are much more common. In fact, if you do something more than once, you should normally do it three times. Thus, if you tear up a piece of paper, try to make exactly three tears. When this is impractical, you can often create a one-two-three pattern artificially. In *The Sigil of Solomon*, for example, you can tear the folded slip only twice. However, you can then add a third gesture by taking the scraps (not the center) into your right hand with a twist of your wrist.

The one-two-three pattern corresponds to some deep psychological factor in all of us. Doing something three times creates a climatic effect. Doing it a fourth time creates boredom. *Fantastic* is a perfect example. Commercial color-changing fans can display four different hues. Thus, you can "dye" four handkerchiefs as easily as three. But this is bad showmanship. Dyeing one is trivial. Dyeing two arouses interest. Dyeing three provides your climax. There is no reason to add an anticlimax simply because you are equipped to do so.

You may occasionally be in doubt as to whether to use the one-two pattern of *I Scry* or the one-two-three pattern of *Fantastic*. The answer depends on the unity of the procedure. *I Scry* contains two separate tests. Either can succeed or fail without affecting the other. The sole function of the second is to prove that the first was not a fluke. A third test would add nothing. *Fan-tastic*, on the other hand, is clearly a unit. If only one handkerchief were dyed, you could not show that the fan changes color, and the effect would be weak. If two handkerchiefs are dyed, the change in the fan presents no mystery, and the routine seems incomplete. The third effect proves that the fan is magical and rounds off the presentation.

I doubt if there is ever a reason for doing something four times. However, there are three cases where more repetitions are needed.

One occurs when we want to express the idea of "very many." Thurston did a magic-fountain number in which water sprang from every point that he touched with his wand. Three jets would have made almost no impression on the audience. He needed to create the illusion that he could draw water from anything. This required some two dozen fountains and a separate wand movement for each.

Multiple repetition is also required for a *running gag*, a bit of comedy which is repeated several times during an act, and which becomes funnier with each repetition. Thus, near the beginning of your act, you might pour water from a lota bowl saying, "This is a desert dew catcher. Nomads in the Gobi Desert, where it never rains, carry them to gather moisture." Use the water in your next routine. When it is over, pour more water from the lota bowl into some waste vessel with the remark, "The only trouble with these things is that you have to keep emptying them. That's fine in the desert, but I find it a bit of a nuisance." At intervals during the rest of your act, murmur, "Excuse me," and empty the lota bowl again. This is mysterious, convincing, and will be extremely funny in the hands of a good comedian.

Finally, we can use multiple repetition when we want to make 'an action uninteresting. Thus, if you use a false shuffle and are unable to execute it indetectably, you can use repetition as a disguise. Make your fair shuffles resemble your false one as closely as possible and make them all alike. After watching a few fair shuffles, the audience becomes bored by the process. You may then be able to slip in one or two false shuffles without having anyone notice the discrepancies.

Observe, however, that this is only a makeshift. Fair shuffles are important points because they convince the audience that the deck is arranged at random. Hence, good showmanship requires you to call attention to them by using a slightly different method each time. False shuffles are made only to keep anyone from suspecting that the cards are under your control. If you make all your fair shuffles alike, you weaken their influence. This may be necessary in order to disguise imperfect false shuffles, but it is a sacrifice.

When you are forced to disguise a false move by making fair moves monotonous, try to compensate for this by finding some other way to give the fair moves prominence. For example, you can stare at your hands and keep silent while making a fair shuffle, but look at a spectator and say something interesting while executing a false one. Here again, variety is the keynote: *use a different attention-getter each time.* One fair shuffle can be stressed by first rapping the deck on the table to square it. Another may be made obviously fair through using the monotonous technique yourself and then inviting some spectator to shuffle again.

DISTRACTION

No technique in directing attention will make an audience watch the source of information when something else is permitted to distract attention. Audiences seem downright perverse about this. If a spotlight picks out your wrist watch, the spectators stare at it and lose the thread of what you are doing. If you let your eyes flick to your assistant to make sure she is in position, half the audience will follow your gaze. When you are the source of information, arrange for the girl to remain motionless but not tense. The most innocent action on her part, even coughing or picking a tray from a table, is enough to rob you of the attention you need at that point. Conversely, be careful not to distract attention from her when she is the source of information.

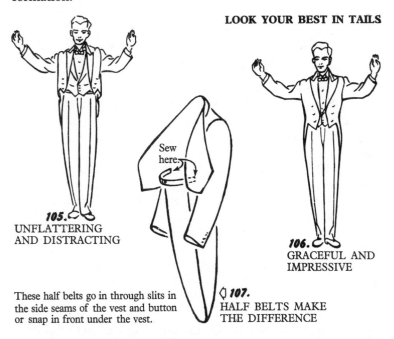

LOOK YOUR BEST IN TAILS

105.
UNFLATTERING
AND DISTRACTING

Sew
here.

106.
GRACEFUL AND
IMPRESSIVE

These half belts go in through slits in the side seams of the vest and button or snap in front under the vest.

107.
HALF BELTS MAKE
THE DIFFERENCE

Go over your act carefully and eliminate all possible causes of distraction—useless movements, jewelry that may catch the light; costume elements that may call attention to themselves at inopportune moments. A skirt that plays hide-and-seek with your assistant's knees is especially bad; her hemline should be at least 8 inches above her knees or at least 4 inches below them. Your own clothes can be equally distracting (Figs. 105 and 106). Your legs may not be pretty, but if some movement reveals a flash of flesh between your socks and your trousers it will draw every eye in the house. If you wear tails, the arrangement in Fig. 107 will keep your coat from becoming shapeless and distracting each time you raise your arms (Figs. 105 and 106).

Chapter 15
MISDIRECTION

There are only three ways in which a spectator can pierce a conjurer's secret. First, he may recognize the effect and know how it is achieved. You cannot fool a brother conjurer with *Ancestral Aid*. Second, the spectator may discover the actual device. If someone watching *Dowsing Test* snatches the napkin off the glasses, he will see the magnet. Third, an astute spectator may deduce the solution by sheer logic. If an observer is sufficiently shrewd, he can decide that *Dowsing Test* depends on a magnet because no other known force will produce the effect that he has observed.

We must guard against these dangers by misdirecting the spectator's mind, his attention, or his eye.

MENTAL MISDIRECTION

Logic requires a "frame of reference" or "context." A successful conjuring theme baffles logic by providing a false frame of reference. *Horoscope* is essentially a conjuring trick. But even the most skeptical observer is likely to mistake it for a misguided attempt to apply a pseudo science. Once he adopts this false frame of reference, he can find no logical explanation for the remarkable accuracy of The Astrologer's character readings.

Success in creating a false frame of reference depends primarily upon your ability to handle your theme, treatment, and atmosphere. The great charlatans were so adept at this that they made indelible impressions on intelligent people although they used only the crudest devices or none at all.

Mock explanations and motivations are deceptive because they create a false frame of reference. Thus, the explanation given for *Lie Detector* raises the question: Is it possible to detect lies from the pulse alone? However, the real question is: How did the performer learn which card was drawn?

Fooling brother conjurers becomes child's play if you can create a false frame of reference. For example:

THE PRESTIDIGITATOR'S PERPLEXITY

This works best on the card manipulator who is really good, but who thinks he is better. You also need an audience of a few other conjurers.

Remove a deck of cards from your pocket and perform one or two sleight-of-hand tricks. The expert will undoubtedly take over the deck and proceed to show off. During this, you make it quite clear that you believe all card tricks should be done with a borrowed pack. Such tricks, you argue, are more convincing. Also, the man who uses prepared cards is in trouble if someone asks for a trick which he cannot perform because he has left the required fake at home.

While your victim is flaunting his skill, inquire what he considers the best method of stacking a deck during the shuffle. No matter what he replies, show enough interest in the subject to get everyone thinking along these lines.

When you are ready for the kill, retrieve the deck. Give it several honest overhand shuffles, and keep the conversation going while you do so. After each shuffle, look at the expert and ask innocently, "Did you catch it that time?" As there is nothing to catch, he will certainly be baffled at this point.

Then say, "Now watch." Put the deck in your inside breast pocket and tell him to reach in quickly and grab a card. When he does so, you name it. Your victim will recognize this device. He knows that the only card he can take by a quick grab is the one farthest from your body.

All you have done so far is to demonstrate your ability to glimpse and control one card. As this is easy, it occasions no surprise. However, you now proceed to let each of the other spectators take a card in the same way. Have eight or nine cards drawn, even if this means that some spectators must draw twice. You name each card and remark, "If I practiced more, I suppose I could stack poker hands that way, but it's all I can do to *cull out* whatever cards I'm able to glimpse."

This would bore laymen, but it astounds the expert. Apparently, you have been able to glimpse, remember, and control eight or nine cards by a shuffle that looks perfectly fair—and you have done it under the nose of a man who thinks he knows all the sleights. The great masters of manipulation can do this, but your victim will hate to admit that you are a master.

The real secret depends on establishing a false frame of reference. The audience must be convinced that the cards are fair. This should be easy as the deck has been used for several tricks over which you had no control. You must also make it clear that you object to tricks which require preparation and that you had no idea of doing this particular trick until after you had watched the other man show off.

Actually, you employ a duplicate deck with the top stock stacked in advance. Use your telephone number as a mnemonic device and fill it out with face cards in the order: Jack, Queen, King. Remember the suits by the word CHaSeD. Thus, if your telephone number is 707-8429, the cards would run like this: JC - 7H - 10S - 7D - QC - 8H - 4S - 2D - 9C - KH.

Lay these on the back of the deck with the Jack of Clubs on top. Place the deck in your inside breast pocket facing your body. The deck you bring out at the start is a duplicate. I created a false frame of reference by lying when I said that you put the fair deck in your pocket. Actually, you drop it down your sleeve and catch it in your right hand. Slip it into your hip pocket. Motivate that by bringing out your handkerchief, and blowing your nose. You have ample time for this as attention is concentrated on your breast pocket.

Add an extra bit of conviction by having a pencil, a pen, and a couple of letters in the pocket with the stacked deck. Take these out just before you pretend to insert the cards. This suggests that the pocket is empty, and that the trick is "impromptu." It also gives you a chance to pull your sleeve away from your armpit, so that you can drop the fair deck down the sleeve without fumbling.

Of course, this routine is only a sample. You certainly cannot use it to fool anyone who has read this book. Nevertheless, it illustrates the principle. You can stump any conjurer on earth if you begin by convincing him that you will use one type of device and then use some entirely different type.

Logic also requires correct identification. When a spectator misidentifies a key factor, he is baffled. In *The Prestidigitator's Perplexity*, the audience mistakes the stacked duplicate for a fair deck. When Dr. Tarbell and his friends attended *The Charlatan*, they misidentified Tilden's confederate as his enemy.

Almost any change in a prop or a sleight may keep spectators from connecting it with knowledge that they already have. Someone who knows *The Wizard* may be thrown off the track in *Dial Information* because coins are substituted for cards. Conjurers who do *The Mind Mirror* themselves may not recognize it in *Psychosomatics* because the cards are displayed face up.

Even the most trivial change may be enough to confuse a spectator for a moment, and that may be enough to keep him from recognizing a device. I have seen fifty performers tie a string onto a solid ring and pull the knot off the ring. But when my friend Gen. Franklin Davis pulled the ring off the knot, I failed to recognize the device. If I had been given two seconds to think, I would have realized what he had done, but Gen. Davis proceeded immediately to the next step in the routine. This occupied my whole mind. As a result, I failed to understand how easily I had been fooled until some hours later. This experience taught me that almost any small change in conventional procedure is definitely worth while—*provided that it is consistent with the theme and does not complicate the presentation.*

A third class of techniques for defeating the spectator's logic consists in confusing the sequence of events. Perhaps the most generally useful of these is the method of *alternative procedures.* As long as the audience does not know what will happen, the conjurer is free to change his routine to meet any situation that may arise. If he can lead everyone to assume that he is following a fixed plan but actually varies his performance to suit some action by a spectator, he can achieve astounding results.

This is best illustrated by a forcing technique known as the *conjurer's choice.* The second divination in *Arithmagic* supplies an ideal example. The Subject chooses either of the two outside packets, you then choose what you will do with them—and adapt your choice to fit his.

This technique is often used when the conjurer has no real choice. Thus, if you show a fair deck and a stacked one, you might tell A Subject to choose either. When he takes the stacked deck, you use it; when he takes the fair deck, you say, "Keep that and I'll use the other one." This is poor policy. When A Subject takes a deck, he expects it to be used. If you merely discard it, you arouse his suspicions. This is entirely different from the situation in *Arithmagic* where something is done with both decks.

Annemann invented a subtle variation on the use-or-discard situation. By applying it to three objects, he made it seem like a process of elimination and, therefore, quite plausible. Let us call the objects A, B, and C. You wish to force B. Tell a spectator to pick up any two of the objects. If he takes A and C, say, "And just lay them aside." If he chooses A and B or B and C, say, "And give me either one." When he gives you B, hold it up and announce that you will use the one that the spectator has chosen. When he retains B and gives you the other one, tell him to hold up his choice so that everyone can see it. This apparently allows him complete freedom, and yet the one selected is always the one you want.

PRESENTIMENT

This is a mental routine that depends almost entirely on the use of alternative procedures.

Make three piles of cards. Each pile should contain a different number, but give the smallest one five cards. While you are doing this, remark that you rarely get psychic information in advance. This evening, however, just before leaving home, you felt compelled to do something that made no sense at the time. You now believe you understand the reason and want to test your theory.

Announce that as it is important to make this a genuine test, you must rule out any suspicion of collusion. Ask one spectator to choose two others whom you will use as subjects. The First Subject chooses one of the piles. He offers it to The Second Subject, who selects one card mentally.

You then say, "I believe you'll agree that unless all three spectators are my confederates, I cannot know the chosen card. Certainly, I could not have known it before I left home. Nevertheless, earlier this evening, I felt impelled to place a card in my pocket. Although I'm not sure, I think now that the one I then chose duplicates the one which has just been selected mentally. As I can't afford to risk having you upset the experiment by changing your mind after I show the card in my pocket, will you name the one you chose?" When he does so, take the matching card from your pocket.

Prepare for this by placing a card in each side pocket of your coat, one in your inside breast pocket, one in the handkerchief in your outside breast pocket, and one in a wallet in your hip pocket. Remember their locations. Have duplicates on top of the deck you use. The five duplicates go in one pile, the other two piles contain one or two more cards. The first pile is forced by Annemann's method. Hence, the Second Subject must pick the mate to one of the cards in your pockets. When he names his choice, you have only to produce the corresponding card.

Still another technique for upsetting the spectator's logic consists in introducing a device at the most unlikely and, therefore, the most illogical moment. Thus, in *The Clairvoyant Die*, the positions of the cards seem fixed before the die is thrown. The idea that it can be altered afterward simply does not occur to most people.

DECEIVING ATTENTION

Standard operating procedure for conjurers requires suppressing interest in everything connected with a device. A spectator who misses a vital clue cannot pierce the secret.

The technique of doing things at the most unlikely moment provides an effective way to suppress interest. It can be recommended for this purpose alone even when its effect on logic is comparatively slight.

Anticipation can be effective at any time before the audience has any reason to expect it. In *Ancestral Aid*, for example, you place the salt after the deck has been cut but before the audience expects you to do anything. In *Dowsing Test*, you anticipate a test by rearranging the magnet each time you replace the napkin.

Premature conclusion is the reverse of anticipation. When a climax is reached, the audience lets its vigilance relax. You can take advantage of this to set yourself up for a higher climax. In *Miniaturization*, for example, the suspicious part of the routine appears to be over as soon as you start producing items from the first cylinder. While the audience watches this, your assistant picks up the second load.

Although the most unlikely moment normally comes before or after the logical moment, some conjurers deliberately choose the logical moment. They feel that boldness is the best disguise and that no spectator will imagine that a performer would take such a risk. In the right hands, boldness can work miracles, but many examples demand more nerve than I possess. Here is one that even the most timid can use.

SECOND SIGHT

This is convincing enough for professional acts and easy enough to work with your wife or sweetheart. She impersonates A Medium, and you play the role of her Manager.

After The Medium is blindfolded, you fan a deck of cards and ask a spectator to touch one. When he does, pull the card half out of the fan to let the whole audience see it. Close the deck with the card still protruding and hold it at arm's length. Be careful to handle the deck so that no one can suspect you of glimpsing the chosen card. In spite of this, The Medium names it at once.

Actually, the card is glimpsed while in the fan. Use the sleight illustrated in Fig. 80, but glimpse the chosen card instead of the one next to it.

The simplest way to convey information to The Medium is by means of a spoken code. Mine is based on a principle invented by Orville Meyer and published in Annemann's *Practical Mental Effects* (p. 323). However, in my version, all remarks are addressed to members of the audience. This is less likely to arouse suspicion than speaking directly to The Medium.

	"O.K. ?"	Club
[*Spoken to Subject*	"Right ?"	Heart
after separating	"'S that it ?"	Spade
chosen card.]	[*Silence.*]	Diamond

[*To Audience while displaying card.*]	"See?"	A, 2, or 3
	"Can you see?"	4, 5, or 6
	"Can you all see?"	7, 8, or 9
	"Everyone see it?"	10, J, or Q
	[*Silence.*]	K

When The Medium announces the color, the conjurer (who presumably does not know the name of the card) asks the audience:

"O.K.?"	A, 4, 7, or 10
"Right?"	2, 5, 8, or J
[*Silence.*]	3, 6, 9, or Q

Thus, to code the 4 of Hearts, the conjurer asks, "Right?," "Can you see?," and "O.K.?" For the Queen of Diamonds, he says, "Everyone see it?" For the King of Spades, he inquires, "'S that it?" As the King of Diamonds is coded by three "silences," the conjurer should give a slight cough to let The Medium know it is time to speak.

CASUAL TREATMENT

The most effective method of deceiving attention consists in handling all devices casually. This is the invariable practice of first-class professionals. They rigorously eliminate any word or action that might direct attention to the device or anything connected with it. Thus, when you take a handful of change from your pocket for *Dial Information* and ask a spectator to choose a coin, act as though this were merely the first thought that popped into your mind. Say something like, "We won't try it with cards, but anything else will do. Here, pick a coin."

Casual treatment should be applied to everything that may arouse suspicion. You are not apt to convince anyone by saying, "This is entirely genuine and unprepared." On the contrary, such a statement reminds the audience that the object may be faked. Once a spectator's skepticism has been aroused, he perversely goes a step further; even when the object is obviously innocent, he convinces himself that something must be wrong with it.

Whenever you can safely do so, let the audience draw its own conclusions. Spectators for *The Strong Man's Secret* can see with their own eyes that cutting the loop and untying the knot divides the string into two parts. Statements like "I will now cut this into two parts" add nothing. On the contrary, they raise a question which might otherwise have been overlooked. Nothing is ever gained by saying, "I will now shuffle the deck." Call attention to the action by pointing or by some bit of business.

Even this should seem casual as though you were shuffling through force of habit and not as though the action had any significance.

Go through each of your routines and weed out everything which is not absolutely necessary but which could possibly raise doubts in the mind of the most skeptical observer.

At the same time, watch for opportunities to introduce casual remarks or items of business which may add conviction without suggesting skepticism. Thus, in *The Strong Man's Secret*, you should say something like, "I'll now put one end of each piece in my fist." This stresses the existence of two pieces, but it takes that "fact" for granted and hence creates no suspicion.

When suspicion is inevitable, assume the position that any doubts the spectators may have are absurd but that you are willing to humor them. Thus, after shuffling a deck of cards, you might offer them to a troublesome spectator saying, "Perhaps you'd like to shuffle these again?" In many cases, he will refuse; the mere offer convinces him that the cards are innocent.

Adopt the same attitude when you feel that the audience may suspect a prop unless it is deliberately offered for inspection. Thus, for a rope routine, you might say, "I've been told that some of my demonstrations of magic bear a superficial resemblance to certain performances offered by professional conjurers on television. For this reason, I want to provide you with every opportunity of assuring yourselves that the apparatus which I shall use is exactly what it pretends to be. You, sir, will you examine this rope and see that it actually is rope such as you yourself might buy at your local hardware store? Perhaps your neighbor doubts your qualifications as a rope expert. Please let him test it."

Contradicting Belief in Confederates

Any volunteer from the audience is apt to be suspected of being a confederate. Ordinarily, this is not serious. However, there are effects, especially in the routines of hypnotists and mentalists, where any hint of collaboration is fatal. In these cases, we must take definite steps to convince the audience that the volunteer is a bona fide spectator.

The difficulty should be acknowledged frankly. For example, you might say, "If this test is to be valid, I need the assistance of someone who cannot be suspected of having any previous contact with me. I therefore propose to select a spectator at random." Toss a playing card into the audience in such a way that it sails up and boomerangs back. Then ask the person who catches it to help you. When the routine involves a card or a number, have it chosen by a combination of several people. *Presentiment* capitalizes on this technique.

MONOTONY, ITS USE AND ABUSE

Monotony kills interest. We have already seen how we can use this to disguise an imperfectly executed sleight (p. 194). However, when you discourage interest in a false shuffle by making all your fair shuffles just alike, you are concealing only the technique. You may (and should) still call attention to the existence of your fair shuffles in other ways, such as fixing your eyes on the cards as you shuffle.

Unfortunately, conjurers sometimes supply misdirection by making an effect monotonous. This is obviously a mistake. The effect is the climax of the routine, and nothing should be allowed to detract from it. For instance, misdirection by monotony is sometimes used to produce a rabbit from a top hat. The performer takes a number of silk scarves from the hat and lets them fall to the floor. He deliberately makes the action repetitious so that the audience will let its attention wander. After this has happened, the conjurer takes advantage of it to sneak his rabbit into the pile of scarves. He then produces the remaining scarves and scoops the whole pile, rabbit and all, into the hat. The ostensible purpose of this is to demonstrate that the scarves are too bulky to go into the hat. However, while apparently trying to press the scarves down, he "discovers" the rabbit and holds it up for all to see. This use of monotony works, but only because the onlookers have lost interest before the rabbit is introduced. Audience apathy is too high a price to pay for concealment.

OPTICAL MISDIRECTION

We use optical misdirection when we fix the eyes of the spectators on one point in order to keep them from watching some other point. There are two ways to do this: we *divert* attention from a device when we focus it on some source of information in the routine; we *distract* attention when we direct it to something outside the routine.

Diversion is merely an intensified form of what a good show-man does anyway when he makes each source of information the focus of attention. The sole difference is that he times his device to occur at a moment when the source of information is especially interesting, and when he can direct attention to it by powerful techniques.

Distraction is poor showmanship. Conjurers are the only performers who employ it deliberately. Other entertainers do all they can to avoid it.

Perhaps the best way to clarify the distinction between di-version and distraction is to compare examples of each.

A routine requires your assistant to pour water into a flat, transparent bowl and carry it some distance. She gets it a little too full. The girl moves gingerly because she is obviously afraid that the water will slop over onto her satin evening gown. Such an "impending accident" is an almost sure-fire eye-catcher. The spectators will follow every step that the assistant takes. This diverts their attention and gives you several sec-onds in which you can perform a complex sleight with little risk of being detected—especially if her movement carries her toward the far side of the stage.

Our example of distraction is only slightly different. Instead of carrying water, the girl fills her bowl with oranges. One orange "accidentally" rolls off the bowl and bounces across the stage away from you. This draws every eye while you per-form your sleight.

The impending accident and the actual "accident" are equally effective disguises for the sleight, but dramatically they belong to entirely different categories. Carrying water is, at that point, the source of information. You would want the audience to watch it even if you had no sleight to conceal. The danger of spilling the water makes it a stronger center of in-terest than its importance warrants but that does no harm. Au-dience attention in the routine is maintained at a high pitch.

Dropping an orange, on the contrary, conveys no informa-tion. The bounding fruit draws every eye by a psychological reflex, but it arouses no real interest. It carries the attention away from the routine, and the audience loses the thread of your demonstration. Points made before the "accident" be-come blurred or are forgotten entirely. You must start again to build interest and re-create suspension of disbelief. Finally, there is a strong chance that spectators may say, "I guess it was a good trick, but I got mixed up at one stage and couldn't follow what went on." This is not an attitude which enhances your credit.

Directing attention toward the source of information is inherently good. If the same action also diverts attention from a false move, this is a free bonus. Directing attention away from the source of information is inherently bad. It may distract attention from a false move, but you pay for it by interrupting the smooth flow of your presentation. The price is too high. Why distract attention to some extraneous action, when a little more thought will reveal some source of information to which you can divert attention in a way that will serve the same purpose as well if not better?

MOTION AS A METHOD FOR CONCEALMENT

Although movement attracts attention, it also diminishes visibility. When a thread is used to support a light object, it can be seen from a surprising distance even when its color matches the background. However, the slightest movement makes it disappear.

A large movement can be used to conceal a small one. For example, the weak spot in *The Strong Man's Secret* is the action of cutting the loop. The technique in Fig. 8 can be made more deceptive if you keep the knife still and force the string against it by a sudden movement of the left hand. The moment the string is taut, twist the knife slightly to snip off the glued piece. The loose ends will then flip toward your left. The large movement of the left hand and the string draws every eye away from the knife so that no one can observe the unnatural way in which the string is cut.

CONTROL AS A DEVICE

When you gain sufficient control of attention, it automatically provides such strong misdirection that you can create powerful illusions by this means alone. No other device is needed. The following routine employs techniques that I have used in several plays when I wanted a supernatural character to appear mysteriously without being seen to enter.

THE MAGICIAN FROM NOWHERE

This is a good opening number for a stage act. The stage is well, but not brightly, lit. The Magician's shapely Assistant enters from *stage left* (the left of the performer), and crosses to a table on the other side of the stage near the footlights. She strikes a match and holds it to a candle, turning toward her left as she does so. At this instant, a spotlight suddenly picks out The Magician, who appears at the center of the stage. He bows, and without waiting for applause, performs some routine with the candle.

The illusion is achieved by five psychological devices which combine to concentrate attention on the Assistant while the conjurer enters unperceived. The girl wears tights and fills them adequately. She moves, and the eye tends to follow a moving object. The stage setting and the conjurer's clothing are dark, but The Assistant's costume is of some pale tint that contrasts sharply with the background. The flames of the match and candle provide spots of even greater contrast. The girl strikes her match as though it were the last source of fire in a frozen world. She then proceeds to devote her whole mind to lighting the candle.

The timing must be perfect. As The Assistant turns toward The Magician, he faces dead front and exposes his white shirt. The spotlight comes on at the same moment.

The effect will not work well if the width of the stage is less than 25 or more than 35 feet. A narrow stage brings the conjurer too close to the girl. A broad stage makes him walk too far to be sure of escaping notice. However, if someone does happen to see him, no harm is done; as far as that person is concerned, The Magician is simply making an entrance.

Chapter 16

DEVISING ILLUSIONS

Complete originality is rare. The most ingenious conjurer can spend a lifetime without hitting on a wholly new device or an entirely novel effect. Fresh illusions are another matter. Almost any worn-out effect can be given new life by supplying it with a different mock explanation. In view of this, I see no reason for endlessly repeating the stock routines that have done duty down the ages. There is certainly no excuse for performing old routines in the old way.

When you appear before a lay audience, an old routine is little better than an old joke. Few people read the same story twice, attend a play the second time, or enjoy reruns on television. Why should we expect them to applaud hackneyed conjuring?

Even if the public prefers conjuring "classics" to novelties, you would be foolish to imitate another performer's routine. It may be perfect for him, but it cannot be perfect for you. Stealing another man's routine is as futile as stealing his false teeth. Neither one will fit.

The routines in this book were chosen to illustrate the principles I intended to present. I made no attempt to be original. In fact, my first plan was simply to dramatize old tricks. However, once I got started, I found that unless a suitable example popped into my head, it was easier to invent a new routine than to hunt for an old one that would serve my purpose.

In order to create your own illusions, you will need familiarity with the standard devices for deception and a knowledge of the proper procedures. No doubt, you will also need a little experience before you get the knack. But once you acquire it, invention is usually plain sailing. Difficult, and even insoluble problems can arise. Nevertheless, many of the routines in this book were invented almost as quickly as I could put words to paper. The chief secret consists in knowing what you want to do. If you asked me to invent a new illusion and gave me a free choice, I might flounder for some time. But if you told me that you needed a particular type of routine, I could probably supply it in an hour. I feel sure that you will have the same experience. Once you have decided what you want to do, you are half way to doing it.

SWITCHING A ROUTINE

The easiest way to create a new routine is to adapt an old one. This is called *switching* and is the technique adopted by comedians when they invent "new" jokes. Do not confuse the mental process of switching a routine with the physical process of switching in which a prop is secretly exchanged for its duplicate.

Arithmagic is merely a switched version of *I Scry*. Both illusions were invented for Chapter 2, before we were ready to consider card sleights. We should now be able to switch them by using a more deceptive device and a new theme. Let us see what we can do with *Arithmagic* if we take *The Monte Carlo Method* for our phenomenon and force a card as our device.

PROBABILITY

Introduce the subject of statistical techniques in operations research. Give a nontechnical explanation of *The Monte Carlo Method*. Force a card. Have The Subject place it on the table without looking at it. Hand the deck to The Subject. Let him deal three piles. Tell three other spectators to shuffle these and turn their top cards face up. Use the numbers of the exposed cards to calculate the denomination of the forced card.

Let us treat this as a lesson. Instead of doing the arithmetic yourself, have The Subject do it. As you decide what numbers to use and what he is to do with them, you control the result just as you did in *Arithmagic*. Note that this is another application of alternative procedures.

This can be used as a follow-up to *The Monte Carlo Method*, or you could offer it as a demonstration when a spectator who has seen you do *The Monte Carlo Method* asks you to repeat it for another group and you are not equipped with a Si Stebbins setup.

As an exercise in invention, try switching *I Scry*. Use any method of learning the name of the card, but find some new phenomena or a new way to reveal the chosen card.

When switching a routine, always try to make it better. Do
not be content to search for features that can be changed. Look
for faults and find ways to correct them. This is simply an
extension of the principle that we should concentrate on the
weakest spots because they offer the best opportunities for improvement. Furthermore, in the great majority of cases, the
harm done by a weak element is far more serious than the benefit derived from a strong one. Even when eliminating a fault
forces us to abandon a spectacular effect, the sacrifice is normally worth while. The best effect will fall flat if it fails to convince your audience.

THE FIVE BASIC ELEMENTS

When we have no old trick to switch, we must follow a different procedure. Every invention starts with an idea of some
sort. This can be almost anything. However, in conjuring, it
usually concerns one of the five basic elements: the phenomenon, the effect, the device(s), the prop(s), or your own
characterization. As you will need all five elements before you
can devise a routine, it makes little difference where you begin.

Strictly speaking, the purpose should be included among the
basic elements. However, purpose is not a fruitful starting
point. Most demonstrations can be reworked to serve as experiments and vice versa. The rarer purposes provide little inspiration, and you will not often encounter a situation where
you need, say, a contest or a lesson. If you do, your best plan
is to go over a list of standard routines until you find one that
you can switch. Sometimes the amount of switching will be very
small. Thus, I did not need much ingenuity to turn *Arithmagic*
into a lesson.

STARTING WITH THE PHENOMENON

Children's books abound in stories of animated objects, and
every child wishes that his toys could come to life and play
with him. Animation will therefore make an ideal phenomenon
for the tots-to-teens set. It has tremendous appeal, and it is
convincing without being deceptive. The most obvious subject
for animation is a doll. It should not be too feminine, or the
boys will resent it. Fortunately, there are plenty of doll-like
toys which appeal to both sexes. I therefore decide to use a
doll as the chief prop. The effect will naturally consist in

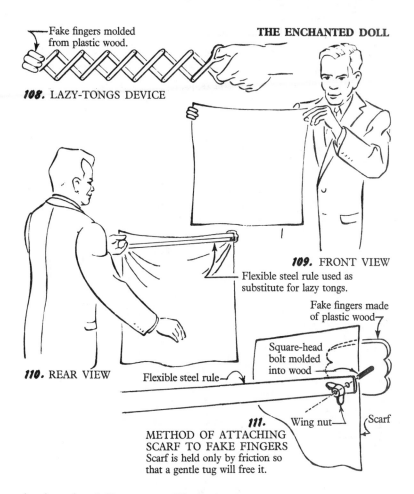

Fake fingers molded from plastic wood.

108. LAZY-TONGS DEVICE

109. FRONT VIEW
Flexible steel rule used as substitute for lazy tongs.

Fake fingers made of plastic wood

Square-head bolt molded into wood

110. REAR VIEW — Flexible steel rule

Flexible steel rule

111. METHOD OF ATTACHING SCARF TO FAKE FINGERS
Scarf is held only by friction so that a gentle tug will free it.

Wing nut

Scarf

having the doll come to life and talk to the young audience. The performer will be A Magician who animates the doll. I now have my theme: "Magician demonstrates his ability to bring doll to life by magic."

The easiest way to animate a doll is to switch it for a hand puppet. Such a puppet is hardly magical. Also, the routine would require a screen over which the puppet could appear. While I was thinking along these lines, I remembered a device invented by nineteenth-century conjurers who often used an imitation spiritualist number in their acts. This device involved a set of fake fingers attached to the end of a pair of lazy tongs (Fig. 108). The performer placed spiritualistic paraphernalia such as a bell and a tambourine on a table. He then used the fake fingers to hold a scarf in front of the table (Fig. 109).

Immediately, the tambourine rattled, the bell rang, and other objects jumped into the air. When the scarf was withdrawn, nothing was visible except the objects themselves.

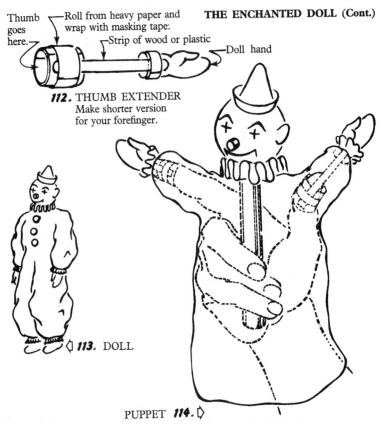

Thumb goes here. — Roll from heavy paper and wrap with masking tape:
— Strip of wood or plastic
— Doll hand

THE ENCHANTED DOLL (Cont.)

112. THUMB EXTENDER
Make shorter version for your forefinger.

◁ *113.* DOLL

PUPPET *114.* ◊

One nice thing about this device is that it has not been used much in recent years and will therefore seem fresh to anyone unfamiliar with the older books on conjuring. Unfortunately, the device is no longer on the market. When I discussed it with my friend Alfred Cohen, he suggested that a flexible steel rule might take the place of the lazy tongs (Figs. 110–111).

For props, I bought two identical dolls. One was satisfactory as it came (Fig. 113). I used the head and hands of the other to construct a puppet (Figs. 112 and 114). Note that mounting the head on a stick makes a much better puppet than the usual hollow head.

I now had all the technical ideas I needed for:

THE ENCHANTED DOLL

Begin by saying, "Most of you have read fairy stories about the elixir of life, but did you ever see it? Not many people have. Last week, I visited the old wizard who taught me all I know about magic, and he gave me a bottle of the elixir. Here it is. It's only a tiny bottle because the elixir takes a long time to make and is very precious. This afternoon, I'm going to bring something to life."

Display the doll. Pretend to pour elixir between its lips. The scarf, fingers, and tape have been assembled in advance (Fig. 111). Pick them up from your table with your real fingers over the fakes. Explain that only magicians who have received the thirty-third degree in thaumaturgy can watch the mystic potion take effect. Stretch the scarf and extend the rule. Divert attention by directing some question at a child on your far left. While he answers, remove your fingers and expose the fake ones. Murmur a spell, and bring the hand-puppet duplicate of the doll up from behind the scarf.

After a brief conversation with you and the children, the doll declares that the effect of the elixir is wearing off. He sinks behind the scarf which is whisked away to show that the doll is no longer animated.

The ventriloquism is accomplished by turning your face toward the doll and talking out of the side of your mouth that is hidden from the audience. Sentences like "Hello, kids. How're you doin'?" which do not contain the letters b, p, f, m, or v, can easily be spoken while facing front, as they do not require you to move your lips.

If the doll is revealed at the end in the position that it held before you hid it with the scarf, the children will realize that you substituted a duplicate. Be sure to avoid this by moving the doll to a noticeably new position.

Note that in working out this illusion, I kept my ideas flexible and changed some of them as I went along. My original effect was Animation. I was later compelled to add Levitation, because my device demanded it. However, this is a defect, and I tried to avoid calling attention to it. Also, when I had trouble finding lazy tongs and searched for a substitute, Alfred Cohen supplied the idea of using a flexible steel rule.

STARTING WITH THE EFFECT

As the effect proves the phenomenon, you will normally find that an idea for an effect automatically suggests a phenomenon. Thus, I might have begun by watching a puppet show and wishing that I could create the same effect by "magic." This obviously calls for animation as the phenomenon. It also suggests using a doll of some description as the chief prop. From there, I could have followed the same line as before and gone on to plan *The Enchanted Doll.*

Even when an effect seems to demand a particular phenomenon, do not take this for granted. When I wanted a character-reading effect for this book, astrology seemed an inevitable phenomenon because I had just met a professional astrologer at a party and my mind was running along those lines. It was not until I read about a routine in which the same effect "proved" the validity of graphology that I realized how many phenomena could be fitted to one effect.

STARTING WITH THE DEVICE

Some reader may have run across the lazy-tongs device in an old book. While seeking for a modern illusion in which it can be used, he realizes that the stretched scarf could serve as a screen for a Punch-and-Judy act. He is about to discard this idea on the ground that Punch and Judy requires two hands whereas he needs his left to manipulate the lazy tongs. However, he suddenly remembers that a ventriloquist uses only one hand. Why not employ a hand puppet in a ventriloquist act? No. That would give the game away. The use of a hand puppet automatically proves that the performer does the animating.

This objection can be overcome by making the children misinterpret the puppet as a doll. If it is successful, it will create the illusion of a magical, animated, talking doll. The misinterpretation can be handled by introducing a real doll. When a scarf is held in front of this, a hand puppet which duplicates the doll will be substituted for the ventriloquial routine. The puppet will then be hidden before the scarf is removed to reveal the original doll.

The scarf must be held shoulder high. How does the doll get up there? Levitation? No, that provides too much magic and weakens the illusion. Why not make a little stage by piling up apparatus? But what excuse is there for the scarf screen? Perhaps the children could be told that the doll is shy about coming to life while anyone except the performer is watching. The dialogue might then run like this:

PERFORMER. [*To Children.*] The elixir of life is working. Toby's twitching already. Now he's moving his arms. Now he's opening his eyes. [*To Toby*]. Speak to me, Toby, speak to me!

THE WITCH AND THE WRAITH

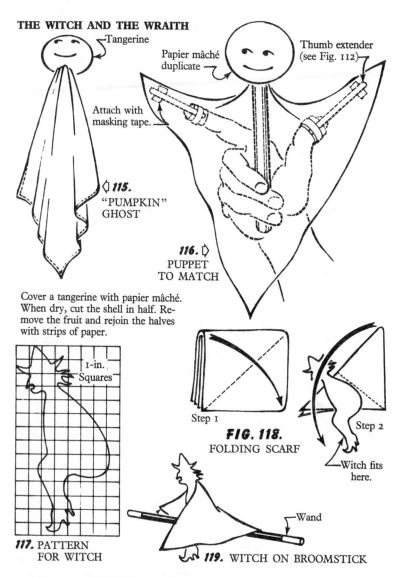

Tangerine

Papier mâché duplicate

Thumb extender (see Fig. 112)

Attach with masking tape.

◁ *115.*
"PUMPKIN"
GHOST

116. ▷
PUPPET
TO MATCH

Cover a tangerine with papier mâché. When dry, cut the shell in half. Remove the fruit and rejoin the halves with strips of paper.

1-in. Squares

Step 1

FIG. 118.
FOLDING SCARF

Step 2

Witch fits here.

117. PATTERN
FOR WITCH

Wand

119. WITCH ON BROOMSTICK

TOBY. [*Still hidden.*] All right, All right. Keep your shirt on.
PERFORMER. Come on up where the audience can see you.
TOBY. I'm coming. I'm coming. But my joints are still stiff. This batch of elixir isn't full strength.
PERFORMER. You always say that.
TOBY. Well, it's always true. [*Appears above scarf but looks at Performer and holds out left arm.*] Look at my arm! Stiff as a

poker. [*Turns and notices Children.*] Hello, kids! Sorry I'm a little stiff, but he's [*Indicating Performer.*] a big stiff.

Skillfully done, this builds suspense and at the same time creates a powerful suspension of disbelief.

STARTING WITH A PROP

Shortly before Halloween, I realize that a tangerine can be presented as a miniature pumpkin. I want to capitalize on this idea for a conjuring routine. A face drawn with a magic marker will turn the "pumpkin" into a jack-o'-lantern. By making a hole in the bottom and inserting one corner of a handkerchief, I can create an amusing toy ghost (Fig. 115). This is hardly magic, but it will amuse children because they realize that they can make such a ghost themselves. Nevertheless, a magician should perform magic. What can I do with my ghost? I can animate it by using a puppet duplicate (Fig. 116) and the device with the fake fingers.

At this point, I face a new problem. I must stretch a scarf to serve as a screen. How can I motivate that? Why not start to make a witch to go with my pumpkin ghost? (Figs. 117–119). I can use a black scarf for this. When I stretch it to show what it is, the ghost can pop up from behind and chat with me and the audience. After the ghost sinks back, I can fold the black scarf into a witch and let her ride my wand as a broomstick.

I now have all the elements required for the basic framework of *The Witch and the Wraith*. Although the effect is recognizably the same as that for *Enchanted Doll*, the presentation will be very different. The ghost routine can be used as a topical number at Halloween, and *Enchanted Doll* can be performed the rest of the year.

Conjurers have shown surprisingly little enterprise in exploring the possibilities of new props. At least 99 per cent of all routines employ such hackneyed articles as cards and coins, cigarettes and silks, doves and rabbits. As the public is more likely to remember a prop than an effect, many people feel that conjurers do only a dozen different tricks and that a person who has seen one performer has seen them all. There is no reason for this monotony. Most of the standard effects can be turned into novelties simply by substituting new props. Furthermore, as the use of a new prop keeps spectators from recog-

THE HAUNTED HANDKERCHIEF

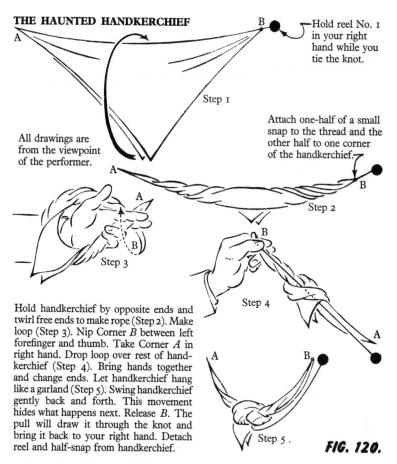

Hold reel No. 1 in your right hand while you tie the knot.

Step 1

All drawings are from the viewpoint of the performer.

Attach one-half of a small snap to the thread and the other half to one corner of the handkerchief.

Step 2

Step 3

Step 4

Hold handkerchief by opposite ends and twirl free ends to make rope (Step 2). Make loop (Step 3). Nip Corner *B* between left forefinger and thumb. Take Corner *A* in right hand. Drop loop over rest of handkerchief (Step 4). Bring hands together and change ends. Let handkerchief hang like a garland (Step 5). Swing handkerchief gently back and forth. This movement hides what happens next. Release *B*. The pull will draw it through the knot and bring it back to your right hand. Detach reel and half-snap from handkerchief.

Step 5 .

FIG. 120.

nizing the effect, it also keeps them from recognizing the device.

In many cases, one prop is as easy to handle as another. Thus, in *Teleportation*, anything that can be put into your square-circle "invention" will work. The more inappropriate it is, the funnier it will be. Why not use an anvil, a boot, a cuckoo clock, a dumbbell, or an eggplant.

The list of possible substitutes for overworked objects is long. Pipe tobacco, sand, or BB shot can take the place of salt or rice. Golf balls, soap, tomatoes, door knobs, or Christmas-tree balls can be used instead of eggs. Poker chips can vary a coin routine. Stick candy or stub pencils may be substituted for cigarettes. Chains, roller bandages, or neckties give a fresh touch to an old rope trick. Take the oldest effect you can think of right now.

Substitute a different prop, and in at least eight cases out of ten, you will have an illusion that will seem completely new to your public.

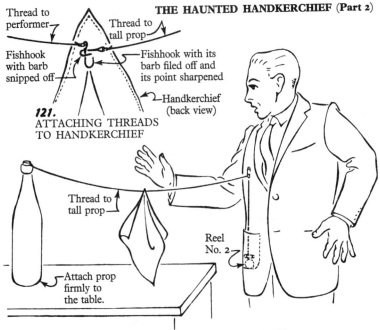

Thread to performer

Thread to tall prop

Fishhook with barb snipped off

Fishhook with its barb filed off and its point sharpened

Handkerchief (back view)

121. ATTACHING THREADS TO HANDKERCHIEF

THE HAUNTED HANDKERCHIEF (Part 2)

Thread to tall prop

Reel No. 2

Attach prop firmly to the table.

122. LEVITATING HANDKERCHIEF

At *A*, the thread runs through the eye of a black safety pin attached to the breast of the performer's coat. It then passes through another safety pin (*B*) in his pocket. This

prevents the reel from pulling itself up. The reel keeps the thread taut, but it permits the conjurer to move back and forth.

STARTING WITH THE CHARACTERIZATION

Perhaps you are attracted by the idea of *The Haunted Conjurer* but feel that you need more "haunted" illusions. Let us begin with A Conjurer Bedeviled by an Obeah Man's Curse and see what sort of routine we can devise to fit.

Why not let The Obeah Man animate one of The Conjurer's props, say a silk handkerchief? The Conjurer ties a knot in this. While he is explaining what he intends to do with it, the handkerchief unties itself with the aid of a concealed reel as shown in Fig. 120. He recognizes this as the work of The Obeah Man but tries to pass it off as an accident by retying the knot, which immediately unties itself again. This causes The Conjurer to give up. He disengages the handkerchief from the thread and drops it on the table while he pockets the reel.

That is only the beginning. It creates a "haunted" atmosphere, but we need much more. The handkerchief has been animated. What other effects of animation can we add?

Figs. 121 and 122 show an old device which uses a second reel to suspend a handkerchief in mid-air. As soon as the handkerchief is on the table, it jumps up and stands erect. The Conjurer slaps it down twice and then grabs it and holds it in his fist where it wriggles realistically (Fig. 123).

Instead of admitting defeat, he decides to take advantage of the situation by putting on a Punch-and-Judy show. "I'll be Punch," he tells The Handkerchief, "and you can be Judy." Note that at this point The Handkerchief ceases to be a mere animated rag and assumes a definite personality.

The Conjurer ties a knot in one corner of The Handkerchief and transfers the hook to this corner while doing so. He returns The Handkerchief to the table where it immediately stands erect.

The Handkerchief says, "If I'm going to be a puppet, I need a puppet box." The performer must jiggle The Handkerchief to animate it while it is speaking.

He replies, "All right, all right. Anything to satisfy you. He stretches a scarf in front of The Handkerchief and gets the

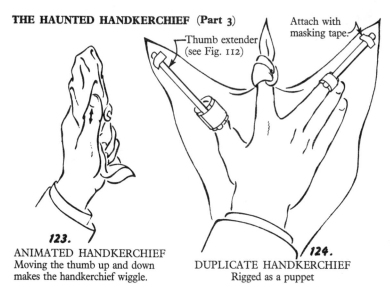

THE HAUNTED HANDKERCHIEF (Part 3)

Thumb extender (see Fig. 112)

Attach with masking tape.

123.
ANIMATED HANDKERCHIEF
Moving the thumb up and down makes the handkerchief wiggle.

124.
DUPLICATE HANDKERCHIEF
Rigged as a puppet

duplicate (Fig. 124) on his right hand. From there on, the procedure follows that for *The Enchanted Doll* and *The Witch and the Wraith*.

Phenomenon, effect, device(s), prop(s), and characterization are more than good starting points when you want to develop a routine, they are the five basic elements that you need before it is worth while to consider going further. When you have these, you can feel that you have invented an illusion. Dramatizing it is another matter.

Chapter 17
DRAMATIC STRUCTURE

Although an illusion does not have a real plot, it requires a dramatic structure. Most tricks are too brief to have much structure. There is a preliminary stage during which certain peculiar things are done. The climax follows abruptly and ends the routine. Some quickies are even simpler and consist in nothing but a climax! Illusions require a more elaborate structure. Quickie illusions are possible, but they cannot stand alone. They exist only as supplementary effects to the main routine and normally share its theme. Thus, if you have already established yourself as A Magician, and if you have just completed a number with three green scarves, you can precede *Twentieth-Century Nylon* with the quickie in which you turn one green scarf red. It then serves as a minor illusion. On the other hand, if you present this before establishing a magical atmosphere, or if you do it at a time when it does not lead up to a more important illusion that requires a red scarf, it is a mere trick and a cheap trick at that.

BASIC STRUCTURE

All illusions follow a standard pattern. This is flexible and may take many different forms. Nevertheless, the underlying pattern must always be there, and you should learn to recognize it when it exists or complete it when a routine falls short. There are nine main stages:

1. *Interest-Catcher*. This commands attention and directs it into the routine. You could get plenty of attention by pronouncing "Mesopotamia" in a loud voice, but that would not aid your illusion.

2. *Introduction*. Once attention has been gained, you must definitely establish the proper atmosphere and fix both your own role and that of your audience.

3. *Statement of Theme.* Although a formal statement of the theme is rarely desirable, the personalities, the phenomenon, and the general nature of the effect should be made completely clear. The statement should be a summary in one or two sentences of ideas already explained in the introduction. Thus, for *Lie Detector*, you might say, "Experts can often dispense with special equipment and detect lies merely by feeling the subject's pulse. I can do it fairly well myself, although I make no pretense of being an expert."

When the effect, or part of it, comes as a surprise, it does not match the theme. Make your statement especially clear in such cases in order to reap the full benefit of the surprise. Thus, in *The Haunted Conjurer*, you must explain that you intend to transpose the two dice. If you fail to make this clear, the audience may not understand that The Obeah Man then turns the dice into guinea pigs.

4. *Kickoff point.* There is always a point where the performer stops dealing in generalities and commits himself to some positive action. This is usually the moment when he agrees to give a demonstration. However, it can come much earlier. In *Chromavoyance*, for instance, you are committed to demonstrate your own sense of color touch as soon as you offer to test the abilities of the spectators. This kickoff point is an important structural element. In most, if not all, cases, it should be marked by a definite statement or clear pantomime. Phrases like, "All right, I'll show you," "Let's try an experiment," and "Try it yourself" are appropriate. In a case like *The Prestidigitator's Perplexity*, simply holding out your hand for the deck gives an implied promise to display your skill.

5. *Preliminaries.* The apparatus is introduced, explained, and rigged during this stage. In *Lie Detector* it consists simply in picking up the deck. On the other hand, the preliminary stages of *Will Power* and *Dowsing Test* are so elaborate that they may be the longest parts of their respective routines.

6. *Instructions.* These are given to volunteers, or, occasionally, to the audience as a whole. Spare no effort to make them brief, clear, and foolproof.

7. *Action.* This is the exhibition proper. Many routines mix the preparations, instructions, and actions. Thus, in *Will Power*, the spectators experiment with the first pendulum while the conjurer prepares two more and gives advice at the same

time. In spite of this, you can usually identify the stage to which each item belongs. Try to be as definite as possible about such things. When you are vague in your own mind, you cannot expect the audience to understand what you are doing.

8. *Effect*. Ideally, this should be short and come as the climax. However, in routines like *Horoscope*, the effect consists of readings which can never be brief and which offer no real climax. In *Dowsing Test*, the effect is repeated and that also weakens any climax.

9. *Ending*. This covers the period from the end of the effect to the point where some completely new subject is introduced.

Most of the elements are obvious, but interest-catchers, climaxes, and endings deserve special study.

INTEREST-CATCHERS

A young performer often has trouble in arousing interest for an "impromptu." If he says, "Would you like to see a trick?" his friends either say, "No" or look bored. But if he does not offer to perform, he cannot get started at all.

The "impromptu" routines in this book show how to secure attention either by introducing a provocative topic such as freak shows, astrology, or telepathy, or by arousing curiosity with a *strange object* such as a toad stone or a clairvoyant die. Almost any small prop can serve as a strange object if it is properly handled. Thus, you might take a piece of unprepared string from your pocket and examine it intently, inch by inch. Such seemingly unwarranted interest in an apparently commonplace article will usually make someone inquire what you are doing. In the unlikely event that it fails to elicit the desired question, you can hand it to the nearest spectator saying, "Do you see anything peculiar about that string?"

Slydini uses the stunt which follows to provide both an interest-catcher and an ending for one of his routines. The version given here serves as an all-purpose way to introduce the idea of magic. Its only limitation is that it cannot be done unless you are seated at a table.

THE PURSE OF FORTUNATUS

Procure a small purse with a metal frame. Remove the bag, leaving only the frame with its clasp. Hold the frame in your left hand at the edge of the table as shown in Fig. 125. Have a cigarette in your left palm. Reach into the purse and extract this. Snap the purse shut and return it to your pocket. Make the whole action completely casual, but speak at the same time to call attention to yourself and to be sure that the move is observed.

Although this is unlikely to deceive anyone, the effect is so surprising that at least one spectator will comment on it. This brings up the subject of magic and gives you an opportunity to present a more ambitious routine. Bring out the purse again and take from it a deck of cards or any other small prop that you intend to use. When you are through, drop the prop back into your purse and catch it in your lap. That provides a nice finish.

The illusions in a formal act need only token interest-catchers. If the performer gives some definite indication that he is about to start a new routine, this will be adequate. In most cases, picking up a new prop is enough.

CLIMAXES

Many routines have built-in climaxes. Showmanship may be needed to dramatize them completely, but the climax itself is clear cut. Unfortunately, some otherwise excellent routines have no real climax. These require special treatment, and the problems involved are seldom easy.

In *Horoscope*, for example, the whole audience will be interested in the first reading and perhaps the second. But after that, everyone except the person being read is apt to be bored. You can correct this to some extent by making your readings amusing and by saving the most interesting points in each reading till the last. However, no amount of skill in wording your readings will provide a climax to the session as a whole. For that, you must contrive to distinguish the last reading in some way and at the same time make it more impressive than the others. In *Horoscope*, this is easy. After three or four Sitters have been

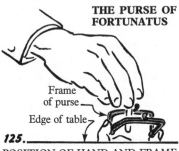

THE PURSE OF FORTUNATUS

Frame of purse.

Edge of table.

125.

POSITION OF HAND AND FRAME

described and identified, memorize the birthday of someone you know fairly well but whom you have not yet analyzed. Suppose it is December 18th. Toss the notebook pages aside and say, "With a little luck, I can work this backward. If I have a good idea of a person's character, I can estimate

FIRST DEMONSTRATION

Hold cord between left thumb and fore-finger. Appear to take it into your right palm, but actually slip your middle finger over it (Step 1), and close your fist (Step 2). Bring thumb end between forefinger and middle finger, and bring the other end between your ring- and middle-fingers (Step 3). Pull cord free. ⟁

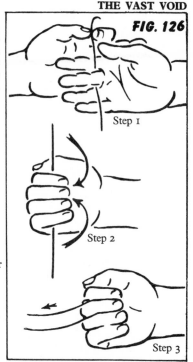

FIG. 126

Step 1

Step 2

Step 3

127.

SECOND DEMONSTRATION

Repeat action in Fig. 126, but cross ends. Give each end to a spectator. Tell your Helpers to pull. Open your hand as they do so. This lets cord pull free.

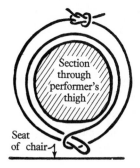

Section through performer's thigh

Seat of chair

128.

THIRD DEMONSTRATION

Appear to wrap cord around your thigh. Actually make loops. Slip one through the other and catch them between your thigh and the seat of your chair. Bring the ends up and join them with a square knot. Pull the knot, and the cord will come free.

his birthday within a day or two either way. Let's see, Bob, I haven't looked at your slip yet, have I?" Mention several of his characteristics and then add, "That combination points to either Sagittarius or Capricorn, but it's a bit more Capricorn, say somewhere between December 16th and 22nd. If I had time to work out a complete analysis, I might get a little closer. But, at a guess, I'd say you were born on December 19th."

When a repeated effect permits rising excitement and a sudden break at the end, the last demonstration may serve as a climax even though it does not differ materially from the others. For example:

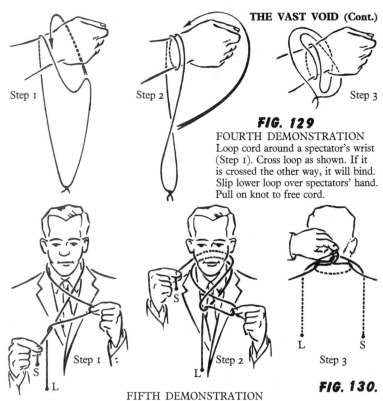

Step 1 Step 2 Step 3

FIG. 129

FOURTH DEMONSTRATION

Loop cord around a spectator's wrist (Step 1). Cross loop as shown. If it is crossed the other way, it will bind. Slip lower loop over spectators' hand. Pull on knot to free cord.

Step 1 Step 2 Step 3

L S

FIG. 130.

FIFTH DEMONSTRATION

Do this with the cord still looped. However, the moves are easier to learn when you have two ends, a long one (L) on your right, and a short one (S) on your left. Draw a loop of L over S as in Step 1. Wrap End S around your neck (Step 2).

Pull on S and raise left hand at the same time till loops cross in back of your neck (Step 3). Pinch the loops between your neck and your collar. When you pull on the ends, the cord will seem to pass through your neck.

THE VAST VOID

Take a piece of string from your pocket and examine it minutely. When someone asks what you are doing, say, "The darndest thing happened to me today. I was riding home in the bus when I suddenly noticed a funny old man on the seat beside me. I didn't see him sit down, but I guess I was thinking about something else. Anyway, he began talking about how everything is just empty space with a few electrons and things floating around in it and great gaps between them. I guess that's true in a way, but the old guy irritated me, so I said, 'If you're right, why don't you fall through the seat of the bus?' He sort of leered at me and replied, 'Let me give you a less catastrophic demonstration.' With that, he took this piece of string from his pocket. He caught it on his finger like this and gave me the ends. He told me to pull. Blest if it didn't come right through his finger" (Fig. 126). "I said 'What's the trick?' He said, "There's no trick—just atoms slipping past atoms. I'll do it on your hand,' and darned if he didn't" (Fig. 127). Continue with the releases in Figs. 128 and 129 and climax the routine by adding, "Finally, he wrapped the string around my neck and told me to pull it myself. I gave it a yank, and it came clear through" (Fig. 130). "That really finished me because, till then, I kept telling myself there was a catch in it. When I got my breath back and turned to look at him, he was gone—and I'd almost swear the bus hadn't stopped anywhere."

Talk all the time and work with increasing speed. When you are through, toss the string to someone saying, "Here, you can play with it if you like. The confounded thing gives me goose bumps!"

Both the impressiveness of this illusion, and its climactic effect depend upon your ability to simulate mounting excitement and an inward struggle between incredulity and conviction. If you can carry your audience with you, this is a splendid routine. Otherwise, it is just a series of puzzling tricks.

When the theme of a repetitive routine provides no climax, we may supply one artificially by adding another effect with a different but related theme. For example, dealers supply several tricks in which The Magician and A Subject each place a bottle or a tenpin in a tube. The tubes are turned over and removed. The Subject's bottle or tenpin is upside down, but the conjurer's remains upright. They first exchange bottles and then tubes. Nevertheless, The Subject's prop is always inverted while The Magician's stays erect.

As this fits into a one-two-three pattern, it has a vaguely climactic effect, but it lacks a punch at the end. We can supply one by offering the following mock explanation while the volunteer returns to his seat.

THE WARLOCK'S FAMILIAR

Begin by saying, "Magicians rarely reveal their methods, but as you've been such an appreciative audience I'm going to let you in on my secret. When anyone asks how I did something, I always reply that I didn't do it—and that's the literal truth. In this case, I can add that my friend who has just left the stage is equally innocent. No, all my magic is actually performed by another, and much smaller, friend. Perhaps you've been told that witches keep cats and toads known as their 'familiars' and that these creatures do the actual witchcraft. Well, we warlocks also have our familiars. Mine is named Pywacket. I put him into the tube, and he kept the bottle (tenpin) from turning upside down. He's rather shy. But if you'll be very quiet, I'll let you have a peek at him."

Place the tube on your hand, lift it, and reveal a pet hamster. The effect is better if you get one which is black or has odd markings. You might even dye a white hamster red, green, or blue with food coloring.

The device, though it hardly deserves the name, is concealed on the principle of premature conclusion. When you thank the volunteer and he starts back to his seat, the audience also assumes the routine is over and ceases to pay close attention. This gives you an ideal opportunity to get the hamster from any convenient place and load him into the tube.

ENDINGS

The climax of an "impromptu" illusion leaves the spectators in the uncomfortable position of not knowing what to say next. Filling in this dead spot is part of the performer's job. He can do it by supplying an ending. The ending is as much a part of the routine as the climax itself, and it should be prepared with equal care.

By far the best way to handle an ending is to perform only one illusion at a sitting and save it until you are ready to leave. The climax of the illusion then becomes the climax of the whole session. As soon as this climax has been reached, you can rise and begin your goodbyes. That provides you with what actors call a *strong exit*. Such an exit makes your climax seem more dramatic than it really is. It also keeps anyone else from topping your performance.

Restricting yourself to one illusion at a sitting has other advantages. When you present several, each one blurs the impression created by the rest. I recently watched a man perform a whole series of brilliant card tricks. When he was through, all I could remember was that he was extremely adept. Later, a friend who had been present described one of these tricks, and I decided that it was the best thing of its kind I had ever seen. Nevertheless, it made a weak impression while I was actually watching it because my mind was confused by all the other tricks that had gone before.

Even illusions which require no sleight of hand are not likely to be successful unless you do them often enough to keep in practice. Hence, few men have a repertoire of more than a dozen items. If you offer three or four at a gathering, you will soon find yourself repeating them before the same audience. A twice-shown illusion falls as flat as a twice-told joke. However, if you do only one at a sitting, ten or twelve routines will last a long time.

Finally, by restricting yourself to one routine you are insured against either monopolizing attention or becoming a bore. Too many performers ignore the need for such insurance.

The do-only-one-and-save-it-till-the-end technique is not always practical. After a highly convincing illusion like *Will Power*, a simple statement that it was all a trick will not disabuse the more credulous spectators. You need at least one anticlimactic illusion-breaker like *Ancestral Aid*.

Again, friends who know that you perform will often ask you to favor them during the early part of a session, and it may seem ungracious to refuse. In such cases say, "All right, but *only* one." If they beg for another, try not to give in. However, when you feel you must, agree to do "only one more." You may ultimately do four or five in this way, but each is a response to popular demand. Stop before your audience has had enough; a wise showman always sends them away wanting still more.

A strong exit after a climax provides all the ending you need. However, when you perform too early to exit, the ending presents real problems.

The first function of a good ending is to give an unmistakable indication that the routine is complete. This is necessary even in a case like *Mental Television*, where the climax seems clear cut. If you fail to show that you are finished, someone may expect you to add more. You cannot blame them for this. Many illusions do add more. *Dial Information*, for example, appears to reach its climax when The Telepath says, "You're thinking about a coin," but he goes on to provide higher and higher climaxes by giving the denomination and the date—and by describing two Participants in the bargain.

In most cases, you should indicate the conclusion by pantomime. Relax, toss your props aside or pocket them, and lean back in your chair. Behave much as you would if you had told a good story and wanted to give somebody else a chance. However, there is one important difference. A story usually leads to another, but an illusion leads nowhere. Except in a group of conjurers, no one can top it and no one is prepared to try. This leaves the spectators with nothing to say. It is your job to introduce a new subject of conversation.

Begin by discussing some phase of the preceding routine. Thus, after any parapsychological illusion you could well bring up some aspect of the supernormal or the supernatural. Try to find a remark that leads in several directions. For example, you might say, "According to the papers, the Russians are attempting to develop telepaths and clairvoyants as spies." This can start a discussion of parapsychology, Communism, or the latest spy thriller.

If someone else picks up the topic you mention, your routine is ended. When this does not happen, make a transition to a new subject which has no connection with your routine. After *Lie Detector*, for example, you could remark, "Of course, the mind also affects the body in many other ways." Pause just long enough for someone to respond. If no one does, add, "That's why people get ulcers from worry, and their hair turns white from fear or grief." Someone is almost sure to comment on the ulcers or argue about the white hair.

You are not ready to perform a routine until you have supplied yourself with: (1) a means of showing that it is finished, (2) an interesting topic which is connected with it and which may start a discussion, (3) a transition which leads to (4) some different, generally interesting topic that is not connected with the phenomena. You may not need the last two, but you are not safe without them.

AVOIDING REQUESTS

If you fail to change the subject, someone else will say the first thing that pops into his head. This is apt to be either, "Do it again" or "Tell us how you did it." Unfortunately, this can happen even when you offer a new topic. You must, therefore, be in a position to refuse either request without seeming rude.

"Do it again" is especially hard to handle. The spectator sincerely believes that he is paying you a compliment and cannot understand that he is really a nuisance. All the good ways of dealing with this request require some preparation during an earlier phase of the routine.

The most positive solution is to destroy an essential part of your apparatus during the performance. For *The Sigil of Solomon*, you might announce that the sigil alone will not suffice for the arcane rite. You must also chant a spell and sprinkle the burning paper with "the powder of inspiration." The powder is actually dime-store incense mixed with some sort of ground spice to provide an aroma which is strange without being unpleasant. You carry this in an oddly shaped vial, but have only a few grains left—"just enough for one ceremony." As you use it all, you cannot repeat the effect.

In mental routines, behave as though the concentration required involves great strain and is extremely fatiguing. That provides ample reason for refusing to repeat the previous effect or to perform another.

In *The Strong Man's Secret*, express doubt as to whether you can succeed. If someone then says, "Do it again," you can retort, "Not a chance. The strings might slip this time. I'm quitting while I'm ahead." The same type of response can be used in *Lie Detector* or any other routine where you do not pretend to be infallible.

When you perform a trick and someone says, "Tell us how you did it," a refusal may appear churlish. After an illusion, however, you can simply embark on a technical discussion of the phenomenon as though it were real. At the conclusion of any mental effect, for example, you could explain the difficulties involved in distinguishing between telepathy, clairvoyance, precognition, and thought control.

Fantastic phenomena are equally easy. Thus, after *The Clairvoyant Die* the conversation might run like this:

"Now tell us how you did it."

"I found the darn thing on the floor in a dime store, of all places. Don't ask me how it got there."

"But how did you work the trick?"

"There's no trick. The silly die just does it. You ought to know. You threw it yourself—both times. If you're asking what makes the thing work, your guess is as good as mine. In fact, if you have even a guess, you're one ahead of me."

By keeping this up and pretending to be serious, you may actually convince the guy!

You can also try a comic treatment. Thus, if someone asks how you did *Ancestral Aid*, you may reply, "Well, I got kind of a head start because I'm old Charlier's grandson umpteen times removed. I got in good with him when I paid Madame la Zouche two bucks to materialize him at a seance. Seems you don't rate much in the hereafter if nobody on this plane asks for you, and Grandpappy was getting burned up because a lot of Indian Guides with names like Prairie Flower and Happy Thunder were in great request, but nobody at a seance ever paged Monsieur Charlier. . . ." It is easy to continue in this strain until your heckler stops asking questions.

When planning an ending, prepare for the heckler who claims to know your secret. If someone makes this claim, feign astonishment and inquire, "You mean that you could imitate this by a *trick*?" As soon as he says, "Yes," put the apparatus in his hands and say, "Show me how." He will almost certainly admit that he cannot perform the trick himself. This makes him look foolish, and you should have no difficulty in shutting him up.

As far as possible, you should also be ready for the heckler who tries to catch you out during the body of a routine. For example, while you have something palmed, a spectator may say, "Let me see your hand." Wink at the others and confide dryly, "This is where I get rich." Turn to the heckler and continue, "Would you like to back your request with a little hard cash, say five or ten dollars? If there's something in my hand, I pay you; if it's empty, you pay me." Show complete confidence in your ability to take the heckler's money. Should he insist on betting, you must expose the palmed object and pay— but few people dare to take the wager. They would be reckless if they did. You know the truth. You have fooled them before. The odds against the heckler's being right are simply too heavy for him to bet.

In some cases, such a challenge produces a certain amount of confusion. People look at the heckler and he looks at them. This may divert attention long enough for you to get rid of the palmed object. Once you do, you can start raising the odds. Offer, "Two to one, five to one, ten to one, hundred to one, thousand to one?" If the heckler finally takes the bet, simply prove him wrong. If he continues to refuse, tell him that he is a poor sport but a wise gambler. Then use your hand in such a way that its palm can be seen, but do not show it deliberately. Never challenge the other spectators. That makes them feel inferior, and a feeling of inferiority is not good entertainment.

Finally, there is always a chance that something will go wrong during the routine—a force fails, someone insists on shuffling a stacked deck, or the only person who has seen a card forgets it. No precaution fits every possible case, but there are a few useful rules: (1) When planning a routine, look for an alternative ending that you can use in case something does go wrong. (2) Try to force a card first; if you fail, you can usually fall back on some control-and-glimpse technique. (3) Always glimpse a chosen card when you can. Even when it is not necessary, it is insurance against accidents.

ACE-IN-THE-HOLE

When you intend to present a take-a-card routine, place the Ace of Clubs, the two of Hearts, the four of Spades, and the six of Diamonds in your pocket. If trouble develops, drop the rest of the deck into your pocket and say, "What was your card?" If The Subject has forgotten it, ask, "What card would you like it to be?" Suppose he calls for the seven of Hearts. Tell him that it would take too long to find that particular card, but you will do the next best thing. Remove the two of Hearts from your pocket and add, "That's the suit." Pull out the four of Spades, "And four is six." Finally, reveal the Ace of Clubs. "And one makes seven."

Ace, two, four, and six can be added together to make any number from one to thirteen. The suit card may or may not be counted. Thus, if the chosen card is the Queen of Clubs, you can show the Ace for the suit and add two, four, and six to make twelve.

Chapter 18

CONTINUITY

Although we must always provide the elements of dramatic structure, this is not enough in itself to create an effective routine. We need to arrange our materials in the way which will make the strongest impression on the audience.

THE INTEREST CURVE

The interest that an audience takes in anything never remains constant. If we do not increase it, it will slump. An audience is entertained only while interest is rising. When interest slacks off, the spectators relax. If the drop in interest continues for more than a few seconds, they become bored. Our success, therefore, depends on our ability to make interest rise for the maximum length of time and fall for the minimum length of time.

We can represent audience interest by curves like those in Figs. 131–133. If we shade the areas under the rising section of the curve, we can see why it is a mistake to start with a bang (Fig. 131). When we do that, we have nowhere to go but down.

Maintaining a steady rise is virtually impossible. We should speed up the increase as in Fig. 133 until we reach the climax. Otherwise interest will peter out as in Fig. 132. This is the weakness of illusions like *Horoscope* and *Dowsing Test*. We may supply an artificial climax to avoid a sag at the end, but routines of this type never permit the ideal curve in Fig. 133. If their themes are strong and their effects are convincing, they may be well worth doing. However, they are less dramatic than an illusion like *Mental Television* which ends at its highest point.

Even under ideal conditions, a rise rarely lasts more than two or three minutes. This explains why most good tricks are short. Plays manage to hold interest longer by making it come in

131. SAGGING INTEREST

132. BILLOW CURVE

133. RISE TO CLIMAX

Shaded sections represent interest; the unshaded sections provide relief from tension. Protracted relief turns into boredom.

The longer the rise, the more interest you can create. Remember the vanishing elephants on p. 31

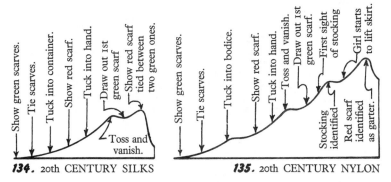

134. 20th CENTURY SILKS

- Show green scarves.
- Tie scarves.
- Tuck into container.
- Show red scarf.
- Tuck into hand.
- Draw out 1st green scarf
- Show red scarf tied between two green ones.
- Toss and vanish.

135. 20th CENTURY NYLON

- Show green scarves.
- Tie scarves.
- Tuck into bodice.
- Show red scarf.
- Tuck into hand.
- Toss and vanish.
- Draw out 1st green scarf.
- First sight of stocking
- Girl starts to lift skirt.
- Stocking identified
- Red scarf identified as garter.

waves. Interest is built up for a few minutes, the audience is given a chance to relax, then the interest is again increased. This continues until the end of the play. Ideally, each wave should have its crest at its end. Furthermore, each crest and each valley should be higher than the one before it, so that the play rises to a main climax. Illusions and whole conjuring acts must also employ the principle of rising waves.

You cannot construct accurate interest curves for your routines, but even rough estimates are worth drawing. If you try it, I suspect that you will be in for some rude surprises. Fig. 134 shows the curve for a performance of the classical *Twentieth-Century Silks* in which the red handkerchief merely vanishes and appears tied between the two green ones. Note that the final climax sags. There is no way to avoid this. If you announce what you intend to do, the fact that the climax is completely expected keeps it from seeming much more miraculous than the disappearance of the red handkerchief. On the other hand, if you do not reveal what will happen, some spectators may fail to appreciate the effect or may have to think for a few seconds before they understand it. In either case, it can make a fair impression, but its interest curve will drop at the climax.

Compare this with the curve for Bob Tilford's *Twentieth-Century Nylon* in Fig. 135. Here, the grand climax gets a

double kick: the girl's legs and the reappearance of the red
handkerchief. Furthermore, there are four waves instead of two,
and the greater length of the routine permits interest to rise
higher.

INTEREST CURVES (Cont.)

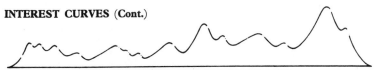

136. CURVE FOR CONVENTIONAL ACT

This act has no pattern. It is simply a series of unrelated tricks. We could add more or drop some without making any real difference. Breaks in the curve show where the performer hopes for applause.

But if an audience is asked to clap too often, it tires. As a result the total amount of applause is much less than it would be if the performer took it only on the main climaxes.

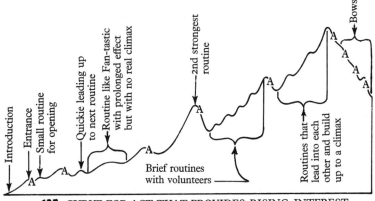

137. CURVE FOR ACT THAT PROVIDES RISING INTEREST

Although this curve is not ideal, it illustrates what can be done by arranging your routines to build interest by creating successively higher climaxes. You will get the greatest total amount of applause if you take it *only* at the points marked "A" and deliberately avoid it after minor routines and quickies.

Most conjuring acts create a fairly level curve (Fig. 136).
No matter how good the individual tricks are, this produces an
over-all effect of monotony. Even when the last item is definitely the best, it cannot create a real climax unless the earlier
numbers have been arranged to provide a curve of rising
interest like that shown in Fig. 137. The techniques for creating
rising interest are a basic part of showmanship. They will do
more to earn applause than all the sleights and gimmicks on
earth.

CONSERVATION

When you try to achieve a rising curve, *keeping the beginning low is as important as making the ending high*. If you start with a strong number, the next few effects will let the curve sag— and you may never be able to make it rise again. Dramatists know this; nearly every play opens with a scene that is deliberately dull. Its only function is to secure attention. If your first effect leaves your audience breathless, you will never be able to top it. Furthermore, if at any time during an act or a routine you let interest rise too high too soon, you create a false climax which makes everything that occurs later seem weak by comparison. Each peak and each valley should be higher than the one before it.

The quickies in Fig. 137 do not break this rule; they are part of the build to the next climax. However, isolated quickies, like those in Fig. 136 definitely let the over-all interest droop.

The need to avoid building too high too soon is the most important case where we must apply the principle of conservation. It is also the hardest lesson in showmanship to learn. Many otherwise gifted performers are unable to resist a temptation to start with a bang or to make a rise so steep that its peak comes before the real climax.

A good opening number should gain attention, establish the personality of the performer and the atmosphere of his act, and convince the audience that the act will be worth watching. If your opening accomplishes these things, the weaker it is in other ways the better.

The Highbrow Lecturer described on p. 51 shows how far this sort of thing can be carried. He stands awkwardly and waits until the audience quiets down. His opening remarks are as dull as he can make them. Then Marvello's Assistant wanders on. One look at the contrast between The Lecturer's face and The Assistant's legs is enough to assure the audience that what happens next is going to repay attention.

Manipulative acts can hardly do better than to begin silently with casual effects like those suggested on p. 33. The only weakness of this lies in the fact that the performer has little control over the timing. When the audience pays attention at once, these effects seem to drag; when the spectators are slow to become quiet, the beginning may be too brief.

"IMPROMPTU" (*Dial Information*)

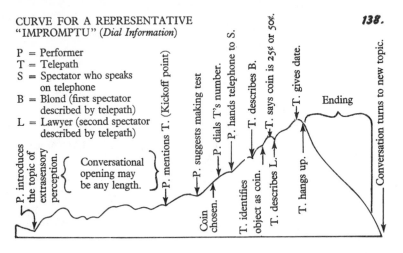

P = Performer
T = Telepath
S = Spectator who speaks
    on telephone
B = Blond (first spectator
    described by telepath)
L = Lawyer (second spectator
    described by telepath)

P. introduces the topic of extrasensory perception.

Conversational opening may be any length.

P. mentions T. (Kickoff point)

P. suggests making test

P. dials T's number.

P. hands telephone to S.

Coin chosen.

T. identifies object as coin.

T. describes B.

T. describes L.

T. says coin is 25¢ or 50¢.

T. gives date.

T. hangs up.

Ending

Conversation turns to new topic.

Strange-object openings are excellent for stage acts. They are strong attention-getters and give you complete control over your timing. Unfortunately, finding just the right one to suit your needs may be difficult. Do not use business in which you seem to be setting up your apparatus or taking care of some other matter that you should have attended to before the curtain. The opening should lead directly into your first routine. The stage setup for *The Instant Incubator* is ideal. No spectator can see that odd conglomeration of equipment without having his curiosity stimulated in a way that automatically provides atmosphere for an act featuring A Crackpot Inventor—and the performer has no difficulty in adjusting his timing to suit his audience.

If you work night clubs where half the audience is drunk, you may need a violent opening to secure any attention at all. My friend John Carlance once played a club on New Year's Eve. Just as pandemonium broke out at midnight, the half-witted manager turned to John and said, "You're on."

I would have murdered the manager. John, however, walked on stage and set fire to a handful of *flash paper*. The resulting flare drew even the bleariest eye in the house. Note that although this seized attention, it was not interesting in itself. In spite of his violent opening, John was able to start his interest curve at the bottom.

The ideal curve for a routine is a simpler and shorter version of the ideal curve for an act. As a routine rarely has a strong introduction, problems of conservation are not apt to arise.

Most "impromptus" begin with conversation (Fig. 138). The audience plays such a large part in this that the performer usually has little control over the shape of the curve. Hence, it wanders up and down until it reaches the kick-off point. However, a few routines, such as *Lie Detector* and *Mental Television* can begin by starting an argument. If this grows more and more heated, the interest curve will rise sharply. The illusion will then come at the top of this rise and achieve a powerful climax. Argumentative introductions are extremely effective, but they require careful handling. Also, they are not suited to cases like *Dial Information*, where the performer impersonates a skeptic, or *Will Power*, where he claims to be completely objective.

Many routines tend to create premature climaxes. Avoiding these may be troublesome. Thus, transportation effects require proving that the object is no longer where it was placed and also that it has arrived somewhere else. This makes the climax double. We must find ways to suppress the first part and strengthen the second so that it will become the real climax.

Each illusion presents different problems, but there are a few general rules: (1) Decide whether the vanish is more dramatic than the production or vice versa, and reveal the stronger one last. (2) Make the first revelation clear, but keep it brief and avoid stressing it in any way; asking for applause at this point is the ultimate in poor showmanship. (3) As soon as the first revelation has been made, start *immediately* to build up to the second. (4) Give the second revelation all the emphasis it will stand.

Techniques for Building Interest

Increasing interest is called *building*. If we had to rely on natural interest, providing an effective interest curve would be a hopeless task. Fortunately, we can call a whole battery of technical devices to our aid.

We build interest by adding more: more movement, more color, more sound, more light, more people, more intensity, more concentration, more excitement. In short, anything whatever that the spectators regard as increasing will also increase their interest.

A stage act gives you plenty of scope. You can start with a bare stage and fill it with production items, or start with black-and-white costumes and apparatus and end with a riot of color. Begin with minor effects like a cigarette vanish and wind up by producing an automobile. Commence with small slow movements and end by racing around the stage waving silken banners. Open silently and close with a shout and a pistol shot. If you have adequate lighting facilities and a *reliable* electrician, nothing is more effective than starting with a fairly dim stage and ending in a blaze of light.

My own pet device for building interest consists in increasing the height of my actors above the stage floor. This works so well that I often introduce steps and platforms merely to make height possible. A conjurer will normally be restricted to a chair and a table, but even these are well worth using. Notice in Fig. 139 how each figure seems more important than the one below him.

The big problem here is one of motivation. If you jump up onto chairs and tables for no reason except a desire to build interest, you will look silly. Much depends on your characterization. An eccentric, uninhibited character might do almost anything; a highly dignified performer would not climb onto a table for any reason whatever. For the average conjurer, a spectacular production of doves or fire might justify a table-top position.

If you could add volunteers one or two at a time, your act would build automatically. That may be possible, and anyone who is accustomed to working with a number of volunteers

The higher your head is from the floor, the more attention you attract.

139. HOW HEIGHT AFFECTS ABILITY TO GAIN ATTENTION

should certainly consider it. In any event, try to use more volunteers in later routines than you do in earlier ones. This does not include the final illusion. Volunteers are a nuisance for this because they interfere with your bows and curtain calls.

Curiously enough, we can build interest by techniques which seem diametrically opposed to each other. In *The Instant Incubator*, for example, the Inventor grows more and more excited and active as he displays his apparatus. When he has carried this as far as possible, he calms down but at the same time becomes increasingly tense as he picks up the egg and deposits it tenderly within the "cathode." He then raises a finger and says dramatically, "Now watch." With a galvanic leap, he jumps to the switch and throws it. His mood alters again, and he tiptoes to the "cathode" and peers in. He looks up with a broad smile and proudly displays the dove. Here we have three shifts: (1) increase of excitement and movement, (2) increase of tension, and (3) a series of abrupt changes in mood.

These techniques do not really conflict. At each point, the performer established the type of build and the audience accepts that as the standard. All the conjurer needs is to be perfectly clear in his own mind what building technique he is using at each point in his routine.

The elements which can be increased during an "impromptu" routine are few and limited. We must, therefore, take full advantage of those we have. Virtually every routine can make some use of all the following techniques:

Increase the intensity of your own interest. Concentrate more and more on the source of information. When the nature of the routine permits, show rising excitement. *Dial Information* and *The Vast Void* lend themselves especially well to such treatment.

Let your movements become broader, quicker, more abrupt, and more varied. As the climax nears, introduce sudden shifts in technique. A shift is stronger than an increase. In *Mental Television*, for example, you might move freely during the early stages and while you are "trying to capture the outline." Then, when the "vision" comes, you could suddenly lock every muscle of your body except those of the fingers used in drawing the design.

Almost any progressive change in speech will build interest. When you talk more and more rapidly and increase in volume, you build interest by force. However, if you speak slower and slower and let your voice drop until it is barely audible, you create an impression that you are losing yourself in what you are doing. If you handle this convincingly, the audience will follow your lead.

THE CONSOLIDATED GUINEA PIGS

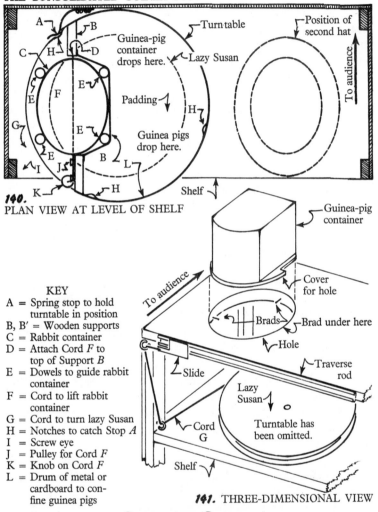

140. PLAN VIEW AT LEVEL OF SHELF

KEY

A = Spring stop to hold turntable in position
B, B′ = Wooden supports
C = Rabbit container
D = Attach Cord F to top of Support B
E = Dowels to guide rabbit container
F = Cord to lift rabbit container
G = Cord to turn lazy Susan
H = Notches to catch Stop A
I = Screw eye
J = Pulley for Cord F
K = Knob on Cord F
L = Drum of metal or cardboard to confine guinea pigs

141. THREE-DIMENSIONAL VIEW

CUMULATIVE CLIMAXES

The best of all ways to build interest is to pile one climax on top of another. For example, if you do a haunted-conjurer

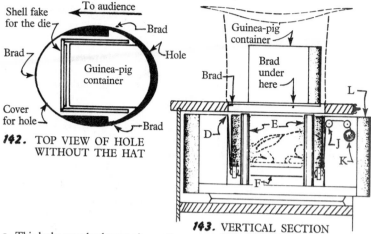

Shell fake for the die — Brad

To audience →

Brad — Hole

Guinea-pig container

Cover for hole — Brad

142. TOP VIEW OF HOLE WITHOUT THE HAT

Guinea-pig container

Brad under here →

Brad →

L

D E J K F

143. VERTICAL SECTION THROUGH TABLE
Both guinea-pig and rabbit containers are shown. Actually, the guinea-pig container drops before the rabbit container is turned into this position.

1. This looks complex because it must be explained in detail. However, if you already have a table, you should be able to make the rest in two or three evenings.
2. The right-hand hat is ungimmicked except that it holds a guinea-pig container (Fig. 16). The left-hand hat is fixed in place. It has no top (bottom when inverted), and a hole the size of the hat is cut into the top of the table (Figs. 141 and 143). The cover for this hole has the second guinea-pig container built on top of it (Fig. 141). The cover rests on three brads and is shaped so that moving it back ¼ in. when you lift out the guinea pig will let the container drop through the hole.
3. As the guinea pigs will be dropped through the same hole, we must get the container out of the way. This is done by a turntable which rests on a lazy Susan. The turntable also contains an elevator to lift the rabbit container into the hat. This

is guided by four dowels (*E*) set into holes bored in the turntable. It is raised by pulling on Knob *K*. This tightens Cord *F*, which is attached at Point *D* Fig. 141, and lifts the container (*C*).
4. The lazy Susan is turned by Cord *G*, which runs through two screw eyes to the slide of a traverse rod of the type used for window curtains. Moving the slide pulls Cord *G*. The amount of turning is regulated by Stop *A* (Fig. 140) which catches in notches (*H*) cut in the edge of the turntable.
5. The rabbit should wear a harness like that shown in Fig. 19.

act, you might save the guinea-pig routine until almost the end. You could then go immediately into:

THE CONSOLIDATED GUINEA PIGS

When you realize that The Obeah Man has once more made you look foolish by turning your dice into guinea pigs, lose your temper. Look upward to your left as though you saw him standing in the air, and gloating over your downfall. Shout, "You think you're clever, don't you? You think you're the only one who can work magic, don't you? All right smartie, let's see you top this!"

As you speak, you cram both guinea pigs into one hat. Make three passes over the hat, saying, "Algon! Orasyn!! Karkahita!!!" Reach into

the hat and pull out a large black-and-white rabbit. Figs. 140–143 show
the mechanism.

THE TRUANT TROUSERS

Hold up the rabbit and challenge The Obeah Man again, "Thought
you had me licked, didn't you? If you're so good, why don't you top this?
Why don't you?" When nothing happens, smirk at the audience and say,
"I guess that left him without a comeback."

As you speak, step from behind your table and reveal that your trousers
have disappeared and that you are wearing yellow shorts with huge
purple spots!

The device is shown in Figs. 144 and 145.

THE TRUANT TROUSERS

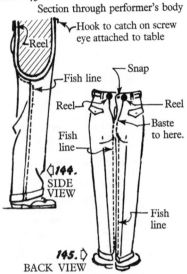

Section through performer's body

1. Remove belt. Rip inseams and back
seam of trousers. Thread two large reels
with 8-lb. monofilament fish line. These
reels must be controlled by brakes. Fix a
heavy snap at the belt to hold the trousers
up until you are ready. Attach the reels to
the waistband as shown. Baste the seams
with the fish lines. Use a large needle to
make holes through which the lines can
run freely. Fasten a hook to the front of
your waistband and a screw eye to the
center-rear of your table top.
2. When you are ready to get rid of the
trousers, catch the hook in the screw eye,
loosen the snap, and release the brakes.
The reels will pull out the fish-line bastings. You can then back out of the trousers
and leave them hanging on the rear of
your table.

Neither of these routines is much by itself, and neither
would justify the mechanism which it requires. However, when
used to top the original guinea-pig transformation they have
tremendous dramatic value. The pace and intensity of the act
are greatly increased. The Conjurer, who has been a meek
underdog, suddenly confronts his tormentor with a challenge.
The consolidation of the two guinea pigs into one rabbit surprises the audience and appears to turn the tables on The Obeah
Man. Properly handled, this strikes a note of drama at the
end of a farcical act. Then, when the performer steps out from
behind his table, we have a second surprise. His momentary
triumph collapses, and the act ends in broad farce.

A three-climax finish like this is probably the most effective
way to close an act. The only thing that could possibly equal

it is a full-scale number such as a levitation or *Sawing a Woman in Half*. However, a large illusion is necessarily slow, and only the climax is dramatic. When three climaxes follow each other in rapid succession, they create a sense of rising tension and excitement which is out of all proportion to their individual importance. Obviously, much depends upon the particular routines and the way they are handled. But if I had to choose between one large climax and a sequence of three small ones, I would decide in favor of the latter.

One other point deserves mention here. The climax of *The Truant Trousers* may seem to violate the rule against an un-expected surprise. Actually, the surprise is expected. In fact, if it were omitted, the audience would feel disappointed and the act would fail. What happens is this: The act has been built around the idea that The Obeah Man will enjoy a series of comic triumphs. There has been no hint that The Conjurer will ultimately win out. Hence, the audience looks forward to The Obeah Man's ultimate, hilarious victory. Again, most spectators will recognize the guinea pigs and the rabbit as the first two elements in a one-two-three pattern. Given these two, they intuitively foresee a third. The whole act has been a farce. The rabbit production is played for drama and would be an inappropriate ending for a comic act. This leads the audience to expect a final twist which will provide a farcical climax. *The Truant Trousers* does just that.

SEQUENCE

With rare exceptions, every conjurer is his own dramatist. He should, therefore, be familiar with at least the rudiments of playwriting. *One of the dramatist's most important jobs is to relieve the audience of all mental effort.* Each step should be clear, and the transition from one step to the next should seem easy and natural. When a step does not logically follow the one before it, the spectators are puzzled. While they are groping for the connection, they miss the next step—or the next few steps. This confuses them still more. Confusion makes the interest curve drop sharply; people who are trying to understand what has happened cannot give full attention to what is happening.

The success of any routine depends largely on how easy it is to follow. This, in turn, depends on the sequence in which the material is presented. In an ideal routine, the first step raises a question. Each succeeding step answers the preceding question and raises a new one. This continues until the climax. That may raise such questions as: Is the phenomenon genuine? Was the demonstration conclusive? or How did he do it? The purpose of the ending is to avoid answering questions of this kind.

The procedure for arranging the steps of a routine in the most effective sequence is best explained by an example. Suppose you like the basic idea of *The Singing Glass* but do not care either for the phenomenon of mass hypnosis or for *Sniff-Sniff*. You, therefore, decide to switch *The Singing Glass*.

Begin by setting down the steps of the routine without worrying whether the sequence is good or bad. Save time and space by writing "C." for "conjurer," "S." for "The Subject," "A." for "the audience," and so on. (See Outline C below.)

OUTLINE C

1. Let S. choose card.
2. Have card replaced and deck cut.
3. Introduce glass, thread, and pencil.
4. Rig glass.
5. Spread deck face up.
6. Move glass along row of cards.
7. Make it sing when it reaches chosen card.
8. Have S. acknowledge card as his.

An outline like this which ignores devices and considers only the points which are presented to the audience is called a *continuity*.

Go over your continuity and ask yourself what question each step answers and what question it asks. Ours has obvious flaws. Step 2, for example, raises the question, "How will the performer reveal the chosen card?" This is not answered by introducing three apparently unrelated props in Step 3. Moreover, Steps 3 and 4 take so much time that The Subject is apt to forget his card. We can eliminate these faults by rigging the glass before the card is drawn.

Further study of our continuity reveals that the climax comes at Step 7, when the glass sings. Having The Subject acknowledge the card in Step 8 is something of an anticlimax. We can correct this by adding an earlier step in which The Subject shows his card to the audience. This lets everyone recognize that the glass sings at the correct moment.

PLANNING ON PAPER

If we had not written out the steps, we might have overlooked the need for these corrections. Also, the fact that we quickly noticed several opportunities for improvement suggests that further study will reveal others—perhaps many others. Making two or three changes in a written continuity is easy enough. But if we make a dozen or more, we may need to rewrite the entire continuity several times. This soon becomes a tedious chore.

Fortunately, there are labor-saving techniques which make the procedure both simpler and more effective. You may need to try these once or twice before you master them. However, after you do, the method will work wonders not only for your individual routines but for whole acts as well.

The first technique employs an ingenious application of the decimal system which is extensively used by library catalogers. This depends on the fact that we can always find a decimal which will fit between any two other numbers. Thus, to add the step in which The Subject shows his card to the audience, we write this at the end of our continuity:

1.1. S. shows card to A.

Obviously, Step 1.1 comes between Step 1 and Step 2.

To move Steps 3 and 4 ahead of Steps 1 and 2, we have only to call Step 3 "0.1" and Step 4 "0.2." Our continuity now looks like the left-hand column in Outline D, but we read it as though the steps were arranged as they are on the right.

OUTLINE D

	1. Let S. choose card.		0.1.	Introduce glass, thread, and pencil.
	2. Have card replaced and deck cut.		0.2.	Rig glass.
0.1.	~~3.~~ Introduce glass, thread, and pencil.		1.	Let S. choose card.
0.2.	~~4.~~ Rig glass.		1.1.	S. shows card to A.
	5. Spread deck face up.		2.	Have card replaced and deck cut.
	6. Move glass along row of cards.		5.	Spread deck face up.
	7. Make it sing when it reaches chosen card.		6.	Move glass along row of cards.
	~~8. Have S. acknowledge card as his.~~		7.	Make it sing when it reaches chosen card.
	1.1. S. shows card to A.			

Although the numbers "3" and "4" have been dropped, the steps still run in numerical order.

A written continuity gives you a clear picture of your routine and helps you to recognize points where corrections and additions are desirable. Even the simplest routine usually offers opportunities for a dozen or more improvements. By the time you have added these, the order of the steps becomes hard to follow. It then pays to rewrite the whole thing and renumber the steps.

Too much rewriting takes all the fun out of planning a continuity. However, a little of it is well worth while because it usually suggests new ideas or reminds you of points that you have overlooked. Compare my rough continuity on the left of Outline E with the rewritten version on the right. The left-hand column includes notes to explain the reason for each change. You would not need these in a continuity that you wrote yourself. Note that the name of the routine has been changed and that Steps 2 and 15 in the new version did not occur to me until I rewrote the continuity.

OUTLINE E

The Mongolian Marble	*The Mongolian Marble*
~~The Singing Glass~~	
1. Let S. choose card.	1. Take small ball from pocket and toy with it until someone asks what it is.
2. Have card replaced and deck cut.	
0.1. ~~3~~. Introduce glass, thread, and pencil.	2. Pass ball around for examination.
0.2. ~~4~~. Rig glass.	3. State that ball is a device used by Mongolian witch doctors, called "shamans," as a kind of divining rod to locate lost articles.
5. Spread deck face up.	
6. Move glass along row of cards.	
7. Make it sing when it reaches chosen card.	
~~8. Have S. acknowledge card as his.~~	4. Offer to show how it is used.
[*Note that as Step 8 has been canceled, we can give its number to the next item.*]	5. Introduce glass, thread, and pencil.
1.1. S. shows card to A.	6. Explain that ball sings when lost object is found and that glass acts as resonator.
0.3. State that demonstration will consist in locating a chosen card. [*This answers the question, "What form will the demonstration take?" and asks, "How will the card be chosen?" It also introduces the cards, which would otherwise have no relation to the glass, the thread, and the pencil.*]	7. Rig glass.

1.01. Tell S. to remember it. [*This should always be said in any take-a-card routine.*]

0.11. Explain that ball sings when lost object is found and that glass acts as resonator.

0.21. Explain that thread keeps sound from being damped out as it would if glass were held in fingers. [*This is a mock explanation to motivate the use of the thread. Most spectators will also accept it as a motivation for using the pencil.*]

0.01. Take small ball from pocket and toy with it until someone asks what it is.

0.02. State that ball is a device used by Mongolian witch doctors, called "shamans," as a kind of divining rod to locate lost articles.

0.03. Offer to show how it is used.

8. Quickly announce name of card. [*This avoids any question as to which card has been located. It also strengthens the climax by adding more sound.*]

9. Talk about shamans while dismantling apparatus. [*This is the first step of the ending.*]

10. Introduce new topic, possibly the effect of Communism on primitive tribesmen.

8. Explain that thread keeps sound from being damped out as it would be if glass were held in fingers.

9. State that demonstration will consist in locating a chosen card.

10. Let S. choose card.

11. Tell S. to remember it.

12. S. shows card to A.

13. Have card replaced and deck cut.

14. Spread deck face up.

15. Have person holding ball drop it into glass.

16. Move glass along row of cards.

17. Make it sing when it reaches chosen card.

18. Quickly announce name of card.

19. Talk about shamans while dismantling apparatus.

20. Introduce new topic, possibly the effect of Communism on primitive tribesmen.

INSERTING DEVICES

Planning a continuity without worrying about devices helps you to see the routine as your audience will. Furthermore, you limit yourself unnecessarily when you decide on a device before you know exactly what it has to do. Thus, *The Mongolian Marble* can be worked by a key card, by a force, by a stacked deck, or by card control and a glimpse—and both the control and the glimpse can take many different forms. Each device has its faults and virtues. You cannot know which one will best serve your needs until you know what those needs are.

In our example, one technique is as effective as another. Choose the one that you can handle most deceptively. Let us suppose that this is control-and-glimpse.

OUTLINE F

*The Mongolian Marble
Continuity*

0.1. [*Begin with device moves*] <u>C</u>, <u>D</u>, <u>E</u>.

1. Take small ball from pocket and toy with it until someone asks what it is.

2. Pass ball around for examination.

3. State that ball is device used by Mongolian witch doctors, called "shamans," as a kind of divining rod to locate lost articles.

4. Offer to show how it is used.

5. Introduce glass, thread, and pencil.

6. Explain that ball sings when lost object is found and that glass acts as resonator.

7. Rig glass.

8. Explain that thread keeps sound from being damped out, as it would be if glass were held in fingers.

6.1 9. State that demonstration will consist in locating a chosen card.

10. Let S. choose card.

11. Tell S. to remember it.

12. S. shows card to A.

13. Have card replaced. [*Follow with device move*] <u>A</u>.

14. Spread deck face up.

13.1 15. Have person holding ball drop it into glass. [*Follow with device move*] <u>B</u>.

16. Move glass along row of cards.

17. Make it sing when it reaches chosen card.

18. Quickly announce name of card.

19. Talk about shamans while dismantling apparatus.

20. Introduce new topic, possibly the effect of Communism on primitive tribesmen.

Devices

A. Push card into deck. Create and hold break.

B. Shuffle, and glimpse card.

C. Have ball in one pocket and pencil in another.

D. Have glass and cards on table.

E. Place thread within reach and find motivation for having it there. [*This will vary with circumstances. If you can perform somewhere near your wife's sewing basket, the problem is solved. But finding a motivation for carrying thread in your pocket will tax your ingenuity. Perhaps you can persuade your wife to carry a miniature sewing kit in her handbag. If you introduce a length of thread without a motivation, you confess that you have come prepared to perform. This greatly weakens conviction.*]

Break the device action up into *moves*. A move corresponds to a step in a continuity, but the use of different terms helps you to avoid confusion. Most routines require preparations. Although some of these may not be, strictly speaking, either moves or devices, it is more convenient to handle them as such. List the moves on a separate sheet of paper as they occur to you. The order does not matter, you will take care of it automatically when you work the moves into the continuity. This is done simply by writing the reference letter of each move after the appropriate step as shown in Outline F on p. 250.

Introducing moves normally requires some rearrangement of the steps. Our example needs only two such changes: Step 9 is renumbered "6.1" to bring it after Step 6, and Step 15 is placed after Step 13.

This procedure gives you a bird's-eye view of the routine and greatly simplifies the problem of making changes. Even if you decide to use a different device, you do not need to rewrite the continuity. Merely erase the reference letters for the old moves and insert those for the new ones.

You will appreciate the value of this method if you try it on some routine with which you are already familiar. That will give you experience in handling the technique—and, in nine cases out of ten, it will show you how to improve a routine which you are accustomed to regard as already perfect.

Chapter *19*

MATERIAL FOR ENTERTAINMENT

Witch doctors, charlatans, and fake mediums perform their marvels for practical reasons. The primary purpose of the honest conjurer is to provide entertainment. He may also be actuated by a desire to show off. However, what the showoff really wants is admiration. The best way to get that is to show off by being entertaining. The man who performs feats which are difficult without being entertaining puts himself in a class with an exhibit in a freak show—he may amaze his audience, but no one admires him.

Entertainment is broader than amusement. Shakespeare's *Comedy of Errors* is amusing; his *Hamlet* is not. Nevertheless, the fact that *Hamlet* is far more popular than the *Comedy of Errors* proves that it is also far more entertaining. By the same token, *Will Power*, properly presented, is better entertainment than *The Haunted Conjurer* can hope to be.

The Mongolian Marble is only a working model for an illusion. All the machinery is there, but its entertainment value is small. How can we make it more entertaining? It is easy to think of "improvements," but how can we be sure they will really improve the routine? Connoisseurs of conjuring constantly complain that certain tricks have been "improved" to death.

The answer is that a real improvement adds meaning by enriching either the theme or the treatment. Padding and digressions are not improvements. For example, you might finish *The Mongolian Marble* by saying, "It takes a magic marble to locate the chosen card from its face. But anyone could tell it from the back." You then turn it over and show that it is the only red-backed card in a blue-backed deck. This would undoubtedly make eyes pop, but it would also ruin the over-all impression created by the routine.

STRENGTHENING THE THEME

Anything that makes the theme stronger intensifies the meaning of the illusion and contributes more entertainment than we can add by improving some detail. The theme of *The Mongolian Marble* is: "Magician demonstrates that shaman's magic marble can locate a chosen card." We should be able to better that.

What does a witch doctor do? He locates lost objects, cures diseases, predicts the future, injures enemies, causes love or hate, and detects criminals. Which of these is most dramatic? Detecting a criminal. What type of criminal is most interesting? A murderer. We cannot detect a real murderer, but we can select a make-believe killer by having all of the spectators draw cards and announcing that the one with the low card is the villain.

This will require changes in both devices and continuity. The conjurer must announce that Ace is high and that suits rank as in bridge: Clubs, Diamonds, Hearts, Spades—with Clubs low. This is necessary to avoid confusion in case two people draw cards of the same denomination. The Murderer's card must be forced. It must be the two of Clubs. Otherwise someone else might get a lower card by accident. The simplest procedure is to locate the Club two during the final hand of a card game. Get it near the top of the deck and remember its position. Make a false shuffle and deal a card to each spectator. Do this in what seems like a random order but actually give the two of Clubs to the person you wish to cast as The Murderer.

This theme makes the routine much more entertaining. Instead of a glorified card trick, we now have an illusion that resembles a miniature detective drama. Furthermore, we have added audience participation; everyone gets a card.

Strengthening a theme often produces several minor improvements as well. This is no exception. Let the spectators keep their cards without showing them to each other. This creates suspense. No one except The Murderer knows who is guilty until the climax. Theoretically, the low card might be a four, or a seven; in that case, The Murderer would not realize his own "guilt." This would be a discrepancy if the routine called for a serious murder story. However, as our Murderer is selected by lot, it does no real harm.

Spreading the cards is no longer enough; we must detect the villain himself. How? Have the spectators hold out their cards face down while you pass the "marble" over them. When you reach The Murderer, make the glass sing. At the same time, grab his card and flip it over so that everyone can recognize it as the low card. This creates a dramatic climax.

EXPANSION

Although padding is always bad, a routine with a strong climax needs time to raise interest to the highest pitch. This time is best filled by a preliminary effect which demonstrates the same phenomenon in a less spectacular way. The pendulum for *The Sympathetic Pendulum* is sometimes said to determine sex. That would be an amusing effect for the shaman's ball, which could sing once for a man and twice for a woman. However, it will spoil the climax unless we find some way to make it mysterious.

Obviously, the performer must be blindfolded. This presents no problem. Prepare yourself with a handkerchief that is large enough to tie around your head and heavy enough to be convincingly opaque when folded. When you are blindfolded, you will find that you can look down the sides of your nose (Fig. 146).

You can still see by looking down your nose.

146. BLINDFOLD

Hold the glass about four inches above the table and close enough so that you can just see the bottom under the blindfold. Have A Subject put his (or her) hand under it palm up. Make the glass sing once or twice according to the sex of The Subject. Repeat with one or two more Subjects.

Whenever you are blindfolded, keep your eyes shut except for the moments when you actually need to see something. While your eyes are closed, your acting is perfect. You do not need to simulate blindness. You are actually blind.

Almost anything that strengthens the atmosphere and is interesting in itself will add meaning. For example, we might make the "marble" of plastic wood. It will still look like clay but will be surprisingly light. The performer can then say, "The thing's a lot stranger than it looks. It's hard as rock but has almost no weight. Feel it yourself." Hand it out and add, "A chemist might be able to analyze the material, though I wouldn't want to bet on his chances." This implies that the ball is made of some unknown and mysterious substance. It will impress many people.

ENRICHMENT

Several types of material enrich a routine by adding meaning appropriate to the theme. If these are interesting in their own right, they make the routine more entertaining and more convincing as well.

Nothing enriches an "impromptu" so much as audience participation. Most tricks permit very little, but the fact that illusions have themes usually provides some way to give the audience a real role. Thus, in *Horoscope*, you can make all the spectators part of the act by saying, "A good astrological reading describes the individual's character so clearly that his friends can identify him. As I give each analysis, try to guess whom it fits. When you think you know, hold up your hand."

This is another case where solving one problem adds bonus values. I thought of it as a way to introduce audience participation, but it also enriches the routine in five other ways as well: (1) It creates an element of contest; each spectator tries to be the one who identifies the sitter. (2) It keeps readings short; you do not need to carry one beyond the point where its Sitter has been identified. (3) Emphasis is shifted from the reading itself to the clues for identification; you can maintain interest even though you are unable to give highly entertaining readings. (4) Each identification provides a climax for its reading. (5) The readings are more convincing because the presentation drives home the fact that they are specific enough to permit identification.

The method used to supply *Horoscope* with audience participation works equally well for *The Mongolian Marble*. Simply say, "A shaman doesn't really need this contraption. The criminal usually loses his nerve and shows it in his face or his hands. While I try to detect our murderer, see if you can spot him by the way he or she behaves."

No routine has a real plot. I have heard many attempts to weave a story around one, but all of them bored me. However, "anecdotal material" can have entertainment value, especially in an introductory explanation. Thus, The Haunted Conjurer's account of his quarrel with The Obeah Man not only prepares the audience for surprises but may also be highly amusing. Something of the sort is needed for *The Mongolian Marble* to explain how the performer obtained such an unlikely object. I suggest the following:

"During the Second World War, the Navy set up a weather station in the Gobi Desert. My uncle was the best crapshooter in the service, so they sent him along to keep him from collecting the pay of the whole Pacific Fleet. He went through the natives of Outer Mongolia like a pestilence and came home with enough loot to stock a museum. He sold most of his trophies to collectors, but this thing [*Holds up "marble"*] isn't a show piece, so he gave it to me."

A limited amount of sugar-coated information adds both authenticity and entertainment. Many of our earlier illusions have contained examples dealing with such diverse subjects as freak shows, magic rituals, and atomic physics. *The Mongolian Marble* can profitably include remarks on the Gobi Desert, shamans, and the Naval Weather Station.

Both the amount and the nature of such material must be adjusted to fit the quality and mood of the audience. A well-educated, serious group may appreciate a lengthy discussion of technical details; frivolous, shallow people will be bored by anything more than a few sketchy remarks.

Fortunately, there is a simple test to guide you: "Avoid anecdotal or informative material unless you feel sure that it would interest the spectators as conversation even if they did not expect any experiment or demonstration."

This test is more important than it may seem at first glance. Many performers indulge in long explanatory anecdotes which bore their audiences stiff. Others, disgusted by these horrible examples, avoid all material of this type—even though they could handle it, and their routines need it.

Material for "impromptu" work can be tested by actually experimenting on an audience. Thus, if you plan a routine along the lines of *The Mongolian Marble*, try telling a group of friends about an imaginary crapshooting acquaintance who cleaned out the Mongolian natives while he was with the Naval Weather Station. See how long you can maintain interest *without* either the mysterious "marble" or any conjuring. Your time will vary from zero to ten minutes, depending on your conversational skill.

Next, prepare the material that you plan to use in your routine. Cut out all phrases which do not either strengthen the atmosphere or earn smiles from your audience. Time the result. If it runs less than half as long as you can hold your audience in conversation, it is safe to use in your routine.

The appearance of difficulty increases interest. Thus, in *Portable Echo*, you should make a point of gripping the saucer firmly and stress how hard it is to adjust it at precisely the correct angle. Make one or two failures before you succeed. Acrobats and jugglers learned long ago that an initial failure exploited with showmanship doubles applause. Conjurers must use this technique with discretion, but it has real value when properly handled.

We could make *The Mongolian Marble* seem more difficult by pretending that the ball is not entirely self-working but requires intense concentration on the part of the operator. However, this would be risky. Any hint that the performer controls the ball mentally may cause some astute spectator to suspect that the performer actually controls it physically. Hence, we should forego the idea of difficulty in the present case unless we can find some better way to introduce it.

Although concentration does not suit our example, it can be used to advantage in most mental routines. It will add an interesting element of difficulty to such illusions as *Horoscope*, *Chromavoyance*, and *Lie Detector*.

Uncertainty is closely allied to difficulty and is even more effective because it introduces suspense. If you present *The Strong Man's Secret* brashly as though you are certain of success, the result is entertaining but rather tame. However, when you suggest that you are not sure you remember just how to work the stunt and are more than likely to fail, the routine becomes almost a miniature drama. Also, the more uncertain you seem at first, the more your audience will be impressed when you win out in the end. It is this element of uncertainty that makes experiments more entertaining than demonstrations.

Danger always adds interest. Much of Houdini's success was due to the fact that his feats were either actually dangerous or were made to appear so. Most routines offer no scope for danger, but we can at least hint at it in any one with a magical or occult theme. Thus, in *The Mongolian Marble*, the performer might admit that although he can work the "marble," he is leery of doing so. The thing is too uncanny. Folklore is full of stories about men like Faust who pried into matters which are best left alone. Probably, there is nothing in the legends, but it is impossible to shake off the idea that something unpleasant just might happen.

Vague hints of this sort influence even the most hardheaded spectator, whereas a straightforward threat of some supernatural disaster would only make him laugh. It is the unknown that terrifies.

Demonstrations or experiments dealing with incredible phenomena must be treated seriously if they are to achieve conviction. In most other illusions, however, a little comedy will add entertainment if you can handle it. The secret lies in treating the phenomenon seriously but jesting about other aspects of the routine. Thus, you can state that shamans sometimes use the pellet to determine the sex of eggs and unborn children, but your uncle says both sexes in Mongolia dress so much alike that it takes a shaman to tell the men from the women.

Touches

Any item of presentation which makes a momentary but powerful impression is called a *touch*. Thus, after holding the string in your fist for *The Strong Man's Secret*, you might say, "Give me a little slack," and then moisten your thumb and fingertips before using them to grip the string again. This touch announces that you will provide a second demonstration. It also explains your need for slack, it creates suspense, and it adds conviction.

A touch may be a bit of business, a prop, a phrase, or an inflection. It may be comic or dramatic, used to clarify a point, introduce suspense, or build atmosphere. It must fit the theme and treatment and be an integral part of the step that it enhances. Pointless bits stuck in to get a laugh or provide a cheap thrill are *gags* not touches.

The more good touches you can add the better. I have occasionally been able to turn the dullest scene in a play into the best, simply because the dull scene offered unusually good opportunities for touches.

The Mongolian Marble is rich in such opportunities. Consider the "marble" itself. The idea of making it of plastic wood is one touch, but a ball is not very impressive. It would be better to use a pellet molded into some strange shape which appears to have a reason but which actually has none (Fig. 147). Paint applied in a definite but unrecognizable pattern adds another touch by suggesting the sort of decoration that we might expect a witch doctor to use. A third touch can be supplied by punching a triangular hole in one side of the pellet with a shoemaker's awl. This will arouse curiosity, and some spectators may suppose that it is the source of the sound.

147. SUGGESTED DESIGN FOR THE PELLET

The idea of Mongolia is itself a touch. It is fresh. It introduces the Gobi Desert (which sounds romantic) and shamans (who will be new to most spectators). Best of all, so little is known about the region that we can invent our "facts" to suit ourselves without fear of contradiction. If you call the pellet in Fig. 147 "Egyptian," some spectator with an eye for art may say, "That doesn't look like Egyptian work to me." You run the same risk when speaking of West African or Voodoo magic, but almost no one in America knows enough about the Gobi to have any opinions.

The blindfold offers an opportunity for a convincing touch. After you rig the glass, set it down with your left hand. When you are blindfolded, grope for the glass with your right hand until someone tells you where it is. Most people will accept this as proof that you are sightless.

The choice of a single word can enrich an illusion. For example, we may make our "criminal" an "assassin" instead of a mere "murderer." When the pellet sings, turn over his card with your left hand. Then, instantly, point your right forefinger at him and hiss, "Assassin!" This provides a triple touch: (1) the unexpected gesture, (2) the melodramatic word

OUTLINE G
The Peculiar Pellet

Notes & Materials

[*Note. Some items in this column are device moves required by changes in the theme. I have given these capital letters to distinguish them from the materials for entertainment.*]

a. Find "murderer" instead of chosen card.

J. Get 2-C near top of deck and note its position.

K. Shuffle, keeping 2-C in position.

L. Choose "murderer." Prefer an excitable woman who may squeal when "detected."

M. Deal cards apparently at random but make sure that "murderer" gets 2-C.

b. Announce that low card is "murderer," that Ace is high, and that suits rank as in bridge.

c. Tell S's. not to show their cards to each other.

d. Tell S's. to place their cards face down in their hands and hold them under the "marble" one at a time.

e. Make "marble" sing over 2-C.

f. Flip card over with left hand.

g. Ball is also used to determine sex of unborn children, and to detect criminals.

h. Decide to demonstrate minor effect and show how "marble" can distinguish sexes. It will sing once for a man and twice for a woman.

i. Have clean handkerchief in pocket.

j. Fold handkerchief. Have someone tie blindfold.

k. Have S. hold hand under ball. Make it sing to announce sex.

l. Repeat with one or two more spectators.

m. Make ball of plastic wood.

n. Stress strange lightness of ball. Doubt if chemist could analyze.

o. Mention uncle's adventures in Gobi.

p. Hint at danger of dabbling in magic.

Continuity & Moves

[*Note. The letters and numerals used in Outline F are repeated here for easy reference. However, when you rewrite your own continuities and moves, give them new numbers and letters to eliminate decimals and gaps in numbering and to put the letters in alphabetical order.*]

0.1. [*Preparations.*] m, q, r, s.

C. Have ball in one pocket and pencil in another. i.

D. Have glass and cards on table.

E. Place thread within reach and find motivation for having it there. L, J.

1. Take small ball from pocket and toy with it until someone asks what it is.

2. Pass ball around for examination. n.

3. State that ball is device used by Mongolian witch doctors, called "shamans," as a kind of divining rod to locate lost articles.

4. Offer to show how it is used.

5. Introduce glass, thread, and pencil. o.

6. Explain that ball sings when lost object is found and that glass acts as resonator. w.

~~6.1 State that demonstration will consist in locating a chosen card.~~

7. Rig glass.

8. Explain that thread keeps sound from being damped out, as it would be if glass were held in fingers. x, t, g, y, h, p, j, u.

~~10.   Let S. choose card.~~
~~11.   Tell S. to remember it.~~
~~12.   S. shows his card to A.~~
~~13.   Have card replaced.~~
~~A.   Push card into deck. Create and hold break.~~

9. 13.1. Have person holding ball drop it into glass. k, l, z, a, aa, ab, K, M, b, c, d, e, f, v.

q. Give ball odd shape. Call it a "pellet."

r. Punch triangular hole with awl.

s. Paint "magic" design.

t. Set down glass with left hand.

u. Grope for glass with right hand.

v. Hiss, "Assassin!" not "Murderer!"

w. Pottery resonators shaped like sleigh bells.

x. Sinew from "left hind leg of yak."

y. Mongols dress so much alike that only shamans can tell men from women.

z. Consent to give more serious demonstration.

aa. Will select culprit by lot.

ab. Chief of tribe has been killed, and shaman has been called in to detect guilty party.

[9.1, *at bottom of column, comes here.*]

~~B. Shuffle, and glimpse card.~~

~~14. Spread deck face up.~~

~~16. Move glass along row of cards.~~

~~17. Make it sing when it reaches chosen card.~~

~~18. Quickly announce name of card.~~

19. Talk about shamans while dismantling apparatus.

20. Introduce new topic, possibly the effect of Communism on primitive tribesmen.

9.1. Remove blindfold.

"assassin," and (3) the hiss (which is also melodramatic). You can easily hiss "assassin," but no one can hiss "murderer." The value of this triple touch is enhanced by the fact that it comes at the climax, which is where a strong touch counts most.

Look for touches that will add conviction to your mock explanations. Thus, instead of stating that the glass acts as a resonator, you might say, "Shamans use pottery resonators shaped something like sleigh bells, but a glass works well enough for our purpose." Such details are extremely convincing. Your audience may not believe in the shamans' magic, but they will never question the sleigh-bell resonators.

The routine lends itself to a blend of comedy and drama. Treat the pellet seriously as an actual magic object, but enliven your remarks with humorous touches. For example, when you come to explain the thread say, "Actually, any sort of cord will do, but the shamans like to be mysterious and never use anything but a special sinew taken from the left hind leg of a yak." This illustrates the fact that some words are comic for no clear reason. "The left hind leg of a yak" will strike most people as funny. "The right front leg of a deer" would not.

INSERTING MATERIAL FOR ENTERTAINMENT

Although we rarely think of material for entertainment in its proper order, this raises no problem. We can handle such material as we did the device moves. List notes and material on a separate sheet, or in a separate column, and designate each item by a small (lower-case) letter. Outline G (pp. 260 and 261) illustrates the procedure. As the routine no longer employs a "marble," I now call it *The Peculiar Pellet*.

In Outline G the continuity is combined with the device moves to save space. However, it is usually better to keep them separate until you have listed your notes and materials for entertainment. I use three parallel columns, but you may prefer to write your lists on separate sheets.

If you try this procedure often enough to become familiar with it, I feel sure you will find that it has many advantages. With its aid, you can correct mistakes, change or rearrange your material, and introduce afterthoughts with a minimum of effort. By keeping the three types of material separate, you can concentrate on one without being distracted by the others. Or you can refer from one to another with ease. Furthermore, if one type of material becomes complicated, you can rewrite it on a separate sheet without having to rewrite either of the other types. When you have several possible devices in mind, you can analyze the moves for each one on a separate sheet and then try to fit them into your continuity one at a time. This test will usually reveal which is the wisest choice.

THE SCENARIO

When you have planned a routine to your satisfaction and decided where the moves and material for entertainment fit into the continuity, write out a *scenario*, which shows the whole presentation in sequence. I have printed moves and notes in italics. If you write in longhand, these items should be in red. If you use a typewriter, they can either be in red or underscored. A scenario for our example might run something like this:

THE PECULIAR PELLET

PREPARATION. Have pellet in right side pocket of coat, pencil in breast pocket, and large, clean but slightly rumpled handkerchief in right hip pocket. Have cards, glass, and thread within easy reach. Find motivation for thread. [*This will vary with circumstances.*] Decide which S. will receive low card. [*A nervous woman is a good choice as she may add to climax by jumping and squealing.*] Get two of Clubs near top of deck and remember its location.

1. Take out pellet and play with it until someone asks what it is.

2. Offer it for examination, saying, "What do you think it is ?"

3. When no one can guess, explain that it is what Mongolian shamans call a "singing stone." However, it is too light to be a real stone. "A chemist might analyze it but I wouldn't bet on that. The darn thing's too eerie."

4. Explain that shamans are witch doctors who use a pellet like this as a sort of divining rod to find lost objects.

5. Consent to show how it works.

6. Introduce glass, pencil, and thread. Explain that a resonator is required and offer to show the arrangement.

7. Rig apparatus. While doing so, tell how "Uncle Luke," the best crapshooter in World War II, won it as part of his loot while serving with the Naval Weather Station in the Gobi Desert. Shamans use pottery resonators shaped like big sleigh bells, but glass will work. Thread keeps the sound from being damped out, as it would be if glass were held in fingers. Any cord will serve, but shamans use a particular sinew from the left hind leg of a yak.

8. Give a dry run, moving glass around. Pellet is still in possession of S.

9. Set glass down with left hand.

10. Add that pellet is also used to determine sex of unborn children and to detect criminals. Mongols dress so much alike that only shamans can tell men from women.

11. Try to get request for actual demonstration. In any case, say that when Uncle Luke discovered that the pellet actually worked, he got leery and gave it to C. Display reluctance but finally agree to show how it can distinguish sexes.

12. Have C. blindfolded.

13. Grope for pencil with right hand. [*Keep eyes closed.*]

14. When pencil is found, hold glass about 3 inches above table and near enough so that bottom of glass can just be seen under blindfold.

15. Have S. drop pellet into glass.

16. Announce that pellet will sing once for man and twice for woman.

17. Have one S. place hand on table palm up under pellet.

18. Make glass sing accordingly.

19. Repeat with one or two more S's.

20. Remove blindfold.

21. Admit that reluctance to demonstrate is silly. Offer to show how criminals are detected.

22. Ask for deck of cards.

23. Shuffle [*Keeping two of Clubs in place.*] while explaining that low card will represent a murderer, someone who has killed the chief of the tribe. Shaman must discover his identity.

24. Deal apparently at random but give two of Clubs to Assassin. During this, announce that Ace is high and that suits rank as in bridge. Tell "Suspects" not to show their cards.

25. Have "Suspects" hold hands in position one at a time.

26. Make glass sing when Assassin's hand is in position.

27. Flip card (two of Clubs) over with left hand. At the same time, point right forefinger and hiss, "Assassin!"

28. Dismantle apparatus and talk about shamans.

29. Introduce new topic, possibly the effect of Communism on primitive tribesmen.

Chapter 20

WORDS

The lines spoken by a conjurer are often called his "patter." As Darrel Fitzkee has pointed out, this is unfortunate. In ordinary use, the word "patter" refers to a rapid stream of speech delivered with little regard for its relation to the topic in hand. This accurately describes a great deal of what conjurers do say, and it also describes what many conjurers believe they should say. Actually, "patter" in its strict sense is appropriate only when the conjurer takes the role of A Pitchman or An Auctioneer.

Patter for tricks is concocted rather than written. The conjurer collects all the bright lines he can find that have any relation to the trick or to each other. He then strings these together so that each one flows more or less smoothly into the next. Thus, the patter for a rope trick might begin as follows:

CONJURER. [*Displays rope.*] They say that if you give a magician enough rope—he'll do a trick. As a matter of fact, this piece wasn't given to me. It's a family heirloom. My granddaddy was a horse thief. I've had this ever since the funeral. Granddaddy would have been seven feet tall if so much of him hadn't been turned up at the bottom. As it was, his feet were so big that he had to pull his pants on over his head. I didn't really learn the ropes myself until I joined the Navy. One day the Captain told me to. . . .

This sort of thing may be adequate for tricks, but it will not do for illusions.

THE PLAYWRIGHT'S APPROACH

You cannot be convincing unless you treat your theme as if it were genuine. To do this, you must talk in character. Typical conjurer's patter is not in character except in cases like *The*

Haunted Conjurer. Even there, you must break down occasionally and speak from your heart when things "go wrong." This means that, in virtually every case, your remarks must sound extemporaneous.

Every word of dialogue in a successful play is in character, and the playwright must keep a dozen or more characters straight while he works. You will find it easy to write lines for yourself and perhaps one or two assistants, if you learn the playwright's method.

Begin with your theme. Write it out to be sure that your ideas are clear. If you are going to do a cut-and-restored rope routine to prove that magic can be useful, your theme might read: "Magician has put his craft to commercial use by inventing a machine which magically unites the pieces of a cut rope. He demonstrates the practicality of his device by letting two spectators operate it to restore a rope that has undoubtedly been cut."

Decide on your treatment. Our example is obviously fantasy intended for a large audience. The treatment should therefore be amusing. Why not pretend that the demonstration is a commercial performed in the hope of selling stock in the invention. The machines could be sold to the Navy for restoring used rope.

With these ideas in mind, your treatment might run as follows: "Treat the demonstration as a genuine attempt to sell stock, but enliven it with humorous remarks and the obvious showmanship of a high-pressure salesman."

Work out your characterization as far as possible without knowing the details of the routine. Our example clearly calls for a light-hearted, talkative type who would be successful selling used cars or vacuum cleaners, but who would be definitely above a street-corner pitchman or the barker for a medicine show. You need not sustain the characterization at this level throughout your whole act but can use it to provide a change of pace. For the rest, you can be A Magician who is sufficiently at home with magic to use its lighter aspects as a source of amusement.

You are now ready to decide on your devices if you have not already done so. In this case, the devices must meet the following rigid specifications: (1) After the cut is made, the pieces must be separated to demonstrate beyond question that the rope was actually cut in half. (2) A "machine" must be used.

(3) The restoration must take place in the hands of Inspectors who are not confederates.

Figs. 148 and 149 explain how the rope is actually cut and restored. However, we must still get rid of the knot. For this purpose, we can introduce a "machine" based on an idea from the fertile brain of U. F. Grant (Fig. 150).

We are now ready to prepare a three-column work sheet showing the device moves, the continuity, and any notes and materials for entertainment that we happen to have. As this procedure has already been explained in the previous chapter, I omit it here.

After the moves and notes have been fitted into their places in the continuity, we write out the scenario. This is shown in the first column of Outline H.

CREATING THE SCRIPT

When you have gained experience as a conjurer-playwright, you can write dialogue directly from the scenario. But, in the beginning, another method is easier and will produce better results. Act out your routine step by step. Make up your remarks as you go along. Speak them aloud to be sure that they sound natural and that they flow smoothly off your tongue. *Do this in character.* You cannot invent lines for A Light-hearted Magician while you think of yourself as a conjurer-playwright.

As your apparatus is not likely to be ready at this stage, provide substitutes. Thus, a pickle jar may serve as a stand-in for the pipe nipple. Have a table handy on which you can set the things that are supposed to be held by volunteers or assistants.

On your first attempt, you will probably stumble a good deal. Some things will go wrong, and you may get new ideas that you must think over. Do not let this trouble you. At least half the rough spots will smooth themselves out during the second round without conscious effort on your part.

Go over your routine repeatedly in this way. Whenever you hit on a particularly effective phrase or bit of business that is not in your scenario, jot it down either in a separate column, as I have done in Outline H or on a separate sheet of paper. As you may want to note devices and touches in the same column, and as these require large and small reference letters respectively, notes for lines should be supplied with reference numerals using either Roman numerals or Arabic numerals in parentheses; e.g., I, II, III or (1), (2), (3).

Make notes of all your ideas for lines even if you cannot find a place for them immediately. Sometimes a line that will not fit as it stands may suggest a better one. Thus, although "Give a man enough rope" did not satisfy me, it suggested "We give the Navy a lot of rope," which I like, and which fits neatly into my routine.

OUTLINE H

The Rope Mender

Scenario	*Ideas for Lines*
0. [*Preparations.*] Prepare rope and hide it behind prop.	I. Use of device by Navy will save taxpayers millions.
0.1. Have thread gimmick in sleeve.	II. Give a man enough rope.
0.2. Place rope mender in full view on table.	III. Need a sailor—or a hangman.
1. M. [*Magician.*] has invented rope mender to commercialize on his magic. XII, XI, I, VII.	IV. "Why should Navy have all the fun?"
2. M. introduces rope. XIII.	V. "Could you do better with a needle?"
3. Will demonstrate.	VI. "Help me balance the budget."
4. Invites 1st I. [*Inspector.*] to help. IV, VIII.	VII. Why saw woman in half if you want her to-gether?
5. Greets 1st I. and asks name.	VIII. Even the tax collectors pay taxes.
6. Introduces scissors and gives them to 1st I.	IX. Hole goes in this side and comes out that side.
7. Tells 1st I. to cut rope. XIV.	X. Patent not yet applied for.
8. He cuts.	XI. We give the Navy a lot of rope.
9. M. holds ropes at arm's length to show that cut was genuine.	XII. Friends criticized magic as useless.
10. M. ties knot. A. M. breaks bastings, catches hook in ring, and gets hold of thread.	XIII. Taxpayers are the cornerstone of our political economy.
11. M. draws both ropes through hand "to see if they are the same length." [*Note motivation for move that is actually unjustified.*] B. M. returns to table and cuts off thread.	XIV. Take a big slice out of the budget.
12. M. introduces rope mender. III, XV.	XV. Oil-well rigger.
13. M. invites 2nd I. to help. VI.	XVI. It starts hard these cold mornings.
14. M. greets 2nd I.	XVII. Get in on the ground floor.
15. M. gives rope mender to 2nd I.	XVIII. Look forward to a nice tax cut next year.
16. M. tells 2nd I. to open it and look inside.	XIX. M. gives free end of rope to 2nd I. and tells *both* I's to keep rope as souvenir.
17. 2nd I. does so. Sees nothing.	
18. M. looks. Says magic machinery is invisible.	

19. M. tells 1st I. to thread rope out through holes.
20. He does so. V.
21. M. tells 2nd I. to replace cap.
22. He does so, X.
23. M. tells 1st I. to pull rope free. XVI.
24. He does so. XVI.
25. M. tells 1st I. to display rope.
26. He does so.
27. M. tells 1st I. to keep rope as souvenir, XIX.
28. M. dismisses I's. XVIII.
29. While they are returning to their seats, M. offers to sell stock. XVII.

No line, however clever, is good unless it sounds spontaneous. Even a line that comes to you naturally while you rehearse may seem forced if you make any change in the business at that point. Discarding an exceptionally funny witticism requires will power, but be firm with yourself. A single out-of-character phrase can kill conviction and spoil the whole illusion.

If you are used to patter concocted by stringing one gag after another, my ideas for lines in Outline H may strike you as weak. However, the comedy comes from the character and the situation. The words merely point it up. Experienced playwrights almost never use lines which are funny in themselves. Many of their lines are brilliant, but they get laughs only because of the situation in which they are spoken and the character of the person who speaks them. The actor's technique is equally important. A momentary pause or the inflection of a single syllable can make all the difference between a line which falls flat and one which is greeted with a roar of laughter. These considerations are so basic that even the most riotous farce may not contain a single line which can be used separately as a joke. This is due to the fact that a joke is normally out of character, or a digression, or both. Either fault will destroy the conviction which is essential to both plays and illusions.

If you work out your lines in rehearsal, you are not likely to invent out-of-character lines or to have trouble fitting lines into place. Furthermore, you are more apt to create comedy which arises from situation, character, and business. Here is my complete script for:

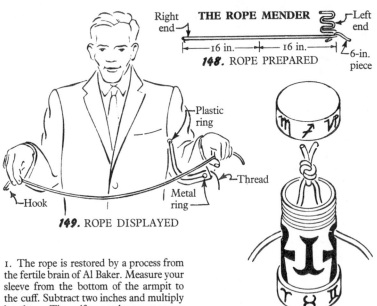

|← 16 in. →|← 16 in. →|
6-in. piece

148. ROPE PREPARED

Plastic ring

Thread

Metal ring

Hook

149. ROPE DISPLAYED

150. ROPE MENDER

1. The rope is restored by a process from the fertile brain of Al Baker. Measure your sleeve from the bottom of the armpit to the cuff. Subtract two inches and multiply by three. Thus, if your sleeve measures 18 in., the rope should be $(18 - 2) \times 3 = 48$ in. This is the proper length for the rope. Shorten the length one-third by folding one end of the rope as shown in Fig. 148. Then, loop a 6-in. piece of rope through the fold and baste it in place with short lengths of white thread. Crush the rest of the rope into a compact bundle and hide it behind something on your table.

2. Sew a plastic ring inside your left sleeve at the bottom of the armpit. Tie a small metal ring to one end of a strong mouse-colored thread. Run this thread through the plastic ring, and let both ends hang down your sleeve. They must hang low enough for you to grip them with your hand.

3. Pick up the rope so that your left hand covers the folded end, and one end of the 6-in. piece sticks out of your hand at the side opposite your thumb. Hold the bunched-up part of the rope in your right hand. When you mention rope, let this part drop. You seem to be holding a 3-foot length of unprepared rope. Take the lower end in your right hand and hold the rope horizontally (Fig. 149).

4. Have An Inspector make his cut nearly in the "middle" (actually about 16 inches from the hook). Hold the ends at arm's length to leave no doubt that the rope was actually cut.

5. Bring the hook to your left wrist and slip it into the ring on the thread that runs up your sleeve. Cover the move by tying a knot in the 6-in. piece. Break the bastings while doing this. Hold the knot with your right hand and take the loose end of the thread in the same hand. Pull on the rope and the thread at the same time. The short end will be drawn up your sleeve and the folds will be drawn out. You appear to be pulling both halves of the rope through your hand to compare their lengths. When the short piece has disappeared up your sleeve, the thread will hang down. Cut this on a razor blade attached to some piece of apparatus.

6. To make the rope-mender, you must secure a 4-in. nipple of 2-in. pipe from a hardware store and get a cap for each end. Bore a $\frac{3}{8}$-in. hole through both sides near one end and paint the prop with a mysterious pattern (Fig. 150). Have A Second Inspector unscrew one cap, thread the ends of the rope out through the holes, and replace the cap. This Inspector then holds the rope-mender while The First Inspector pulls the rope free. The knot remains in the prop, and the rope comes out in one piece.

THE ROPE MENDER

MAGICIAN. [*Comes forward holding rope.*] Some of my friends have criticized magic as useless. They ask what good it does to saw a woman in half and then glue her back together again. If you want her together, why saw her in half in the first place? I thought the matter over and had to admit that they had a point. So I began wondering how I could commercialize on my magic. I finally came up with an invention that's going to save the taxpayers millions of dollars. We give the Navy a lot of rope. [*Display rope.*] But after it gets all cut up into little pieces, what good is it? I decided to invent a magic rope mender which would put all the cut rope back together again, and take some of the strain off the taxpayer's pocket. [*Step to footlights.*] As I am doing this for the taxpayers, and as they are the cornerstone of our political economy, I think they should have a representative during this demonstration. [*Indicate George, a spectator.*] Are you a taxpayer, sir?

GEORGE. Unfortunately.

MAGICIAN. Who isn't? [*To Audience.*] It's getting so these days that even the tax collectors pay taxes. [*To George.*] Will you be kind enough to step up onto the stage and cut the rope? Why should the Navy have all the fun? Thank you, sir. May I have your name?

GEORGE. George.

MAGICIAN. [*Shaking hands.*] Glad to meet you, George. [*Takes scissors from pocket and hands them to George.*] Now, George, you're about to take a big slice out of the budget. Let's cut it right in half. [*Magician holds up rope and George cuts.*] Don't you wish Congress had courage enough to do that? Now let's tie them together. [*He does so and draws both ropes through his left hand.*] Have to make sure they're about the same length. My invention isn't perfected yet, and it won't work if one piece is much longer than. . . . Yes, they're nearly equal. [*Gives them to George.*] I hereby appoint you Official Custodian. [*Holds out hand.*] Could I have my scissors back, please. [*Takes them, returns to table and places scissors on it. Cuts thread.*] And now, my friends, be prepared for the wonder of the age. [*Picks up rope mender. To Audience.*] This is it. This is the amazing little device that's going to keep some of the tax money right in your pockets, where it belongs. I am afraid that if I demonstrate my rope mender, you'll think I work the magic myself, and that the rope mender is just a piece of pipe with a hole through it. So I'll tell you what I'm going to do. I'm going to have a sailor come up here and mend this rope without my touching it. Is there a sailor in the house? [*Pauses for reply.*] If there aren't any sailors, I could use a hangman, [*Pauses hopefully.*] or a cowboy, or an oil-well rigger. [*Becoming discouraged.*] I could even use another taxpayer in a pinch. [*To Joe, another spectator.*] You look like a taxpayer to me, sir. Am I right?

JOE. Ain't we all?

MAGICIAN. Wouldn't you like to help me balance the budget?

JOE. Okay. [*Starts to come up on stage.*]

MAGICIAN. And what is your name, sir?

JOE. Joe McInnis.

MAGICIAN. [*Shaking hands.*] Thanks for helping. [*Hands Joe the rope mender.*] Unscrew the top, Joe, and look at the machinery. [*Joe takes off one cap of rope mender and peers in.*]

JOE. There's nothing in this.

MAGICIAN. What's that? Oh, yes, there is. Let me look. [*Peers into rope mender.*] It's there all right. Only it's magic machinery. I told you that in the first place. How can you expect to see magic machinery? Now, Joe, you hold the rope mender, [*To George.*] and George, you thread the ends of the rope through these holes—one end through each hole. That's right. [*To Joe.*] Put the cap on, Joe, and screw it tight. I haven't applied for my patent yet, and I can't afford to let anyone see all that invisible machinery in operation. That's the stuff. Now grab the rope mender with both hands. [*To George.*] George, you pull the rope. Give it a good jerk. It starts hard these cold mornings. [*George draws rope free. It is all one piece.*] Thanks, gentlemen, you put on a magnificent demonstration. You can both look forward to a nice tax cut next year. [*He takes the free end of the rope in his right hand and hands it to Joe while he relieves Joe of the rope mender with his left. This leaves both Inspectors holding ends of the rope.*] Keep that as a souvenir of this memorable occasion. [*As they cannot both keep it, this should produce comedy. When they start for their seats, Magician steps to footlights and addresses Audience.*] If any member of the audience would like to get in on the ground floor of a million-dollar invention, there is still a little common stock available at a hundred dollars a share. [*Takes stock certificates from pocket and fans them.*]

If you go over the above presentation carefully, you will see that—except for the comic approach and the allusions to magic—it is exactly what a salesman might do and say while demonstrating a model of a real rope mender in order to sell stock in the company. This is much more impressive than announcing, "Ladies and gentlemen, with your kind permission, I would like to show you my improved version of the cut-and-restored-rope trick."

MEMORIZATION VS. EXTEMPORIZATION

Many expert conjurers recommend memorizing lines. This has important advantages. You use the best phrase that you have found for each spot. You can polish your timing so that words and actions match exactly. Best of all, your memory supplies your remarks and frees you to concentrate on holding the interest of your audience.

However, you must pay for these assets. Memorization will probably decrease your illusion of spontaneity and can destroy it completely. Also, if anything goes wrong, the man who depends on memory may fail entirely. The conjurer who extemporizes is less polished, but he is always spontaneous. He may be embarrassed when something goes wrong, but his embarrassment is not aggravated by the fact that he has nothing to say.

If you compose your lines while rehearsing in character, you can have the best of both methods. You will memorize the sequence of steps and the gist of your remarks at each step. You will also memorize lines which depend for their effect on the exact wording or which affect the timing of important business. Other remarks will be flexible. You will change the wording slightly at each performance.

This is the technique of the expert who tells jokes. He remembers the continuity, a few key phrases, and the point. The rest he rewords each time. When you apply the same method to conjuring, you retain your spontaneity. You vary your remarks to fit each audience, and your memory does not let you down when some accident occurs.

The technique works equally well for "impromptus." The spectators do more of the talking, and their remarks cannot always be foreseen. Nevertheless, working your own lines out in advance makes you familiar with the things you have to say. You will usually have to improvise a little, but you rarely need to do much of it.

Learn all you can about the backgrounds of your illusions. Investigate water-finding for *Dowsing Test* and statistical procedures for *The Monte Carlo Method*. In cases like *Arithmagic*, where no real background exists, make up your own. You will then be prepared to talk glibly about "The Science of Number."

When you are not armed with facts, real or imaginary, confess ignorance frankly. If you improvise "information" about Professor Rhine's experiments while presenting *Will Power*, some spectator may make you look foolish by exposing your mistakes. But if you admit that you are ignorant, you can still propose an experiment—and that is all you really need.

Words and the Audience

It is not enough to conceive your lines in character. You must also consider how they will affect the audience. Train yourself for this by noting how you react to remarks made by other conjurers.

When a performer puts a coin in one hand and closes both fists, he often asks, "Which hand is it in?" This challenges the audience to solve a puzzle and creates the very frame of mind that you should be most anxious to avoid. A still more serious objection is that any question of this type forces the spectator to give an answer which he knows will make him appear either naive or foolish. Nothing is gained by embarrassing a member of the audience in this way. It is so easy to say, "Now some of you may think the coin remains in my right hand, and some may think it has traveled to my left. Actually, ..."

Thoughtless conjurers deliberately poke fun at volunteers to make them seem ridiculous. How does that impress you when you are part of the audience? Most spectators sympathize with one of their own number rather than with the performer. They may titter at the victim's discomfiture because they are a little embarrassed themselves. However, they rarely laugh aloud unless they feel sure that the victim is taking it good-naturedly. But think of the guffaw if the victim suddenly turned the tables and made a fool of the conjurer!

The usual rule about vulgarity is: *When in doubt, don't.* This is good, but I suggest a more detailed test. Does it grow naturally out of the theme? If not, it has no place in your act whether it is clean or dirty. If it does grow out of the theme, is it funny enough to raise a real laugh? When the most you can hope for is a giggle, the joke is not worth the risk of offending even one narrow-minded spectator. If it grows out of the theme and is really funny, how many people is it likely to offend? Can you be sure that you will not use it by force of habit when working before a more sensitive audience? Can you find a clean gag which would be equally funny and certain not to offend anyone? If you apply all of these tests to every questionable gag you use, and turn down all that fail to pass, you will not go far wrong.

SPEECH

The impression that you make on an audience depends almost as much on your voice as it does on your words. A trained speaker can make a poor line sound like profound wisdom.

Every sentence should be worded clearly, and each word should be spoken distinctly. Performers in all fields often assume that casual remarks which are not essential to understanding can be missed by the audience without real loss. This might be true if the performer displayed a placard which read, "My next statement does not really matter." Without some such warning, the spectator believes that the line is important. He asks his neighbor what was said. This makes them both lose the next few lines, which may contain some key point in the routine.

Each word should carry to the furthest spectator. The use of a microphone is a confession of incompetence. If well-coached high-school students can make themselves heard in the senior play, you can do the same thing. A microphone restricts your movements so drastically that you should do everything in your power to free yourself from the necessity of using one.

Your voice must fit your characterization. If you talk like a New England schoolmaster, you cannot hope to succeed as a loud-mouthed Pitchman. If you have a Brooklyn accent, do not wear tails and bill yourself as "Society's Favorite Sorcerer."

A monotonous voice is a major liability. Nothing holds attention like vocal variety. Almost any variety is better than none. This is the great secret of political orators and popular preachers. They rarely have much to say, but their vocal gymnastics hold the ear and hypnotize the mind.

Unfortunately, there is not much that you can do about speech yourself. Most speech faults call for exercises which, if overdone, will lead to the opposite fault. Thus, an attempt to make your voice carry may cause strain which results in a harsh tone. A good teacher can correct this, but the field is full of quacks who will do you more harm than good. If you can find someone who has really benefitted his pupils, by all means seek his aid. However, do not select one without convincing proof of his ability.

The following exercises are safe. I have used them extensively myself and with my actors and students. Practice each one for three or four minutes every day. This need not take any working time; I do my exercises while driving my car.

What counts is not the sound that you make in your throat but that which comes out of your lips. You can improve both the clarity and the carrying power of your voice by opening your mouth as much as possible when you pronounce each vowel. Start with the "i" in "his." Sing it on a continuing note and open your mouth wider and wider until the vowel changes its character and ceases to be a clearly recognizable "short i." You will find that your mouth is much more open than it usually is when you pronounce this vowel. Do the same thing with the vowels in "the," "bird," "an," "of," "odd," "fraud," "old," "you," "could," "tale," and "tell." Each of these permits you to open your mouth wider than the "short i" does, but only the vowel in "odd" lets you open it to its fullest extent.

After you learn your limits for the individual vowels, practice with this sentence. "The old fraud could tell you an odd tale of his bird." Open your lips as far as possible for each vowel, but be sure that you pronounce it clearly.

This exercise will develop the habit of opening the mouth. While you practice, you will feel that you are making faces but that is because you are carrying the movements to extremes. In your act, and in daily life, you will subconsciously modify this to a point where no one will feel that you are grimacing while you talk. None of my actors or students ever had any trouble in this regard.

Clarity depends to a surprising extent on three consonants: "p," "t," and "k." Forming the habit of pronouncing each one with a sharp click will do wonders toward helping your audiences understand what you say. Steele's exercise is invaluable here.

p - - -, p - - -, p - - -, p - - -;
p p - -, p p - -, p p - -, p - - -;
p p p -, p p p -, p p p -, p - - -;
p p p p, p p p p, p p p p, p - - -.

Pronounce the sound crisply as "p" not "pee" or "puh." Count mentally for each dash—"p, two, three, four, p, two, three, four. . . ." Use the same exercise for "t" and "k."

Exercises for variety are more elaborate, but they are also more interesting. My actors and students usually show improvement before the end of the first week, even though they rarely practice more than five minutes a day. Memorize some speech which takes about a minute. Anything will do, but Shakespeare is especially good. I can recommend The King's speech in Act III, Scene 2, of *Richard II* which begins, "Let's talk of graves, of worms, and epitaphs." Recite your speech, varying the volume as much as possible. Shout some passages and whisper others. Do not worry about making sense. After you have repeated the speech a dozen times in this way, you will find that you subconsciously distribute your soft, medium, and loud tones just where the meaning requires.

Next, forget volume and recite the speech for variety of pitch. Use your deepest base notes in some spots and occasionally rise to a shrill falsetto. When you can do this adequately, try varying your tempo; race through one passage and plod through another.

After you acquire some skill with volume, pitch, and tempo, use the memorized passage to vary the quality of your voice. Speak one passage in a mellow tone, be harsh for the next, and whine for a third. Snarl, rant, and coo. Try to invent vocal tones that you never used before.

Finally, vary your smoothness. Let one word flow into the next here; separate them sharply there. Introduce abrupt changes in volume, pitch, tempo, and quality. Also, experiment with gradual changes.

These exercises will be fun if you use all your ingenuity to find new ways to introduce variety. But even if you practice them mechanically, they cannot help making your voice more interesting and giving you greater control over the attention of your audiences.

You may seem to be overdoing variety while you practice, but you need not fear that this will carry over to your speech on stage or in daily life. Several hundred of my actors and students have used this exercise, but none of them ever developed even half the variety that they could have used with profit.

Exercises can help you form good speech habits. Do not let them cause you to think about your voice while you are performing. Never practice in public.

Chapter 21

BUSINESS

Each routine demands business, and some of this is obvious. Thus, if you plan to discover a card, you must first have it chosen. Misdirection may call for one or two other bits of business. These types are essential, but the showman goes much further. He adds touches to make necessary business expressive, and he invents additional business to provide atmosphere, characterization, clarity, comedy, and drama.

PANTOMIME

When we speak of doing something "in pantomime" we usually mean that we do it in pantomime alone. However, pantomime is not necessarily silent. It may accompany speech. In fact, you should try to supplement your words with actions that express the same ideas, phrase by phrase.

There are several reasons for this. When the pantomime does not duplicate the meaning of the words, you are saying two different things at the same time. If your audience tries to follow both, it will become confused. But when you say exactly the same thing in two different ways at once, each supports and reinforces the other. The combination makes a much stronger impression then either could make by itself.

Some people are eye-minded; they understand what they see better than what they hear. They are also more likely to believe what they see. Others are ear-minded; they may be unable to follow your actions unless these are described in words.

Again, your words may not be entirely clear, or they may be missed because of some noise. If the spectators understand your pantomime, they can follow the continuity in spite of missing a sentence or two. On the other hand, a spectator who momentarily turns his head away for some reason, or who happens to look at the wrong part of the stage through your failure to control his attention, can, nevertheless, keep in touch with the routine because he hears what you say.

There are, however, two exceptions to the rule that pantomime should duplicate speech. Material like the introduction to *The Rope Mender* cannot be expressed effectively by pantomime. You would only make yourself ridiculous if you copied the nineteenth-century elocutionists and cupped a hand behind an ear when you said, "Listen!" or shaded your eyes when you said, "I see." Modified versions of such pantomime have occasional uses, but they must be employed with discretion.

The other exception occurs when the business is purely routine, such as rigging the glass in *The Peculiar Pellet*. Describing each step in words would be boring. Instead, you should take advantage of this dull business to work in explanations which do not lend themselves to pantomime. In *The Peculiar Pellet*, for example, you can relieve the tedium of rigging the glass by telling about your uncle and the Gobi weather station. Even in these cases, try to make words and business work together as much as possible. Thus, in *The Peculiar Pellet*, mention resonators while handling the glass and talk about yak sinews while you tie the thread.

In ideal pantomime, each movement should express the exact idea that you want to convey, no more and no less. Train yourself to make your actions significant by going through exercises without props. For example, try spreading imaginary jelly on imaginary bread and then eating the bread. Imagine the knife, the jelly jar, the bread plate, and the table on which they rest. Practice with these until you can handle them without letting the knife miss the jelly jar or shoving the bread through your cheek.

After you are adept at that, invent expressive touches. Let the jelly run off the bread onto your fingers and lick them, wipe up a spot of jelly that has dripped onto the table, and so on.

When you can do these and a few similar exercises that you invent for yourself, go through one of your routines without the props. Then try the same thing without using either props or words. Get a friend to watch you. He should be able to follow each step of the routine with no explanation from you. This last exercise is extremely difficult. Complete success is not always possible. Nevertheless, it is a goal toward which you should always strive in every presentation.

BUSINESS AND APPARATUS

Each piece of apparatus should be clearly visible to the most distant spectator under the light in which it is shown. This includes not only the apparatus itself but also every important feature of it. For example, if the spots on the dice used in *The Haunted Conjurer* cannot be seen from the back row, the illusion is a poor choice for that auditorium.

However, the visibility of a prop depends largely on the way it is handled. There are many ways to go wrong. Some men produce a small prop, such as a billiard ball and then hide it with their fingers (Fig. 151). Others stand on the same floor with a seated audience and work at waist level, so that only the spectators in the first row can see what is happening. I have watched a performer keep his face under a spotlight while he did card manipulations in the surrounding darkness. I have even seen a man saw a woman in half while he was hidden behind a table piled shoulder high with bulky apparatus!

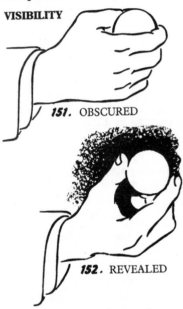

VISIBILITY

151. OBSCURED

152. REVEALED

When handling a small prop, show as much of it as possible and display it against a contrasting background.

This sort of thing is a dead bore. Make sure that your small props are clearly visible and contrast with the background (Fig. 152)—and remember that your audience sees things from a different angle than you do and hence against a different background than yours. Display objects in the best light available. Hold them high, preferably at shoulder level. Keep them still long enough for everyone to get a good look.

As you introduce each prop, identify it by name. No matter how commonplace it is, never assume that the spectators can recognize it. Some of them may be nearsighted. Try to work the name in unobtrusively. Thus, you might say, "With this egg, I shall demonstrate . . ." or "Have you ever stopped to wonder how an egg gets inside its shell?" If you cannot find a smooth description, it is better to state flatly, "This is an egg" than to let some inattentive spectator mistake it for a golf ball.

When a prop, or some detail is too small to be seen clearly, you may find business that will convey the essential information through the reaction of a volunteer. I recently watched a stage performer rub "magic" ashes on the palm of his hand and announce that he would blow them onto the hand of a woman volunteer. When he blew, she looked at her palm. Her start of surprise announced his success as plainly as though the whole audience had seen the spot of ash. Note that the woman's reaction was involuntary. This is an entirely different thing from merely showing someone a card and having him acknowledge it as his.

Skillful pantomime on the part of the performer can convey a good deal of information about details that are too small to be seen clearly or even about matters which are completely invisible. When you handle an egg, your pantomime should make your audience clearly aware of its weight, its texture, its fragility, and the nasty mess that it will make if dropped. An expert can make a wooden egg seem much more egg-like than a real egg would appear in the hands of a less adept performer.

In fact, the expert can go even further. He can convince the spectators that a small prop exists although it is actually imaginary. Slydini does an eye-popping vanish by first persuading his audience that his empty hand holds a coin and then opening the hand to show that it is empty. This sort of skill can save you from embarrassment if you discover at an awkward moment that you have mislaid some small but essential prop.

Pantomime is not limited to the hands; it includes the face and body as well. It also includes your mind. In fact, what you do with your mind is even more important than what you do with your hands. Conjurers frequently pour milk out of transparent glass pitchers. Unfortunately, few of them think of it as milk. Instead, they regard it as merely a white fluid suitable for use in a conjuring trick. When you use milk, or anything else, think about it. What is it like? What is it good for? How do you feel about it? How will the audience feel about it?

Think up things to say about the milk even if they do not suit your act. "Personally, I never touch the stuff." "They say it's good for babies, but when I offered my baby a glass, she told the waiter she wanted champagne." Make yourself as milk-conscious as you can. Then, while you are pouring milk, remember that it is milk you are pouring.

An expert pantomimist can create many routines which are highly entertaining, but which would fall flat if he depended on words alone. Although the example which follows contains only one minor routine, it illustrates how pantomime can supply atmosphere, comedy, and an all-purpose mock explanation that can turn a whole series of "impromptu" tricks into illusions.

THE GENIAL JINNI

Introduce a small bottle of unusual appearance. Explain that it contains a captive jinni whom you have bent to your will and imprisoned by the irresistible power of Solomon's Seal. This jinni will perform marvels at your behest. Actually, he is entirely imaginary and is created by your words and pantomime. That is not easy, but it can be done and is extremely effective. Here are a few hints:

Give your jinni a name. Any Arabic name, such as Agib (Ah-zheeb), Baba, or Djmal (Jem-all) will do. Create his character. Make him clever or stupid, servile or rebellious, but keep him consistent. Know him so well that you can foresee how he will act under any circumstances. Imagine his appearance. The easiest way to do this is to study a picture of a jinni in an illustrated copy of *The Arabian Nights*. If a spectator asks, "How wide is his sash?" or "What color is his beard?" you should be able to answer without thinking. You cannot make your jinni convincing until you can see him in your imagination—and you cannot see him if some important detail, such as his turban or his slippers, is missing.

Take pains with the bottle. A miniature brass one marked with Arabic inscriptions is ideal, but a glass bottle of some strange shape will do. A glass bottle should be rubbed with emery cloth to make it look old and worn. Then copy an Arabic symbol on it with paint. If your bottle has a brass or glass stopper, seal it in place with wax. When you must use a cork stopper, cover the whole top with wax and impress this with some sort of seal.

Take the bottle from your pocket and break the seal. Watch the jinni emerge and speak to him as he does so. Treat him exactly as though he were real, and remember that jinn are giants. Even a small one has to stoop under an ordinary ceiling. Work up your routine as carefully as you would a ventriloquist act. When the jinni speaks, listen. Know what he is saying. Give him time to say it and let your facial expressions indicate his remarks, word by word. This is what a good actor does when he talks on the telephone. No one is on the other end of the line, but the actor knows what his imaginary caller says—and he uses timing and facial expressions to convey this information to his audience.

Discuss your jinni's powers in a matter-of-fact way as though you were completely accustomed to them. If, for example, you reverse a card in the deck, you might say, "Agib claims that he can pass solid through solid, but I think that's a lie. I believe he just makes the card invisible, turns it over and slides it back in the deck face up—like this!"

A tame jinni is especially handy when something goes wrong. Suppose, for example, that you have lost control of a chosen card and do not know either its location or its name. Place the deck confidently on the table and tell someone to "Look at the top card." If it happens to be right, take credit for a miracle. If you are told that it is wrong, glance around you, saying sternly, "Agib, A-gib!" Turn to the audience and say, "He likes to play tricks. Sometimes he steals a card right out of the deck."

Look at the person who chose the card and ask, "What was it?" When you are told, run through the deck as described for *Psychosomatics*, but hold the cards up so that the audience cannot see their faces. Break the deck after the named card. Square this packet and place it on the table face up. Run through the rest of the deck to the end and place it on the first packet. Turn the deck over. The named card is now on top of the deck. While doing this, say, "I thought so, it isn't here. Agib has it." Look at him sternly and say, "All right, this is your last chance. Return that card before I count three, or it's back in the bottle for you—and no rice for a week!"

Ask the nearest spectator to turn over the top card. Before he can do so, look up at the invisible Agib and say, "And if it isn't the right one this time, old boy, you'll be sorry." Your words and actions will draw every eye upward for a moment, and this lets the audience accept the idea that Agib has had a chance to return the card unseen.

When the card is revealed, ask, "Is that correct?" As soon as you are told that it is, look up and say, "All right, Agib, I forgive you this time. But I'm getting tired of your foolishness and I don't want this sort of thing to happen again."

You have done three things here. You have discovered the chosen card, you have made it vanish, and you have made it reappear. Whether or not you can convince the spectators with these effects will depend upon how thoroughly you have led them to accept Agib as a fairy being from a fantastic world.

Do not present your jinni to your brother conjurers. He will bore them to death. Laymen, however, would rather watch a weak trick turned into an illusion by a convincing jinni than an amazing but pointless trick with no jinni.

Symbolic Pantomime

So far, we have been discussing *realistic pantomime*. It may deal with imaginary or fantastic objects, but the actions are performed as though these objects were real. *Symbolic pantomime* is quite different. It is used to describe an object or explain an

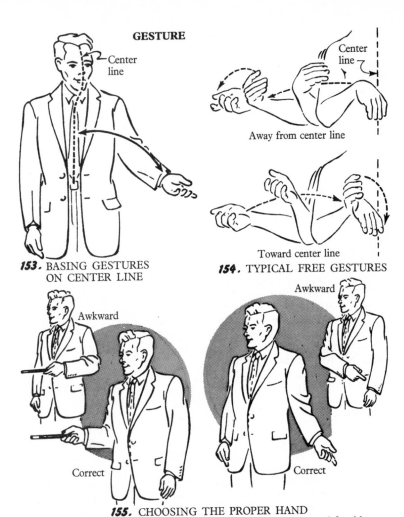

GESTURE

Center line

Away from center line

Toward center line

153. BASING GESTURES ON CENTER LINE

154. TYPICAL FREE GESTURES

Awkward

Awkward

Correct

Correct

155. CHOOSING THE PROPER HAND

Gestures which cross the center line, as seen by the audience, tend to be awkward and hard to understand. Avoid these faults by gesturing toward your left with your left hand and toward your right with your right hand.

idea. When a GI in Germany or Japan pats his stomach and then pretends to eat, he is employing symbolic pantomime to say, "I am hungry." The "expressive gestures" of the old elocutionists were symbolic pantomime. However, they overdid it to the point where they made themselves ridiculous.

Conjurers can use symbolic pantomime to enliven and clarify speech. It is especially valuable when giving directions or recapitulating a series of event. In these cases, you do not imitate real actions exactly. Instead, you exaggerate your

284

movements to make them more vivid, and you leave out unimportant details to save time. In *Dowsing Test*, for example, you should illustrate the use of both the forked-stick and the coathanger types of divining rod by going through the appropriate motions without props while you talk. Later in the routine, when your first subject is about to test his dowsing ability, you will need to recapitulate your explanation of the procedure to make sure that it has been understood. The glasses, napkin, and miniature divining rods are available. However, a verbal résumé accompanied by symbolic pantomime without the props will usually be both quicker and clearer than an actual demonstration. It also avoids any danger of fumbling and thus assures that the presentation will flow smoothly at this point.

Note that although realistic pantomime is worthless unless it is convincing, symbolic pantomime is frankly artificial.

Symbolic pantomime is used chiefly to explain and emphasize your remarks. It can be employed instead of words, but it is a poor substitute. If you do a silent routine, try to make your realistic pantomime so clear that your actions explain themselves. You may occasionally need to convey information by a bit of symbolic pantomime, but keep this to a minimum.

Gesture

The ability to gesture freely is almost a necessity for the stage performer and a great asset to the close-up worker. Fortunately, it is easy to acquire by means of a simple exercise.

Before you try this, however, let me remind you that the rule—*Never practice in public*—applies here with especial force. Practice gesture exercises in private until the correct action becomes habitual. Then depend on the habit to take care of you in public. If you think about what you are doing and try to avoid mistakes, you cannot avoid self-consciousness. That, in turn, is sure to make you stiff and awkward.

You cannot expect to avoid all mistakes in your early performances. Do not attempt to correct them while before your audience. Merely make a mental note that you need more practice on that point. Thinking about an acting technique in public never pays. If you find yourself unable to avoid such thoughts, abandon the exercise. Its sole purpose is to form attractive habits. When you must think about something, it is not a habit.

Gestures are of two types, *free* and *controlled*. Free gestures are basic. Virtually all of them move either away from or toward an imaginary *center line* which runs from your forehead to your belt buckle (Fig. 153). Note that this twists when you turn your head.

To make a free gesture, think of your wrist as a weight. Toss it in the desired direction and let your hand and arm follow behind. When the wrist stops, the hand flips over in an extremely graceful fashion (Fig. 154). There should be no sign of strain or stiffness in your hand, elbow, or shoulder. If your elbow sticks out, the gesture is not free. Ballet dancers gesture with their elbows, but this is not desirable in the other performing arts.

An outward gesture need not begin at the center line. In fact, most of them start five or six inches from it. The point is that they should move in a direction away from the center line and not away from, say, a shoulder or a hip. This rule applies only to the beginning of the action; as all free gestures curve, none of them can continue to move away from the center

PASSING A PROP ACROSS YOUR BODY

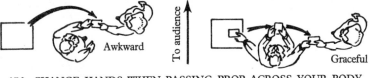

156. CHANGE HANDS WHEN PASSING PROP ACROSS YOUR BODY

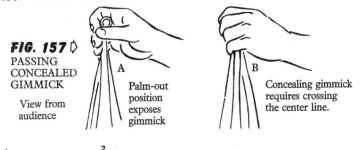

FIG. 157 ◊
PASSING
CONCEALED
GIMMICK

View from
audience

Palm-out
position
exposes
gimmick

Concealing gimmick
requires crossing
the center line.

Swing into profile on Step 1. Pass the prop and gimmick with your left hand. Continue walking to Position B without hesitation. Your assistant should *give stage* by taking one step in the direction of the arrow marked *C*.

158. FOOTWORK FOR PASSING GIMMICK

line. The reverse holds for inward gestures. They need not end at the center line but should be aiming toward it when they stop.

Extremely broad gestures must start from shoulder or hip to give room for the widest possible swing. However, such gestures are so rare that few performers ever have occasion to use one. Except for these exaggerated gestures, try not to let your wrist cross your center line. (Fig. 155). This rule is especially important when you take a prop from somewhere on your right and pass it to your left or vice versa. That cannot be done gracefully without changing hands (Fig. 156).

Actors have no reason to break the rule. However, a conjurer may need to pass a visible prop and some concealed object to his assistant. He cannot do that secretly if the palm of his hand is exposed, as it must be in *A*, Fig. 157. There does not seem to be any ideal solution to this problem. The best expedient is to swing your whole body into a profile position and bring up your hand at the same time (*B*, Fig. 157). Then cross in front of your assistant. Fig. 158 shows the footwork.

Practice both outward and inward gestures until you eliminate any suspicion of stiffness. Move your wrist in different directions including up, down, and straight forward. Try gestures of different lengths and at different speeds. Work first with one hand and then with the other. Also make a few gestures in which both hands move simultaneously in opposite directions. Do not spend much time at this; two-handed gestures have their place, but they should be used sparingly.

159.
GETTING OUT OF THE
PUMP-HANDLE POSITION
The two actions should blend
into a single smooth movement.

Many people tend to get into a position where one hand sticks out like a pump handle (Fig. 159). They can find no way out of this awkward pose without dropping the hand. That is a weak gesture and is normally undesirable. The solution is simple. Toss your wrist toward your center line at the level of your stomach. When it is about six inches away, let it drop to your side. This movement is inconspicuous and gets rid of the pump-handle effect without seeming weak.

After you master free gestures, experiment with controlled ones. A controlled gesture can be made with any part of the body. Figs. 101–103 show examples. If the girl in Fig. 98 moved into her position with an emphatic action, she would gesture with her left hip.

Concentrate your entire attention on your *leading part* and let the rest of your body take care of itself. Controlled gestures made by a part of the hand usually move toward or away from the center line.

The strength of a controlled gesture depends largely on its ending. Die-away gestures are weak. Those that stop abruptly are strong. Another method of emphasizing a gesture consists in making some movement with the fingers just as the main gesture stops. For example, you might extend your closed fist and then suddenly open your hand.

Never practice a controlled gesture. They should be completely spontaneous. When a controlled gesture becomes a habit, it ceases to have any meaning. In a carefully rehearsed act, you will normally use the same gesture at every performance. Nevertheless, such a gesture is not a habit. You should think the same thought each time and let the thought inspire the gesture. When you do that, the gesture is truly spontaneous. This may seem metaphysical, but it is solid fact. If you memorize a gesture and use it without thinking, it is lifeless—and everyone in the audience recognizes it as such. Watch other performers and note how easy it is to distinguish memorized gestures from those that express what the performer is actually thinking. This is one reason why it is so important to provide yourself with a silent script.

FACIAL EXPRESSIONS

Your facial expressions are an important element of both your personality and your characterization. They are vital in close-up work and can be recognized from a surprising distance in an auditorium.

Facial expressions, like controlled gestures, should always be spontaneous. Never practice specific expressions such as smiles or frowns. If you do, you will end with a set of fixed grimaces that will repel spectators instead of attracting them. The proper procedure is to experiment by making faces in your mirror like a schoolboy. Do not hold an expression or make the same one twice. Merely note the effect and then try something different. The best time for such experiments is while you are preparing to shave.

Making faces benefits you in several ways. It relaxes inhibitions; most of us are afraid to let our faces mirror our thoughts. This is foolish. A good actor has as much control of his expression as a poker player, but he is far more attractive. By making faces, you give tone to your facial muscles and train them to be responsive. Finally, by watching your experiments in a mirror, you build up a subconscious vocabulary of expressions. This enables you to invent the best expression for each situation spontaneously. *Never think about your face while you are performing.*

TIMING

The effectiveness of any piece of business depends largely on how precisely it is timed. Timing is especially important when an action must be coordinated with a speech. Thus, in *Twentieth-Century Nylon,* you might say, "The red handkerchief will leave my hand invisibly on the count of three. One, two, three!" Open your hand exactly on the word "three." If it is a fraction of a second too soon or too late, the impression will be spoiled.

Coordination is not confined to such obvious examples. For example, the climax of *The Peculiar Pellet* should be done while you mentally count three. Grasp the two of Clubs as you think "one," turn it over as you think "two," and hiss "Assassin!" when you would think "three," if you were not thinking "Assassin!"

When an action accompanies a speech, they should start and stop together. If this is impossible, start the speech and movement together and end them separately, or start them separately and end them together.

One way to learn timing is to beat time while you speak your lines. After a little practice, you will be able to make the important words fall on the beats, thus:

"Sóme of my friénds have críticized mágic as úseless. ' They ásk what good it dóes to saw a wóman in hálf and then glúe her togéther agáin." Note that the beat before "They" falls on a pause.

Do not think about timing while you try this; simply speak the words and tap a pencil or pat your foot as you do so. If you have any feeling for rhythm, you will soon find that key words automatically fall on the beats—though not necessarily on the ones I have marked. This is an exercise; do not think about rhythm or timing during your act except when you make a dead pause. You should then count silently, so that you can begin your next move or speech on a beat. A good showman uses many one-beat pauses. He may occasionally need a three-beat pause. I cannot imagine a case where a conjurer could afford to pause for more than three beats.

After you have learned to match your words to beats, rehearse some piece of business without the usual words, but count aloud as you do so. Count from one to ten and repeat. The names of the numbers do not matter; they simply provide a convenient way of marking the rhythm. Try to make all important actions coincide with a number. Most people do not need to try very hard, the mere fact that they are counting tends to make them move in rhythm.

Do not worry about the speed of counting. This comes intuitively; none of my actors ever had any trouble with it.

Silent actions between two spoken passages should just fit the gap, like this: "$\overset{1}{\text{Glad}}$ to $\overset{2}{\text{meet}}$ you, $\overset{3}{\text{George}}$. [*Takes scissors from pocket and hands them to George.*] $\overset{6}{\text{Now}}$ George, ..." The business of getting the scissors should take exactly three beats. Hence, if we count "Glad" as the first beat, your hand should go into your pocket on the fourth beat, come out on the fifth, and offer the scissors to George on the sixth at the exact moment when you say, "Now George. . . ."

Although it was an accident that the business in this example took three beats, it will nevertheless pay you to arrange short actions to fit three beats whenever that can be done without strain. This is another case where the one-two-three pattern is effective.

MATCHING BUSINESS AND LINES

The length of an act or a single routine should be governed by your ability to make your audience want more. The time allotted to each individual point is determined on an entirely different basis. A spectator is interested in a point for the precise length of time he needs to grasp it. If you offer new material before he has grasped the old, he loses the thread of the routine—and his interest in it as well. On the other hand, the moment a point is clear, it ceases to be interesting. Waste half a second more on it, and you begin to become boring. This gives us our rule: *Spend exactly enough time on each point to make it clear.* Any less will be dull because it is confusing; any more will be dull because it conveys no information.

Inexperienced conjurers sometimes neglect an audience entirely while they dispose of apparatus from the previous routine or prepare something for the next. This creates what is known in the theater as a *stage wait*. A stage wait of thirty seconds will do more to kill an act than two minutes of dull patter.

Try to have the lines and business for each step match in length. If they fail to do this, it is better to cut the long one than to pad the short one. Brief bits of business rarely need cutting. The trouble comes in cases like *Dowsing Test* and *The Peculiar Pellet* where you appear to improvise fairly complex equipment. Such business can always be shortened by one or more of the following techniques.

Prearrange the items so that you can reach them quickly. You can perform *The Singing Glass* completely impromptu. But if you do, you may be compelled to let interest sag for several minutes while you assemble the necessary glass, thread, and pencil.

Find efficient methods of handling matters which might otherwise slow you down. The first time you try to tie a glass to a pencil, it will be a slow job. However, practice will teach you how much thread to use, how to break it off the spool, and the quickest way to tie the knots. Sometimes one good idea can cut a minute or two off your time. Hanging a pendulum on a thread for *Will Power* would ordinarily take four or five minutes. By using a threaded needle and a penknife as in Fig. 65, you can cut this to thirty seconds.

Try to divide any long piece of business into several parts. If you then do only one part at a time, the process will seem shorter and you will have less trouble making your words match your business. In *Dowsing Test*, for example, you must find two clips, a piece of paper, two rubber bands (or two pins), several glasses, water, and a napkin. You must then bend both clips, supply them with handles, see that one glass has water and that the rest are empty, and cover all the glasses with a napkin. Even if all the apparatus is within easy reach, you can hardly rig it in less than five minutes. Handled that way, it is apt to drag.

The proper procedure is to break the business up into parts:

1. Make first "rod," without its handle, and pass it around.
2. Ask someone else to bring glasses, water, and a napkin.
3. Make second "rod," complete with handle, and pass it around.
4. Make handle for first "rod."
5. Attach handle to first "rod."

When this plan is followed, the spectators are kept busy examining the "rods" and arranging the glasses. Conversation flows freely, the action never drags, and no one will think you are monopolizing attention.

Occasionally, you may find that even after your business has been streamlined, it still takes more time than the accompanying words. When this happens, try to use words from some step where the lines are longer than the business.

When you can neither streamline a piece of business nor shift lines to cover it, you will normally be wiser to invent more lines than to work in silence. This does not mean that you should talk all the time. Some steps go best without speech. However, these are apt to be those in which you present a long effect, such as producing a series of scarves from a hat. Routines or whole acts in pure pantomime are usually crowded with effects, and the time taken to rig apparatus is negligible. As rigging is rarely entertaining, even dull talk is apt to be better than none at all.

Apply the same principles in reverse when you must give a lengthy explanation and have no business to accompany it. Most "impromptu" routines can be arranged to let you work your explanation in during a preliminary conversation. Or you can save at least part of the explanation until you have some business to go with it.

In a formal act, words that do not cover essential business should be kept to a bare minimum. Single comic lines may be inserted between actions, but anything approaching a monologue is dangerous unless it is very funny indeed. A line that is amusing without getting a laugh may be worth while if it goes with some action, but it is not justified when it makes a long speech longer.

When you need a lengthy explanation and cannot combine it with business, you can always break it up with movement. The first speech of *The Rope Mender* illustrates this. It takes forty seconds, and almost none of the essential business can be introduced during the speech. Nevertheless, a competent showman can find plenty to do. Here is the speech with a complete set of stage directions:

MAGICIAN. [*Standing back of table.*] Some of my friends have criticized magic as useless. [*Pick up folded rope.*] They ask what good it does to saw a woman in half and then glue her back together again. [*Step out from behind table.*] If you want her together, why saw her in half in the first place. [*Take three short steps toward audience.*] I thought the matter over and had to admit that they had a point. So I began wondering how I could commercialize on my magic. [*One more step.*] I finally came up with an invention that's going to save the taxpayers millions of dollars. We give the Navy a lot of rope. [*Suddenly let rope dangle.*] But after it gets all cut up into little pieces . . . [*Use fingers like scissors to pantomime cutting rope into short lengths. Make about seven cuts in rapid succession. This can be funny; it is unexpected, there is something inherently comic about the scissor movement, and it creates a mental image of sailors sitting on deck cutting rope to bits with scissors. Note also that this is an example of repeating a movement to express " Very many."*] . . . what good is it ? [*Gathering up rope.*] I decided to invent a magic rope mender which would put all that cut rope back together again and take some of the strain off the taxpayer's pocket. [*Moving to footlights and looking around audience as though seeking a representative taxpayer.*] As I'm doing this for the taxpayers, and as they are the cornerstone of our political economy, I think they should have a representative during this demonstration. [*Indicates George, a spectator.*] Are you a taxpayer, sir ?

Although none of these movements has much significance or is especially interesting, they give the audience something to watch. They also break up the speech and keep it from being an uninterrupted flow of words. This is the sort of thing an actor does in a well-staged play. Without it the long speeches in Shakespeare would be unbearable.

Chapter 22

THE PERFORMER AND THE STAGE

All the performing arts, except conjuring, regard a director as a necessity. A director can be as useful to the conjurer as he can to the actor, the dancer, or the musician. However, as directors who understand the technical requirements of conjuring are scarce and are not likely to be cheap, a few suggestions on how to be your own director and dramatic coach may not come amiss.

Before making them, however, let me point out that directing yourself is a poor substitute for hiring an outside director. The director views you from the same angle and distance that the audience does. You cannot see yourself in this way. A mirror will help you to practice sleights, but it is a liability during rehearsals. Rehearsing before a mirror is apt to make you self-conscious. Few mirrors are large enough to show your whole body, even when you sit still. This may explain why close-up workers rarely make broad gestures; they are afraid to let their hands move out of sight beyond the edges of the mirror! Finally, you must keep your eyes fixed on the mirror in order to watch what you are doing. That seriously restricts your movements.

Another reason why you cannot hope to compete, even with a poor director, is that no director shares either your prejudices or your attitude toward yourself. Most performers assume that any routine, witticism, or bit of business that pleases them must also please an audience. Unfortunately, a conjurer's viewpoint differs so widely from that of his audience that even experienced performers are often blind to their own mistakes. I know one who persists in closing his fine act with a trick that cannot fool the youngest spectator. Another of my friends interrupts his clever tricks with a joke which has fallen flat every time I have heard it.

VARIETY AND THE STAGE

The stage is an asset which few performers have learned to exploit. This is a whole art in itself, but there are certain basic principles which you cannot afford to ignore—even when your stage is only one end of a living room.

STAGE GEOGRAPHY

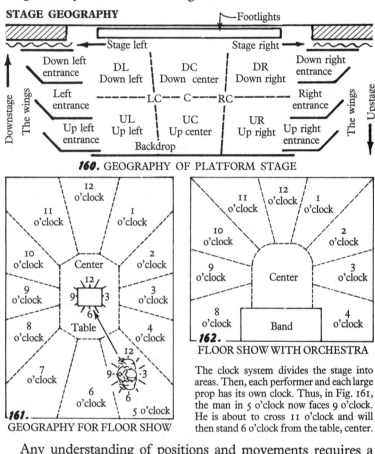

160. GEOGRAPHY OF PLATFORM STAGE

161. GEOGRAPHY FOR FLOOR SHOW

162. FLOOR SHOW WITH ORCHESTRA

The clock system divides the stage into areas. Then, each performer and each large prop has its own clock. Thus, in Fig. 161, the man in 5 o'clock now faces 9 o'clock. He is about to cross 11 o'clock and will then stand 6 o'clock from the table, center.

Any understanding of positions and movements requires a knowledge of stage geography (Fig. 160). This is simple, but you should study it until it is as familiar as the arrangement of your own bedroom. If you work night clubs, or other places where you are more or less surrounded, you need to master the "maps" in Figs. 161 and 162.

Variety adds interest and makes it easier for you to hold attention. The easiest way to gain variety is to do each routine

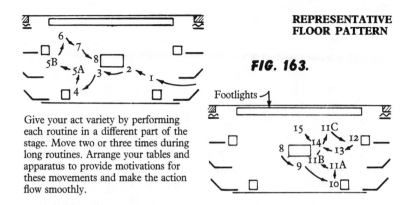

REPRESENTATIVE
FLOOR PATTERN

FIG. 163.

Footlights

Give your act variety by performing each routine in a different part of the stage. Move two or three times during long routines. Arrange your tables and apparatus to provide motivations for these movements and make the action flow smoothly.

in a different spot. Fig. 163 shows how you can motivate the necessary movements by arranging apparatus on tables or chairs set in the corners of the stage.

Areas vary in strength. The order is up left (weakest), up right, down left, down right and up center (about equal), and down center (strongest). You can build interest by arranging your routines so that the *floor pattern* will cover the areas in roughly the order of their increasing strength. The act in Fig. 163 does this adequately but still motivates the performer's movements and lets them seem casual. Save down center for your climactic routine. You may walk through this area earlier or perform some minor bit of business there, but do not waste its value by making serious use of it until you reach your main item.

POSITION

The actor's rule—*Never turn your back on an audience*—applies even more strictly to the conjurer. When you turn your back, you cannot see the spectators and they cannot see your face. Under these conditions, you are in danger of losing control. Furthermore, if you speak with your back to the audience, your words are muffled, and your lips—which are the visual source of information—are hidden.

The rule permits any position from full front to profile (Fig. 164). It does not apply to the body but merely to the head; the man in Fig. 165 is not breaking the rule. Furthermore, the rule applies only while a performer is the source of information or is displaying or describing some prop which is the source of information. When you are claiming the attention of the audience, your assistant may, and often should, turn

297

slightly away from the footlights; when attention is focused on her, you may turn away yourself. However, no performer should turn his back squarely to the audience except in the special cases where he wants to demonstrate that he cannot observe what is going on.

Although you do not break the back-to-the-audience rule by a position like that in Fig. 165, a conjurer should normally *turn out* slightly more than the mechanics of the situation require. In Fig. 166, for example, the conjurer and his assistant are talking to each other. This would ordinarily lead them to face each other directly and stand profile to the audience. Actually, they have turned their bodies 45° and their faces 20° toward the audience. This device makes them more prominent. Although it is unnatural, it does not seem so. Actors do this habitually, even in highly realistic plays.

RELATION OF PERFORMER TO AUDIENCE

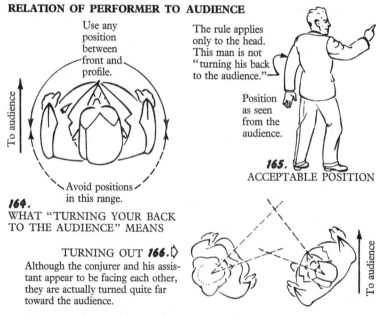

Use any position between front and profile.

To audience

Avoid positions in this range.

164.
WHAT "TURNING YOUR BACK TO THE AUDIENCE" MEANS

The rule applies only to the head. This man is not "turning his back to the audience."

Position as seen from the audience.

165.
ACCEPTABLE POSITION

TURNING OUT *166.*
Although the conjurer and his assistant appear to be facing each other, they are actually turned quite far toward the audience.

To audience

When you work surrounded, as you do in a night club, you have your back to some spectators all the time. Arena directors have solved this by three rules: (1) Turn frequently; never keep your back on anyone for long. (2) Never stay in the same area for more than a minute or two; arrange your floor pattern so that you will be close to each group of spectators at one time and

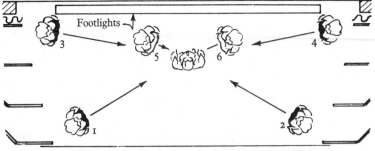

167. POSITIONS FOR INACTIVE ASSISTANT

These are the best positions for an assistant to take when she is not busy. The numbers indicate the order of preference, No. 1 being the least obtrusive. However, there is not a great deal of difference between them.

far from it at others. (3) Zigzag; do not merely move around the clock. These rules may seem to require unnatural movements. However, arena players soon become adept at making the necessary actions appear to be completely motivated. If they can do it, so can you.

Technique for Assistants

An assistant raises few problems as long as she is kept busy. However, in most acts, there are several periods when she has nothing to do and must be made as inconspicuous as possible. The ideal solution is to have her exit and return just in time for her next scene. If she continually bobs back and forth, however, the effect may be comic. Furthermore, when either an exit or an entrance requires more than three steps, the movement itself distracts attention.

When she must remain idle on stage, try to have her retire to one of the corner positions shown by the shaded figures in Fig. 167. If this involves distracting movements, let her stay near you but keep her slightly downstage (unshaded figures in Fig. 167). That turns her back slightly toward the audience and makes her less distracting.

The rule against making any movement without a motivated purpose applies even more strongly to the assistant than it does to the conjurer. When she is idle, she should be erect but not rigid and should avoid making any movement whatever. Small, restless actions are especially bad.

Whether an assistant is active or inactive, *she should keep her eyes on whatever happens to be the source of information at the moment.*

Your assistant is slightly less likely to attract attention when she is on your left. However, keeping her on this side the whole time tends to make the act monotonous. Changing sides presents no problems. You may have been told that a performer should never pass between another performer and the audience. This is a false rule. The true rule depends on which performer is the source of information. When the stationary performer is the source, the moving performer will distract attention whether he crosses in front or in back (Fig. 168). *Crossing* in front is worse because it is both awkward and rude. However, there is little choice as far as distraction is concerned. On the other hand when the moving performer is the source of information, he should cross in front of the other. Crossing behind a stationary performer is always a mistake unless the latter is seated or stooping so that the moving performer's face can be seen by the audience as he passes (Fig. 169). These considerations apply equally to conjurers, assistants, and volunteers. The only distinction is that conjurers are more often the source of information. Hence they have more opportunities to cross.

PASSING ANOTHER PERFORMER

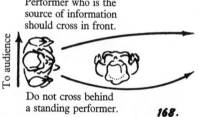

Performer who is the source of information should cross in front.

To audience

Do not cross behind a standing performer.

168.

CROSSING BEFORE AND BEHIND

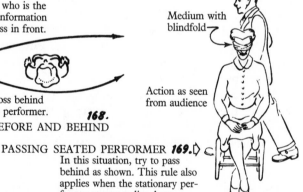

Medium with blindfold

Action as seen from audience

PASSING SEATED PERFORMER *169.*
In this situation, try to pass behind as shown. This rule also applies when the stationary performer stoops or lies down.

Color, Light, Music

Manufacturers of apparatus appear to be color blind and their customers make matters worse by combining hues at random. This is one reason why women dislike conjuring. They are more sensitive to colors than men are, and they refuse to be entertained by a performer who displays red and orange "flowers" against a maroon scarf. Buying colors by mail is as risky as marrying a mail-order wife.

Your act will be much more acceptable to the distaff side of your audience if you have two or three women friends help you select your colors. Display all your apparatus while they are advising you. Colors can be judged only in relation to other colors. No color is ugly in itself, and no color is beautiful.

If you play a character role, see that every detail of your costume is appropriate. If you play Yourself, make sure that both you and your clothing are clean and that your suit is pressed. The better you look, the more impressive your illusions will be.

Your assistant's costume and grooming are equally important. Unless she takes a broad character role, she should be dressed as becomingly as possible and should wear high heels; women never look their best in flat heels.

Colored lights and music have great entertainment value. However, they present problems that the average performer finds insuperable. Lighting must be designed and music must be selected. Equipment must be available. Stagehands and musicians have to be secured and rehearsed. They must be skilful and reliable. They must also be able to improvise when something goes wrong. It is nearly impossible to satisfy all these requirements for an act that plays short runs in a variety of clubs, halls, and theaters. If even one is lacking, the result can be disastrous. An orchestra which plays the wrong tune, or a stagehand who misses a light cue, can make the most brilliant routine appear ridiculous. Unless conditions are exceptionally favorable, the value of an orchestra and special lighting are more than offset by the difficulties and dangers that attend any attempt to use them.

Silent acts need music, and the canned variety is the safest type to use. Unfortunately, there is a lot more to it than buying equipment and recording a tape. The equipment is expensive and cumbersome. Even when it is of high quality, it does not sound natural unless the speakers are properly placed. The correct volume varies with the size of the audience and cannot be set in advance. Finally, if the act must synchronize with the music, the least hesitation at any point will be painfully obvious and may throw the rest of the performance out of step.

Head high — Shoulders hang free — Spine almost straight — Knees straight but not stiff — Let weight fall here.

◁ **170.**
POISED AND RELAXED

Head hangs — Back bent — Spine sags — Knees slack —

◁ **171.**
DREARY DROOP

Shoulders forced back — Buttocks project — Knees locked —

Chin drawn in — Chest puffed up —

◁ **172.**
STIFF AND STARCHED

Weight too far back —

◁ **173.**
FORCE YOUR CHEST UP
This is an exercise to relax your chest muscles. Expand chest as far as possible (dotted lines). Hold for half a minute. Relax. Your muscles will bring your chest to the position shown by the solid lines. This is the ideal chest position. Do not exert any effort to force out more air, and do not let your chest sag.

174. ◁
STRETCH UP
Do this three times a day

Rock head forward.
Do not tip head back.

Lie flat on your back on the floor. Stretch your arms over your head. Let your muscles relax and wait for your spine to straighten. This may take three or four minutes at first.

Touch here.   Not here.

STRETCH OUT **175.**

POISE

Poise is even more valuable to the conjurer than it is to the actor. Physical poise helps you to achieve the mental poise that you need to dominate an audience. Unfortunately, most of us suffered in our youth from attempts to teach us "correct posture" by people who were wrong on almost every point.

Physical poise comes from keeping each part of your body in balance (Fig. 170). It is easy and comfortable. You cannot acquire ease, comfort, or balance by straining to force your chin in, your shoulders back, and your chest out (Fig. 172). Walking around with a book on your head is equally harmful. You may balance the book, but the book will not balance you.

Physical poise is effortless, but attaining it may require work —especially if you have let yourself fall into a permanent slump like the man in Fig. 171. Fortunately, you will not have to work either very hard or very long at a time.

The exercises illustrated in Figs. 173–175 and described in the accompanying captions are easy to do and require only a few seconds each. By devoting five minutes a day to them, you can improve your appearance in less than a week. This is so true that if you fail to notice any improvement, you can be sure that you are not doing the exercises correctly.

It is not enough to make improvements; you must retain them; you must continue to practice the exercises throughout life, just as you practice sleights. Fortunately, once you master the exercises, you will find that all three of them take less than two minutes a day.

FOOTWORK

Good footwork will do wonders both for your appearance and for the smoothness of your presentation. It begins with the foot position in Fig. 176. This stance is basic. Form the habit of falling into it each time you stand still. It is even more important for your assistant than it is for you because it shows a girl's legs to the best advantage. Make sure that you both master it before going further.

When you walk, follow the simple rule: *Always take your first step with the foot nearest the goal.* Fig. 177 demonstrates that you can observe the rule no matter in which direction you move.

An entrance from the wings of the stage should begin with the upstage foot.

When you cross from one place to another, try to take either one step or three (Fig. 178). The extra half step needed to bring your feet together does not count in the rhythm. When you perform on a stage, this one-or-three rule will leave you turned slightly toward the audience—especially if you have followed a gentle curve like that in Fig. 178. I have not had enough experience with arena staging to say whether or not these considerations apply when the performer works surrounded by an audience.

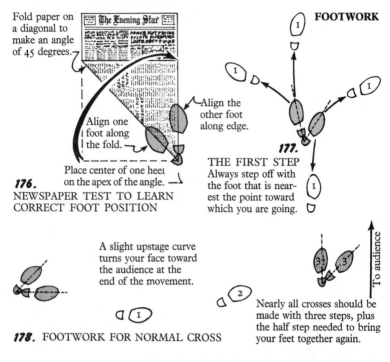

Fold paper on a diagonal to make an angle of 45 degrees.

The Evening Star

Align one foot along the fold.

Align the other foot along edge.

Place center of one heel on the apex of the angle.

176. NEWSPAPER TEST TO LEARN CORRECT FOOT POSITION

FOOTWORK

177.

THE FIRST STEP
Always step off with the foot that is nearest the point toward which you are going.

A slight upstage curve turns your face toward the audience at the end of the movement.

To audience

Nearly all crosses should be made with three steps, plus the half step needed to bring your feet together again.

178. FOOTWORK FOR NORMAL CROSS

A well-planned act should not require you to take more than three steps at a time. Longer crosses tend to be dull. If you must make one, you can escape monotony in two ways. One is to break the rhythm by taking either short, quick steps or exaggerated strides. The second, and more useful, technique consists in doing something to add fresh interest as you take your fourth step. If, for example, you enter from the wings of a wide stage and cannot present your first number until you reach the center, you will need five or seven steps. On the fourth, turn your face toward the audience, smile, and make some gesture with your wand.

There are several techniques for moving upstage without turning your back on the audience. You cannot consider yourself a finished performer until you have mastered them.

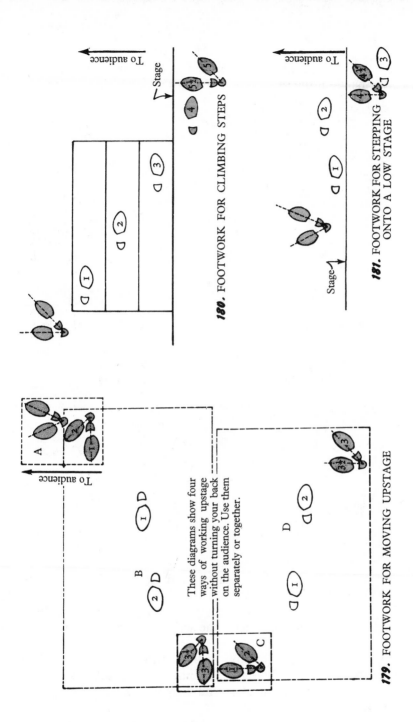

180. FOOTWORK FOR CLIMBING STEPS

181. FOOTWORK FOR STEPPING ONTO A LOW STAGE

179. FOOTWORK FOR MOVING UPSTAGE

These diagrams show four ways of working upstage without turning your back on the audience. Use them separately or together.

To audience

Stage

305

1. Take a single step backward as you make a gesture with the hand on the same side as the foot with which you step.

SITTING

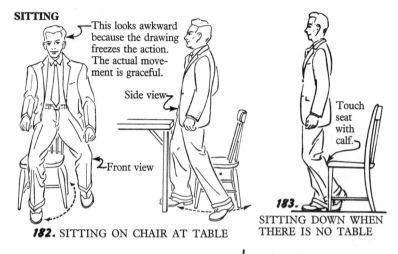

This looks awkward because the drawing freezes the action. The actual movement is graceful.

Side view

Front view

Touch seat with calf.

182. SITTING ON CHAIR AT TABLE

183. SITTING DOWN WHEN THERE IS NO TABLE

Avoid slumping when you reach.

Keep your body erect and rock forward on your hip bones.

184. REACHING (Awkward)

185. REACHING (Graceful)

2. Take a backward step as you bow.

3. Have your assistant cross in front of you. Take three steps back to give her room.

4. Walk upstage at an angle of 45° using the footwork in *B* or *D*, Fig. 179 and looking at the audience over your downstage shoulder.

5. Use the same footwork without turning your head while another performer holds the attention of the audience.

6. Work upstage while turning (footwork in *A* or *C*, Fig. 179).

7. Combine techniques 4. and 6. with pauses between to work upstage along a zigzag path (whole pattern in Fig. 179).

Many conjurers turn their backs when they mount steps from the auditorium to the stage. As this usually occurs just before the climax of a routine, the performer throws away his control of the audience at the very moment when he needs it most. Fig. 180 shows how to apply the diagonal technique to stairs. Fig. 181 illustrates the method of stepping onto a low stage when there are no stairs.

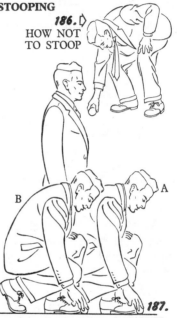

STOOPING

186. ◊

HOW NOT TO STOOP

SITTING, RISING, AND STOOPING

The performer who works tables at a night club makes his first impression on his audience when he sits, and leaves it with the impression that he makes when he rises. Fig. 182 illustrates the proper techniques.

Other conjurers rarely need to sit. If you do, place yourself in front of your chair and move one leg slightly backward until you can feel the seat with your calf. This tells you that it is safe to sit (Fig. 183). Never glance back at your chair before sitting; audiences regard this as funny. Rise as in Fig. 182, but step forward with the foot at the side instead of backward with the foot in front.

187.

STOOP BY TAKING ONE STEP FORWARD OR BACKWARD

A forward step (*A*) is more graceful. But when you stoop to pick up a dropped object, you must normally step back (*B*). For some reason, learning to do this subconsciously requires quite a bit of practice.

When you reach for something while seated, rock forward on your hip bones (Fig. 185). Slumping creates a poor impression (Fig. 184).

Stage conjurers stoop fairly often, and most of them do it like the man in Fig. 186. The proper technique is illustrated in Fig. 187.

APPLAUSE

Conjurers throw away more applause than they get. The amount of applause that a performer receives is governed as much by his technique as it is by the quality of his act. Some techniques encourage applause, others kill it. You cannot expect an audience to express approval if you use the wrong technique at the wrong time.

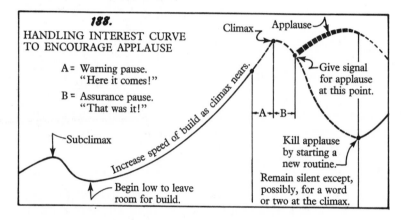

188.
HANDLING INTEREST CURVE
TO ENCOURAGE APPLAUSE

A = Warning pause.
"Here it comes!"

B = Assurance pause.
"That was it!"

Increase speed of build as climax nears.

Subclimax

Begin low to leave room for build.

Climax

Applause

Give signal for applause at this point.

←A→←B→

Kill applause by starting a new routine.

Remain silent except, possibly, for a word or two at the climax.

Many performers feel that applause corresponds to "*A* for effort." If they devote time and energy in an attempt to entertain, the least the audience can do is to reward them by clapping. This view is unfounded. Whether the spectators pay in cash or attention, they have acquired the right to be entertained. The performer who succeeds merely balances the account; one who bores his audience puts himself more deeply in its debt.

People who have been entertained want to applaud. When they do so spontaneously, they form a higher opinion of your act. Each spectator hears the rest clapping and says to himself, "If they like it this much, it must be better than I thought."

On the other hand, when a performer begs for applause or tries to bully his audience into providing it, he lowers himself just as any other beggar or bully does. Even a spectator who has enjoyed the performance thinks, "I liked it. But if this guy has to high-pressure people into clapping, he can't be much good."

There is no need for either begging or bullying. If your act justifies any applause at all, you can get more than it deserves by using the proper technique.

The first step is to go over your act and decide where the applause should come. At least half the men I watch are vague on this vital point. If you do not know when you want the spectators to clap, you cannot expect them to find out for themselves.

Spot your applause immediately after the climax of each major wave (points A in Fig. 137). You may be able to get a little applause after each quickie. But if you do, the spectators' hands will grow tired and the clapping will dribble away to a polite flurry at the end (Fig. 136).

Premature applause in the middle of a routine, or a progressive series of routines, will rob you of any chance for a real hand after the climax. If you let your audience clap after *The Haunted Conjurer* and *The Consolidated Guinea Pigs*, interest will sag instead of rising—and *The Truant Trousers* will not produce the ovation that it should when properly handled.

On the other hand, if you make people want to applaud but keep them from doing so, the desire will grow stronger and stronger. When it reaches a peak, let it come and take a well-deserved bow.

Learning when to stifle and when to encourage applause is more than half the battle. The other half consists in providing clues to which the audience can respond.

Avoid applause by indicating plainly that you have not reached a climax. When you create some minor effect, pause just long enough for the audience to appreciate it, and go immediately into your next routine. If possible, say something at the point of transition. That will make the spectators listen instead of applauding. If you must be silent, keep moving, avoid facing the audience directly and give some definite sign—such as walking toward a different table or picking up a new prop—that you are going on with your act and that it is not time to applaud.

Getting applause is no more difficult but is a trifle more complex. The technique begins with the build which immediately precedes the climax (Fig. 188). Handle this in such a way that your audience knows you are approaching a revelation of some sort. Your technique will vary with the routine and with your personality. However, if you are keenly aware of the fact that a miracle is about to happen, you will subconsciously transmit this information to the audience. Just before reaching the climax, pause for a count of "One." The spectators will recognize this as a signal that the big moment has arrived. Present your climax. Pause for another count of "One." During this pause neither you nor your assistant should make any sound or movement. Face dead front, and give the audience a cue to applaud.

This clue can be any small action such as a flick of your wand, a slight bow, or a sudden smile. It announces that the routine is complete and that some sign of appreciation will be welcome. It also acts like the downbeat of a conductor's baton and helps all the spectators to start clapping at the same instant. Applause that begins raggedly never becomes enthusiastic.

If you need proof that this technique is important, watch your fellow conjurers. Time and again one of them will fail to indicate that his routine is over and that it is time to clap. The spectators are uncertain whether to applaud or to wait attentively for some further development. As a result, they do nothing. The performer looks disappointed and says, "I usually get a hand at that point." He intends this as a reproach, but the spectators interpret it as an apology for not being up to his usual standard.

Never let applause die out. If it does, people will tire their hands and use up their tendency to applaud. The instant the clapping begins to fade, kill it. You can do this by turning away and giving some definite sign that you are starting your next routine. Unless you do a silent act, begin to talk at this point. Do not attempt to be heard over the applause. Speak in a normal tone. The audience will quiet down to avoid missing anything. As your remark will probably be lost, it should not contain important information.

You may have trouble timing this technique at first. But once you master it, you can get a bigger hand from a weak routine than the average conjurer gets from a strong one.

Unfortunately, the technique requires a clear-cut climax. Many excellent routines lack such climaxes. In *Fan-tastic*, for example, the climax starts when the first handkerchief is "dyed." The second and third handkerchiefs round off the routine but add little or no build. I doubt if any technique will gain a real hand after an effect of this type, even though the audience may find it highly entertaining. Your best plan is to avoid applause at that point, let the tendency to clap build up, and reap the full benefit after the climax of your next routine (Fig. 137).

TAKING BOWS

This can be developed into a fine art, but a few words about the rudiments may not come amiss.

Face dead front for small bows. Incline your head slightly, but keep your eyes on the audience; people are more inclined to clap when they feel you are watching. If the hand warrants more than one bow, make a second nod to your left and a third to your right.

When you use the first nod to cue applause, think, "I hope I have pleased you," as you make it. This acts as a silent script and takes care of your facial expression and any subconscious bodily movements. For second and third bows, say, "Thank you. Thank you." You can say this to yourself or speak in a fairly loud tone depending on the amount of applause. Never make the mistake of saying, "Thank you" before the applause comes.

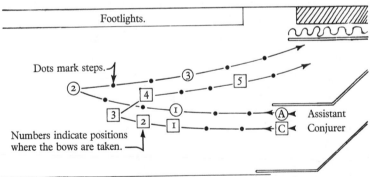

189. TAKING BOWS WITH YOUR ASSISTANT

A real hand deserves a real bow—from the waist. Keep your head up so that the audience can see your face. Bow first to the center and say, "Thank you!" If the audience continues, bow left, saying, "You're very kind," and bow right, saying, "Thank you!" again.

Even the strongest routine in the middle of an act will rarely rate more than three bows. After that, the applause will begin to fade and should be killed. However, at the end of your act, you should take all the applause you can get without straining.

Judging by the questions that I am asked when I lecture on showmanship, many conjurers have never learned the art of taking a curtain call with an assistant. The secret lies in the footwork (Fig. 189).

Vaudeville performers developed hundreds of techniques for *milking* applause at the end of an act. Some of these were as clever as the acts themselves. An expert could double his quota of earned bows simply by his use of milking techniques. These deserve your best thought. Managers judge the quality of your act by the amount of applause that you receive at the end.

The secret behind all milking techniques consists in doing something unexpected at the precise moment when the applause begins to die. This provides what is known as a *kicker* and starts another wave of clapping. Clever "kickers" are best. However, almost any small action, such as a sudden grin or a shrug, will work if it is appropriate and perfectly timed.

Perhaps the best example of a kicker is the *walk-off*. The act is over, the audience looks for nothing more. But, then, the performer adds an extra comic touch and walks off while the audience is still laughing. This is rewarded with a curtain call.

For example, if you end a haunted-conjurer act with *The Consolidated Guinea Pigs* and *The Truant Trousers*, you could display the rabbit, boast of your triumph over The Obeah Man, put the rabbit back in the hat, count "One," and step from behind the table. Count "One" again. Bow to give a cue for applause, but not so deeply that you can see your bare legs. Instead of the ovation that you expect for consolidating the guinea pigs, you will be greeted by a burst of laughter.

This is the point at which the walk-off technically begins. Appear puzzled and upset. Look around to see what is causing the laughter. When you can find nothing, appear indignant at such an unappreciative audience and stalk off the stage.

If you have handled this properly, the laughter will turn to applause as you exit. Come out and take a deep bow. For the first time, you notice your legs and are both embarrassed by your nudity and chagrined by The Obeah Man's triumph. Search frantically for something to do. Bow and produce a scarf bearing the words "The End" (Figs. 190–191). Wrap this around you and exit. That will certainly make the audience bring you back for another bow.

Now let me take my bow and wish you "Many happy curtain calls!"

QUICKIE FOR ENCORE

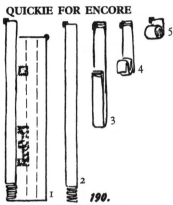

190.

METHOD OF FOLDING SCARF

191. FRONT VIEW OF SCARF

1. Sew buttons on the upper corners of the scarf. They should be different shapes so that you can tell them apart by touch. Place the scarf face down. Fold it into 2-in. accordian pleats (Step 1). This creates a long, narrow strip (Step 2). Fold up one-third of this and accordian pleat it (Steps 3 and 4). Roll up the rest from the bottom (Step 5). Put a rubber band around the bundle and drop it into your pocket.

2. On your first exit, take out the scarf and remove the band. Hide the scarf in your hand and enter. Bring your hands together and grasp the buttons. When you separate your hands, the scarf will open all at once and seem to appear magically in mid-air.

ROUTINES

References in parentheses indicate basic descriptions. References in italics indicate pertinent illustrations. All other references are either to variations or suggestions on presentation. Cases where routines are cited merely as examples are not listed.

INDEX

References in italics indicate illustrations.

A CATALOG OF SELECTED
DOVER BOOKS
IN ALL FIELDS OF INTEREST

A CATALOG OF SELECTED DOVER
BOOKS IN ALL FIELDS OF INTEREST

CONCERNING THE SPIRITUAL IN ART, Wassily Kandinsky. Pioneering work by father of abstract art. Thoughts on color theory, nature of art. Analysis of earlier masters. 12 illustrations. 80pp. of text. 5⅜ x 8½. 23411-8 Pa. $4.95

ANIMALS: 1,419 Copyright-Free Illustrations of Mammals, Birds, Fish, Insects, etc., Jim Harter (ed.). Clear wood engravings present, in extremely lifelike poses, over 1,000 species of animals. One of the most extensive pictorial sourcebooks of its kind. Captions. Index. 284pp. 9 x 12. 23766-4 Pa. $14.95

CELTIC ART: The Methods of Construction, George Bain. Simple geometric techniques for making Celtic interlacements, spirals, Kells-type initials, animals, humans, etc. Over 500 illustrations. 160pp. 9 x 12. (USO) 22923-8 Pa. $9.95

AN ATLAS OF ANATOMY FOR ARTISTS, Fritz Schider. Most thorough reference work on art anatomy in the world. Hundreds of illustrations, including selections from works by Vesalius, Leonardo, Goya, Ingres, Michelangelo, others. 593 illustrations. 192pp. 7⅛ x 10¼. 20241-0 Pa. $9.95

CELTIC HAND STROKE-BY-STROKE (Irish Half-Uncial from "The Book of Kells"): An Arthur Baker Calligraphy Manual, Arthur Baker. Complete guide to creating each letter of the alphabet in distinctive Celtic manner. Covers hand position, strokes, pens, inks, paper, more. Illustrated. 48pp. 8¼ x 11. 24336-2 Pa. $3.95

EASY ORIGAMI, John Montroll. Charming collection of 32 projects (hat, cup, pelican, piano, swan, many more) specially designed for the novice origami hobbyist. Clearly illustrated easy-to-follow instructions insure that even beginning papercrafters will achieve successful results. 48pp. 8¼ x 11. 27298-2 Pa. $3.50

THE COMPLETE BOOK OF BIRDHOUSE CONSTRUCTION FOR WOODWORKERS, Scott D. Campbell. Detailed instructions, illustrations, tables. Also data on bird habitat and instinct patterns. Bibliography. 3 tables. 63 illustrations in 15 figures. 48pp. 5¼ x 8½. 24407-5 Pa. $2.50

BLOOMINGDALE'S ILLUSTRATED 1886 CATALOG: Fashions, Dry Goods and Housewares, Bloomingdale Brothers. Famed merchants' extremely rare catalog depicting about 1,700 products: clothing, housewares, firearms, dry goods, jewelry, more. Invaluable for dating, identifying vintage items. Also, copyright-free graphics for artists, designers. Co-published with Henry Ford Museum & Greenfield Village. 160pp. 8¼ x 11. 25780-0 Pa. $10.95

HISTORIC COSTUME IN PICTURES, Braun & Schneider. Over 1,450 costumed figures in clearly detailed engravings–from dawn of civilization to end of 19th century. Captions. Many folk costumes. 256pp. 8⅜ x 11¾. 23150-X Pa. $12.95

STICKLEY CRAFTSMAN FURNITURE CATALOGS, Gustav Stickley and L. & J. G. Stickley. Beautiful, functional furniture in two authentic catalogs from 1910. 594 illustrations, including 277 photos, show settles, rockers, armchairs, reclining chairs, bookcases, desks, tables. 183pp. 6½ x 9¼. 23838-5 Pa. $11.95

AMERICAN LOCOMOTIVES IN HISTORIC PHOTOGRAPHS: 1858 to 1949, Ron Ziel (ed.). A rare collection of 126 meticulously detailed official photographs, called "builder portraits," of American locomotives that majestically chronicle the rise of steam locomotive power in America. Introduction. Detailed captions. xi + 129pp. 9 x 12. 27393-8 Pa. $13.95

AMERICA'S LIGHTHOUSES: An Illustrated History, Francis Ross Holland, Jr. Delightfully written, profusely illustrated fact-filled survey of over 200 American light-houses since 1716. History, anecdotes, technological advances, more. 240pp. 8 x 10¾. 25576-X Pa. $12.95

TOWARDS A NEW ARCHITECTURE, Le Corbusier. Pioneering manifesto by founder of "International School." Technical and aesthetic theories, views of indus-try, economics, relation of form to function, "mass-production split" and much more. Profusely illustrated. 320pp. 6⅛ x 9¼. (USO) 25023-7 Pa. $9.95

HOW THE OTHER HALF LIVES, Jacob Riis. Famous journalistic record, expos-ing poverty and degradation of New York slums around 1900, by major social reformer. 100 striking and influential photographs. 233pp. 10 x 7⅞. 22012-5 Pa. $11.95

FRUIT KEY AND TWIG KEY TO TREES AND SHRUBS, William M. Harlow. One of the handiest and most widely used identification aids. Fruit key covers 120 deciduous and evergreen species; twig key 160 deciduous species. Easily used. Over 300 photographs. 126pp. 5⅜ x 8½. 20511-8 Pa. $3.95

COMMON BIRD SONGS, Dr. Donald J. Borror. Songs of 60 most common U.S. birds: robins, sparrows, cardinals, bluejays, finches, more–arranged in order of increasing complexity. Up to 9 variations of songs of each species. Cassette and manual 99911-4 $8.95

ORCHIDS AS HOUSE PLANTS, Rebecca Tyson Northen. Grow cattleyas and many other kinds of orchids–in a window, in a case, or under artificial light. 63 illus-trations. 148pp. 5⅜ x 8½. 23261-1 Pa. $5.95

MONSTER MAZES, Dave Phillips. Masterful mazes at four levels of difficulty. Avoid deadly perils and evil creatures to find magical treasures. Solutions for all 32 exciting illustrated puzzles. 48pp. 8¼ x 11. 26005-4 Pa. $2.95

MOZART'S DON GIOVANNI (DOVER OPERA LIBRETTO SERIES), Wolfgang Amadeus Mozart. Introduced and translated by Ellen H. Bleiler. Standard Italian libretto, with complete English translation. Convenient and thoroughly portable–an ideal companion for reading along with a recording or the performance itself. Introduction. List of characters. Plot summary. 121pp. 5¼ x 8½. 24944-1 Pa. $3.95

TECHNICAL MANUAL AND DICTIONARY OF CLASSICAL BALLET, Gail Grant. Defines, explains, comments on steps, movements, poses and concepts. 15-page pictorial section. Basic book for student, viewer. 127pp. 5⅜ x 8½. 21843-0 Pa. $4.95

THE CLARINET AND CLARINET PLAYING, David Pino. Lively, comprehensive work features suggestions about technique, musicianship, and musical interpretation, as well as guidelines for teaching, making your own reeds, and preparing for public performance. Includes an intriguing look at clarinet history. "A godsend," The Clarinet, Journal of the International Clarinet Society. Appendixes. 7 illus. 320pp. 5⅜ x 8½. 40270-3 Pa. $9.95

HOLLYWOOD GLAMOR PORTRAITS, John Kobal (ed.). 145 photos from 1926-49. Harlow, Gable, Bogart, Bacall; 94 stars in all. Full background on photographers, technical aspects. 160pp. 8⅜ x 11¼. 23352-9 Pa. $12.95

THE ANNOTATED CASEY AT THE BAT: A Collection of Ballads about the Mighty Casey/Third, Revised Edition, Martin Gardner (ed.). Amusing sequels and parodies of one of America's best-loved poems: Casey's Revenge, Why Casey Whiffed, Casey's Sister at the Bat, others. 256pp. 5⅜ x 8½. 28598-7 Pa. $8.95

THE RAVEN AND OTHER FAVORITE POEMS, Edgar Allan Poe. Over 40 of the author's most memorable poems: "The Bells," "Ulalume," "Israfel," "To Helen," "The Conqueror Worm," "Eldorado," "Annabel Lee," many more. Alphabetic lists of titles and first lines. 64pp. 5$\frac{3}{16}$ x 8¼. 26685-0 Pa. $1.00

PERSONAL MEMOIRS OF U. S. GRANT, Ulysses Simpson Grant. Intelligent, deeply moving firsthand account of Civil War campaigns, considered by many the finest military memoirs ever written. Includes letters, historic photographs, maps and more. 528pp. 6⅛ x 9¼. 28587-1 Pa. $12.95

ANCIENT EGYPTIAN MATERIALS AND INDUSTRIES, A. Lucas and J. Harris. Fascinating, comprehensive, thoroughly documented text describes this ancient civilization's vast resources and the processes that incorporated them in daily life, including the use of animal products, building materials, cosmetics, perfumes and incense, fibers, glazed ware, glass and its manufacture, materials used in the mummification process, and much more. 544pp. 6⅛ x 9¼. (USO) 40446-3 Pa. $16.95

RUSSIAN STORIES/PYCCKNE PACCKA3bl: A Dual-Language Book, edited by Gleb Struve. Twelve tales by such masters as Chekhov, Tolstoy, Dostoevsky, Pushkin, others. Excellent word-for-word English translations on facing pages, plus teaching and study aids, Russian/English vocabulary, biographical/critical introductions, more. 416pp. 5⅜ x 8½. 26244-8 Pa. $9.95

PHILADELPHIA THEN AND NOW: 60 Sites Photographed in the Past and Present, Kenneth Finkel and Susan Oyama. Rare photographs of City Hall, Logan Square, Independence Hall, Betsy Ross House, other landmarks juxtaposed with contemporary views. Captures changing face of historic city. Introduction. Captions. 128pp. 8¼ x 11. 25790-8 Pa. $9.95

AIA ARCHITECTURAL GUIDE TO NASSAU AND SUFFOLK COUNTIES, LONG ISLAND, The American Institute of Architects, Long Island Chapter, and the Society for the Preservation of Long Island Antiquities. Comprehensive, well-researched and generously illustrated volume brings to life over three centuries of Long Island's great architectural heritage. More than 240 photographs with authoritative, extensively detailed captions. 176pp. 8¼ x 11. 26946-9 Pa. $14.95

NORTH AMERICAN INDIAN LIFE: Customs and Traditions of 23 Tribes, Elsie Clews Parsons (ed.). 27 fictionalized essays by noted anthropologists examine religion, customs, government, additional facets of life among the Winnebago, Crow, Zuni, Eskimo, other tribes. 480pp. 6⅛ x 9¼. 27377-6 Pa. $10.95

FRANK LLOYD WRIGHT'S DANA HOUSE, Donald Hoffmann. Pictorial essay of residential masterpiece with over 160 interior and exterior photos, plans, elevations, sketches and studies. 128pp. 9¼ x 10¾. 29120-0 Pa. $12.95

THE MALE AND FEMALE FIGURE IN MOTION: 60 Classic Photographic Sequences, Eadweard Muybridge. 60 true-action photographs of men and women walking, running, climbing, bending, turning, etc., reproduced from rare 19th-century masterpiece. vi + 121pp. 9 x 12. 24745-7 Pa. $10.95

1001 QUESTIONS ANSWERED ABOUT THE SEASHORE, N. J. Berrill and Jacquelyn Berrill. Queries answered about dolphins, sea snails, sponges, starfish, fishes, shore birds, many others. Covers appearance, breeding, growth, feeding, much more. 305pp. 5¼ x 8¼. 23366-9 Pa. $9.95

ATTRACTING BIRDS TO YOUR YARD, William J. Weber. Easy-to-follow guide offers advice on how to attract the greatest diversity of birds: birdhouses, feeders, water and waterers, much more. 96pp. 5³/₁₆ x 8¼. 28927-3 Pa. $2.50

MEDICINAL AND OTHER USES OF NORTH AMERICAN PLANTS: A Historical Survey with Special Reference to the Eastern Indian Tribes, Charlotte Erichsen-Brown. Chronological historical citations document 500 years of usage of plants, trees, shrubs native to eastern Canada, northeastern U.S. Also complete identifying information. 343 illustrations. 544pp. 6½ x 9¼. 25951-X Pa. $12.95

STORYBOOK MAZES, Dave Phillips. 23 stories and mazes on two-page spreads: Wizard of Oz, Treasure Island, Robin Hood, etc. Solutions. 64pp. 8¼ x 11. 23628-5 Pa. $2.95

AMERICAN NEGRO SONGS: 230 Folk Songs and Spirituals, Religious and Secular, John W. Work. This authoritative study traces the African influences of songs sung and played by black Americans at work, in church, and as entertainment. The author discusses the lyric significance of such songs as "Swing Low, Sweet Chariot," "John Henry," and others and offers the words and music for 230 songs. Bibliography. Index of Song Titles. 272pp. 6½ x 9¼. 40271-1 Pa. $9.95

MOVIE-STAR PORTRAITS OF THE FORTIES, John Kobal (ed.). 163 glamor, studio photos of 106 stars of the 1940s: Rita Hayworth, Ava Gardner, Marlon Brando, Clark Gable, many more. 176pp. 8⅜ x 11¼. 23546-7 Pa. $14.95

BENCHLEY LOST AND FOUND, Robert Benchley. Finest humor from early 30s, about pet peeves, child psychologists, post office and others. Mostly unavailable elsewhere. 73 illustrations by Peter Arno and others. 183pp. 5⅜ x 8½. 22410-4 Pa. $6.95

YEKL and THE IMPORTED BRIDEGROOM AND OTHER STORIES OF YIDDISH NEW YORK, Abraham Cahan. Film Hester Street based on Yekl (1896). Novel, other stories among first about Jewish immigrants on N.Y.'s East Side. 240pp. 5⅜ x 8½. 22427-9 Pa. $6.95

SELECTED POEMS, Walt Whitman. Generous sampling from *Leaves of Grass.* Twenty-four poems include "I Hear America Singing," "Song of the Open Road," "I Sing the Body Electric," "When Lilacs Last in the Dooryard Bloom'd," "O Captain! My Captain!"—all reprinted from an authoritative edition. Lists of titles and first lines. 128pp. 5³/₁₆ x 8¼. 26878-0 Pa. $1.00

THE BEST TALES OF HOFFMANN, E. T. A. Hoffmann. 10 of Hoffmann's most important stories: "Nutcracker and the King of Mice," "The Golden Flowerpot," etc. 458pp. 5⅜ x 8½.   21793-0 Pa. $9.95

FROM FETISH TO GOD IN ANCIENT EGYPT, E. A. Wallis Budge. Rich detailed survey of Egyptian conception of "God" and gods, magic, cult of animals, Osiris, more. Also, superb English translations of hymns and legends. 240 illustrations. 545pp. 5⅜ x 8½.   25803-3 Pa. $13.95

FRENCH STORIES/CONTES FRANÇAIS: A Dual-Language Book, Wallace Fowlie. Ten stories by French masters, Voltaire to Camus: "Micromegas" by Voltaire; "The Atheist's Mass" by Balzac; "Minuet" by de Maupassant; "The Guest" by Camus, six more. Excellent English translations on facing pages. Also French-English vocabulary list, exercises, more. 352pp. 5⅜ x 8½.   26443-2 Pa. $9.95

CHICAGO AT THE TURN OF THE CENTURY IN PHOTOGRAPHS: 122 Historic Views from the Collections of the Chicago Historical Society, Larry A. Viskochil. Rare large-format prints offer detailed views of City Hall, State Street, the Loop, Hull House, Union Station, many other landmarks, circa 1904-1913. Introduction. Captions. Maps. 144pp. 9⅜ x 12¼.   24656-6 Pa. $12.95

OLD BROOKLYN IN EARLY PHOTOGRAPHS, 1865-1929, William Lee Younger. Luna Park, Gravesend race track, construction of Grand Army Plaza, moving of Hotel Brighton, etc. 157 previously unpublished photographs. 165pp. 8⅞ x 11¾.
23587-4 Pa. $13.95

THE MYTHS OF THE NORTH AMERICAN INDIANS, Lewis Spence. Rich anthology of the myths and legends of the Algonquins, Iroquois, Pawnees and Sioux, prefaced by an extensive historical and ethnological commentary. 36 illustrations. 480pp. 5⅜ x 8½.   25967-6 Pa. $10.95

AN ENCYCLOPEDIA OF BATTLES: Accounts of Over 1,560 Battles from 1479 B.C. to the Present, David Eggenberger. Essential details of every major battle in recorded history from the first battle of Megiddo in 1479 B.C. to Grenada in 1984. List of Battle Maps. New Appendix covering the years 1967-1984. Index. 99 illustrations. 544pp. 6½ x 9¼.   24913-1 Pa. $16.95

SAILING ALONE AROUND THE WORLD, Captain Joshua Slocum. First man to sail around the world, alone, in small boat. One of great feats of seamanship told in delightful manner. 67 illustrations. 294pp. 5⅜ x 8½.   20326-3 Pa. $6.95

ANARCHISM AND OTHER ESSAYS, Emma Goldman. Powerful, penetrating, prophetic essays on direct action, role of minorities, prison reform, puritan hypocrisy, violence, etc. 271pp. 5⅜ x 8½.   22484-8 Pa. $7.95

MYTHS OF THE HINDUS AND BUDDHISTS, Ananda K. Coomaraswamy and Sister Nivedita. Great stories of the epics; deeds of Krishna, Shiva, taken from puranas, Vedas, folk tales; etc. 32 illustrations. 400pp. 5⅜ x 8½.   21759-0 Pa. $12.95

THE TRAUMA OF BIRTH, Otto Rank. Rank's controversial thesis that anxiety neurosis is caused by profound psychological trauma which occurs at birth. 256pp. 5⅜ x 8½.   27974-X Pa. $7.95

A THEOLOGICO-POLITICAL TREATISE, Benedict Spinoza. Also contains unfinished Political Treatise. Great classic on religious liberty, theory of government on common consent. R. Elwes translation. Total of 421pp. 5⅜ x 8½. 20249-6 Pa. $9.95